"Dr. Keck's writing style presents a down-to-e_____ easy to identify with sticky situations that unc_____ adoptees and their loved ones. Having experienced gaping emotional wounds as a former foster youth, this groundbreaking book has brought me to a new level of understanding in my own healing and is sure to be an eye-opening tool for any child welfare professional or advocate."

—TRAVIS LLOYD, RN,BSN, motivational speaker; rap artist; cofounder, Band of Christians, www.BandOfChristians.com, www.travislloyd.net

"Every adoptive parent should read this book. There is so much good and useful information here, it's like getting the instruction manual on how to build a family. I wish I'd had this book sixteen years ago. (I'd have had my son read it too.) It's an important addition to the library of necessary books."

—DAVID GERROLD, author of *The Martian Child*

"Often people feel as if there is a chasm between themselves and their adolescents. The extra complexities for adopted adolescents can make that gap feel like the Grand Canyon. Dr. Keck offers a meaningful way to bridge the gap through his skillful weaving together of adolescent development and adoption issues with practical, reliable suggestions. This valuable resource will find its way to a place of prominence on parents' bedside tables for frequent reference."

—VICKY KELLY, Psy.D., LCSW, MHA, former president, ATTACh

"Dr. Keck brings a down-to-earth, commonsense approach to parenting the adopted adolescent. Parent your adolescent who suffers from trauma and loss nonintrusively rather than in a controlling manner. Parent your adolescent with empathy and patience and not like you are a dictator. Parent your adolescent with the power of your example rather than by the example of your power. Dr. Keck is right on!"

—PAT O'BRIEN, LMSW, founder and executive director, You Gotta Believe! The Older Child Adoption and Permanency Movement, Inc.

"As a mother, I would have found this book to be particularly helpful when parenting and adopting teens. As the manager of an adoption agency that places many older kids into adoptive families, I am delighted to have such a wonderful resource to share with our clients. Dr. Keck normalizes the issues we fear and helps us see that every experience does not have to be catastrophic. This book is not only helpful, it is humorous and enjoyable to read."

—MARY LOU EDGAR, MSS, LCSW, program manager, Upper Bay Adoption and Counseling Services, Wilmington, Delaware; mother of five children by birth and adoption

"This is a must-read book for any parent of an adolescent, adopted or not! With the wisdom of a seasoned adoption clinician, Dr. Gregory Keck compassionately steps into the shoes of the adolescent, providing insights about the complexities that adoption and adolescence present. With humor, Keck enables parents to laugh at themselves while learning how to gain and maintain a balanced perspective, even when their adolescent is rocking the boat. *Parenting Adopted Adolescents* is a great book for anyone, including grandmothers like me who long to relate effectively to the adolescents in their lives. Thank you, Greg, for writing this book."

— SHERRIE ELDRIDGE, speaker and author of *Twenty Things Adopted Kids Wish Their Adoptive Parents Knew, Forever Fingerprints... An Amazing Discovery for Adopted Children, Questions Adoptees Are Asking, Twenty Things Adoptive Parents Need to Succeed*

"The thing I loved about this book is its compassionate and positive tone. It provides an approach to parenting that is both well researched and clear to follow. As we as a country move in the direction of placing adolescents in families rather than institutions, this book is an essential support for parents."

— SARAH GERSTENZANG, MSW, executive director, NYS Citizen's Coalition for Children; author of *Another Mother: Co-Parenting with the Foster Care System*

"Gregory Keck knows what he is talking about and has the experience to back it up. This book is full of helpful insights about teens both adoptive and biological. Instead of filling my head with terms and facts I can't use, I was given practical advice and knowledge to inspire my adolescents to get through the most difficult journey of their lives."

— TAMMY MAHAN, foster/adoptive mom and social worker; founder, Elevate (a group of young people who seek to inspire others to new levels of compassion to the life connection needs of foster care and adoptive teens)

"This book for adoptive parents of older children is extremely important to read and read again. The author gives interesting and fruitful advice, and his examples of the striking behavior of adolescent adoptees are to the point."

— RENE HOKSBERGEN, PhD, adoption professor; author of fifteen books on adoption

"Dr. Keck accomplishes an impressive feat in *Parenting Adopted Adolescents*: He combines decades of clinical knowledge with a wealth of everyday experience, and he does it in an accessible, readable way. The result is an important book and an invaluable tool for parents."

—ADAM PERTMAN, executive director, Evan B. Donaldson Adoption Institute

PARENTING ADOPTED ADOLESCENTS

UNDERSTANDING AND APPRECIATING

THEIR JOURNEYS

Gregory C. Keck, PhD

Edited by L. G. Mansfield

A NavPress resource published in alliance
with Tyndale House Publishers, Inc.

NavPress is the publishing ministry of The Navigators, an international Christian organization and leader in personal spiritual development. NavPress is committed to helping people grow spiritually and enjoy lives of meaning and hope through personal and group resources that are biblically rooted, culturally relevant, and highly practical.

For more information, visit www.NavPress.com.

Parenting Adopted Adolescents: Understanding and Appreciating Their Journeys

Copyright © 2009 by Greg Keck. All rights reserved.

A NavPress resource published in alliance with Tyndale House Publishers, Inc.

NAVPRESS and the NAVPRESS logo are registered trademarks of NavPress, The Navigators, Colorado Springs, CO. *TYNDALE* is a registered trademark of Tyndale House Publishers, Inc. Absence of ® in connection with marks of NavPress or other parties does not indicate an absence of registration of those marks.

Developmental editor: L. G. Mansfield
Cover design by The DesignWorks Group
Cover images: Left image: Shutterstock
                      Middle image: Getty
                      Right image: iStock

This publication is designed to provide accurate and authoritative information in regard to the subject matter covered. It is sold with the understanding that the author and the publisher are not engaged in rendering legal, accounting, or other professional service. If legal advice or other expert assistance is required, the services of a competent professional person should be sought. From a Declaration of Principles jointly adopted by a Committee of the American Bar Association and a Committee of Publishers.

Scripture taken from the Holy Bible, *New International Version,*® *NIV.*® Copyright © 1973, 1978, 1984 by Biblica, Inc.® Used by permission. All rights reserved worldwide.

Some of the anecdotal illustrations in this book are true to life and are included with the permission of the persons involved. All other illustrations are composites of real situations, and any resemblance to people living or dead is coincidental.

Library of Congress Cataloging-in-Publication Data

Keck, Gregory C.
  Parenting adopted adolescents : understanding and appreciating their
journeys / Gregory C. Keck.
      p. cm.
  Includes bibliographical references.
  ISBN 978-1-60006-281-0
  1. Adopted children. 2. Teenagers--Psychology. 3. Parenting.
4. Adoptive parents. 5. Adoption--Psychological aspects. I. Title.
  HV875.K43 2009
  649'.145--dc22
                                      2008055588

Printed in the United States of America

21 20 19 18 17 16 15
10   9   8   7   6   5   4

To my sons, Brian and James—

Thanks for including me in your journeys. You have changed my life forever.

Broken Love

Sitting quietly on the steps
I seem normal to the world, but inside I'm torn
Lacking attachment to my loved ones by whom I was born
I cling to the hope that someday . . . maybe someday
I will feel what it means to be whole.
These are the words of a ten-year-old boy
suppressed by medications who acts out with acts of hatred
because that's all he knows.
As he stares in the mirror, tears drop to the floor
and he births a new version of himself
to disguise the lonely ten-year-old boy filled with fear.
The only love he knows torn from his soul and he cries on the inside,
seemingly, the end is near. He's lost all control.
So he takes it out on those who try to help him
and in the midst of the pressure they lose track of the fact
that he's still a ten-year-old boy filled with fear
needing nothing more than the comfort of a loved one
who doesn't change how they treat them because of fear.
Now it is time to evade these presumptive perceptions of who a foster kid is.
Broken? No.
In need of guidance to find how he is whole.
We stand by his side and uphold these values praying that someday
they will bond with his soul.
And though it seems we have lost it, we never had control
as we pour our love into a child that yearns for more.
The years pass by and we realize . . .
The hardest thing to do is let go.

—TRAVIS LLOYD

CONTENTS

Download the free discussion guide for
Parenting Adopted Adolescents at NavPress.com.

FOREWORD

Parenting your adopted adolescent is a little like sailing a new boat on a large, unfamiliar lake. It can be a scary journey. You thought you knew something about sailing, but this boat is so complicated and the whitecaps are larger and more treacherous than anything you have ever experienced. This was supposed to be fun, but now you wonder whether you will ever be able to navigate the sandbars and rocky passage that lead to the safe harbor you see in the distance.

If only you had someone on board who had actually sailed a boat like yours and knew which areas of the lake are hazardous and which call for smooth sailing. Although you are the sailor, you desperately need a navigator who can tell you when to relax and enjoy the ride and when to pay attention to the frequent wind changes. You need a navigator who will tell you how silly it is to spend time scrubbing the deck when you need to concentrate on trimming the main sail.

You need direction and encouragement to stick with the time-honored fundamentals of sailing that do not change with each new boat model. You need to know that the boat you are sailing is constructed to weather the waves and that you have every chance of reaching that distant harbor. You need to know that others have weathered the storm and are now firmly anchored.

In this informative book, Dr. Gregory Keck is the navigator who has personally and professionally experienced the demanding, enriching, sometimes perplexing, and inspiring journey of parenting adopted adolescents. He will teach, encourage, challenge, and confront you, enabling you to laugh and let go of the need to control the things you cannot manage and concentrate on those areas of your relationship with your child that have lasting significance.

He will guide you through the confusing mystery of adolescence by helping you consider the issues that are normal expressions of adolescent development. He will then assist you in combining that knowledge with the specific concerns that apply to your child. This might include loss and grief issues, such as loss of culture, religion, connections, siblings, birth order, language, family traditions, and identity. Your conversation with Dr. Keck will provide the encouragement and considerations necessary to support your adopted adolescent in his search for personal identity during this stage of combining genetic heritage and possible past environmental deficits with the present-day nurturing potential of adoption.

Parents of adopted adolescents especially need a navigator to supply the knowledge that will help them stand up to the outside world of friends, school officials, family, and professionals who may form critical judgments based on incorrect and irrelevant suppositions.

As your personal navigator, Dr. Keck first teaches and illustrates so you can begin to see the world through the eyes of your adolescent. He then invites you to examine your own convictions and motivations as he anticipates your many questions: *Why does my adolescent have such a need to control, and why do I feel compelled to win irrelevant battles? What about the onset of puberty? What should I be doing about my adolescent's sexual interest, behavior, and energy?*

As a parent, do you go with the flow and accept the norms of a culture your adolescent can view on cable TV or the Internet? What if your child looks like an adolescent but is emotionally still a child? Is there anyplace for your personal, faith-based convictions in today's world? Are morals still important, and if they are, how do you impress the importance of morality and standards on your adopted adolescent? When do you trust your child, and when do you monitor and impose controls? How does your adopted adolescent incorporate a different culture or race in the necessary search for identity? When is it important to seek professional help that is really helpful? How do you progress from feelings of frustration and failure to building or maintaining a lasting connection with your adopted adolescent?

Your conversation with your navigator will include some magnificent stories of adopted adolescents who are now firmly anchored in a safe harbor. I think you will agree that their challenging ride was worth the effort.

Although this book has explicit meaning for parents of adopted adolescents, it is really a book that has a message for parents of all adolescents. It is a courageous book that combines humor and a relaxed parental attitude with strong convictions and data that encourage and persuade parents to model standards and morality that are enduring. Enjoy!

—JOANNE MAY, PhD
founder, Family Attachment
Counseling Center of Minnesota

ACKNOWLEDGMENTS

Anyone who undertakes writing a book ends up with many people to acknowledge. I dedicated this book to my sons, both of whom were adopted during adolescence. Their journeys *did* change my life forever, probably much like any child impacts his parents. Their histories became part of my life, and my history became part of their futures. I thank them for sharing their lives in a way that enriched me and helped me remain sensitive to the needs of the many adoptive families with whom I work.

As I was thinking about writing this book, Kris Wallen, managing editor at NavPress, encouraged and invited me to submit my proposal to her. She was always responsive to me and consistently solicited my input throughout the entire process, from the proposal phase through the final stages of publishing. One of the most critical questions Kris asked was, "Who would you like to edit the book?" It took me a millisecond to say, "Lynda Mansfield!" Thanks, Kris, for making things happen.

Lynda (or Elle, depending on who's talking about her) is an adoptive parent, an author, and a friend. Her personal understanding of adoption was an additional bonus. She edited *Adopting the Hurt Child* and *Parenting the Hurt Child*, books I coauthored with Regina Kupecky, with much grace and sophistication. Again, in *Parenting Adopted Adolescents*, Lynda has enriched my voice, fine-tuned my writing, and made important suggestions and changes that have led to a reader-friendly and useful book. Thanks, Lynda—you did it again!

I would like to offer a special thanks to Sharon Kaplan Roszia, MS, and Deborah Silverstein, MSW, for sharing their seminal work on the seven core issues of adoption, which addresses so many critical points relative to what adoptees experience. They have contributed enormously to the field of adoption, and I sincerely appreciate their permission to use their work.

Katherine Petefish, MS, LPC, has contributed a heartwarming piece of work related to the use of animals in therapy. What an important addition to this book! Animals can truly help children and adolescents develop empathy. Thank you, Kathy.

I have learned so much from the families with whom I work. As they share their joy and their pain, they strengthen my belief that every child deserves and needs a family. A family provides the foundation upon which the child will build the rest of his life. For that reason, we must support all families as they embark on a journey to shape the futures of their children. I thank the many people who have chosen to work with me and with the therapists in my office. You bring to us some of the most difficult challenges in life, and when real change occurs, we are as thrilled as you are.

The therapists in my office are superb! They face extremely challenging situations, and rarely do I hear complaints. Every adoptive family we see has chosen to parent a child who has had some level of trauma (for example, abandonment, sexual abuse, physical abuse, institutional care, multiple foster-home placements). People who adopt a hurt child share the child's pain; the professionals who work with hurt families often share that pain as well. Thanks, Arleta, Bonnie, Linda, Mariann, Paula, Regina, Susan, and Virginia. Thanks, Marita and Chris, for keeping administrative things in order.

Thanks to my friends Di and Molly, who've had to listen to me talk about this book and my writing progress—or lack thereof—for many months. The answer to their question "So what have you been doing today?" was almost always "Writing!" I appreciate your ears and I enjoy your humor!

Throughout the writing process, I periodically needed computer coaching, given that I suffer from Excessive Clicking Disorder. (When in doubt, I just keep clicking on things.) My friend Matt's southern voice saying, "Rot click, double rot click," will forever resonate in my mind when I'm trying to use spell-check or find a synonym. Thanks, Matt.

I extend special thanks to my parents and grandparents for being such an extraordinary family. I'm so glad to have grown up in an era when adults knew that kids do foolish things—they almost expected it! These days, things that were once considered merely witless and thoughtless are now deemed criminal. I had a lot of fun growing up, and my parents and grandparents were a part of that fun. I particularly appreciate the fact that my mother did not greet me every day after school with a directive that seems to be at the heart of today's family communication: "Do your homework!" Thanks, Mom.

I enjoy watching my sister, Sue, and her husband, Ted, parent their adolescents, Greg and Jennifer, their children by birth. They share many experiences with parents who have adopted adolescents. I am always encouraged when they share their journeys — they're not so different after all.

Many adoption professionals have been supportive of my work, writing, and training. Thanks for your ongoing confidence in me, and thanks for all of the good work you do with adoptive families.

Thanks to Dr. Joanne May, founder of the Family Attachment Counseling Center of Minnesota, for writing an excellent foreword. I have known her for a long time, and I value her friendship as well as her professional insights and contributions. There were many people whom I felt could lend their voices in a foreword that would energize and excite readers as they began to read *Parenting Adopted Adolescents*. However, I knew that Dr. May's review would grasp not only the details of the book but also the tone and context of it. Joanne, you didn't miss a thing, and you captured exactly what I hope all who read this book will take away with them. Thanks so much.

I especially want to thank Travis Lloyd for his moving poem, "Broken Love." Travis wrote this on very short notice just after reading *Parenting Adopted Adolescents*. His work on behalf of America's children who are in foster care is to be applauded. Thanks, Travis.

Finally, thanks to the people who so graciously offered their written endorsements of this book and to the readers who've added it to their bedside stacks. I hope you find wisdom and comfort in its pages.

INTRODUCTION

The mere mention of adolescents pushes some people, particularly parents, immediately into panic mode. Moms and dads constantly ask me, "If he's like this at six, what will I ever do with him when he hits fourteen?" Their fear of what might happen eight years down the road is indicative of how powerful the image of "teen" has become for some parents. Their assumption that they will have a completely unruly, rebellious, sexualized junior adult on their hands often paralyzes them. Their perceived impotence renders them unable to realize that while most adolescents have some rough spots, they do not automatically stumble into the out-of-control persona characteristically described in the media. Most adolescents don't even come close to being as "bad" as their parents think they could be.

Adoptive parents often find themselves wondering if their child will start to become more like his birth family during the identity-seeking adolescent years. If he came from an abusive background—complete with criminal activity, drug or alcohol addiction, or other kinds of dysfunction—their fear may be even greater. After all, adolescence is the time when children start to morph into young adults. They make bold, confident proclamations about who they are, what they like, what they know (and they're convinced they know a *bundle*), and what they will become. Although such statements of brazen independence tend to throw parents into a spiral of terror, these assertions are actually rather benign, even useful. Their purpose is to help the adolescent begin to establish a sense of self that is separate from his family's identity.

Throughout this book, I will address issues based on the following assumptions:

- All adolescents have some things in common, such as stages of development.
- Some adolescents have some things in common, such as gender, race, culture, and socioeconomic class.
- All adolescents have unique qualities that they share with no one.

Of course, the same assumptions apply to adoptees. The only difference is that the child who has joined his family via adoption must address both adolescent-developmental issues and adoption-related issues, either simultaneously or alternately. Amidst the psychological and physiological transformations, the adolescent might appear to be intentionally driving his parents crazy—at least from their perspective.

It is important for parents not to overreact to the changes that arise during adolescence. Turning each new and questionable behavior into cause for controversy not only complicates the adolescent's life but also compromises the parents' capacity to be what their child needs them to be: parental yet friendly. I will talk more about this later because I can already hear some of you saying, "I'm not here to be his friend!" But please note that I didn't say *friend*; I said *friendly*.

Parents often believe that controlling their adolescent is critical, and they are afraid of losing the power to be "the boss." In some cases, they overcompensate by becoming hovering micromanagers of their adolescent's life. The fact is, control is elusive. The only behavior that people can truly take charge of is their own. Most individuals are not in control of anything beyond their own responses to others. It therefore follows that parents have the freedom to be creative, thoughtful, fun, and, yes, *friendly* toward their adolescent. Once parents come to understand what they don't control, they are free to figure out precisely what they do control: themselves.

Adoptive parents sometimes feel a heavy burden to be the "perfect" parent, even though there is no such thing. They are well aware that they are held to different standards than are birth families. Adoptive parents consistently report that they experience being judged by professionals, extended family members, and the community at large in a manner that sees them as different from "real" families.

In spite of such perceptions, the truth remains that all families are real families regardless of how they were formed. Adoptive parents must stand up for themselves and become comfortable with the task of addressing the second-class-citizenship issues each time they are presented. If a school report describes the meeting with "Sean and his adoptive mother," Sean's mom has every right to point out to teachers and administrators that "adoptive" is an unnecessary and prejudiced distinction. After all, would a teacher note that she had a meeting with "Sean and his overweight mother"? With "Sean and his badly-in-need-of-a-haircut mother"? Somehow I doubt it.

Sometimes parents cannot see their adolescent as others do, and an adolescent does not see his parents as his peers do. Even his own friends may not think his parents are as weird as he does. While there seems to be a societal assumption that adolescents do not want to be around adults, I do not believe this to be true. Adolescents often develop very close relationships with coaches, teachers, members of the clergy, and the parents of their friends. They act as if they don't want to be around their own parents, but it's perfectly okay—and maybe even cool—to hang out with other kids' parents.

Because other adults do not have the kind of connection to an adolescent that his parents do, they are able to interact with him as a person, not as the child he used to be. People outside the family perceive him without all the nuances his own parents often cannot shake. Others can laugh at the adolescent's irreverent jokes without feeling they need to correct him or give him a tutorial on the "real world."

Parents sometimes are so consumed with making sure that everything the adolescent says or does is world-appropriate that they forget to enjoy his emerging self. They may not see the process of the developing person if they are overly focused on ensuring propriety. I believe that parents want to enjoy their children and adolescents. I also think they are a bit afraid of enjoying their kids too much, lest they lose control—which they probably don't have anyway.

Some adoptive parents may experience feelings of not being good enough: *Is my child's pulling away related to adoption? To loss? If this were my birth child, would he be seeking an identity so separate from mine?* As these thoughts and concerns are disturbing the parents, their adolescent may be having a parallel experience: *Would my birth parents be this awful? This strict? This controlling?* He might think that if he were with his birth family, they would understand him better.

The truth for both sides is that things would probably be very similar under just about any set of circumstances. Adolescents who were removed from their birth families as a result of abuse or neglect would almost always be facing huge challenges if they had remained in their homes of origin. History continues to be the best predictor of the future, and if an adolescent grows up in a situation where he is maltreated, it is probable that he will have significant difficulty moving into a productive young adulthood.

In *Parenting Adopted Adolescents*, we will take a look at the adolescent in general and, more specifically, the adolescent who was adopted. I will visit a diversity of adolescent and adoption issues and help to simplify their intertwined relationship as it becomes more complicated and exaggerated over the course of time.

As you read each chapter, you will find sense emerging from your confusion. You will discover humor blessedly rising up from your pain. And you will experience some relief when you realize that most of us made it through the energized years of adolescence to return to what could be called "normal."

The journey through this book will give parents hope. It will give professionals the insight to help parents and adolescents in a manner that will allow them to remain close even while their relationships are being challenged by biology, sociology, and psychology. Professionals will see that all adoptive families have some things in common, some of them have some things in common, and, finally, each family has its own uniqueness. In helping parents and professionals, this book will give adolescents the kind of adult guides they need to steward them through what is a traumatic time for many of them — an experience that most of us would not choose to relive anytime soon!

While *Parenting Adopted Adolescents* is theoretically based and sound, I have made an effort to write this book in a casual and conversational tone. My intent is to enable readers to feel as if they are involved in an exchange of ideas, as opposed to being subjected to countless endnotes and theoretical references. It is my hope to stimulate thinking and creativity that can be translated into effective interactions between parents and their adopted adolescents.

ONE

ADOLESCENCE

What's It All About?

Adolescents are often referred to as teenagers. That will not be the case in this book because adolescence, as a discrete developmental stage, encompasses more than the teenage years. Studies continue to indicate that the onset age of puberty is much earlier than it was thirty years ago. I contend that puberty is when adolescent development begins, and recent research about the adolescent brain suggests that it may not be adult-like until the midtwenties.

The adolescent brain is very much a work in progress — just like the adolescent himself — and is responsible for both fueling and dousing the fires that are so typical at this age. One part of the adolescent brain, the limbic system, is responsible for impulsivity, risk-taking, sexual drive, and emotional responses. Another part of the brain, the prefrontal cortex, is responsible for emotional and behavioral regulation, task accomplishment, organization, planning, rational thinking, and decision making. Imagine that these two components are engaged in an ongoing tug of war throughout adolescence.

Brain research is exploding, and it is revealing that the prefrontal cortex — the reasoning regulating device — is not fully developed until after age twenty. As a result, it's easy to see what is happening in the adolescent brain. The seat of emotion, the limbic system, is fully fired up, and the prefrontal cortex that's supposed to mitigate what the limbic system produces is still asleep at the wheel, not fully capable of doing its job. No wonder adolescents sometimes appear not to have any good sense at all, and no wonder they calm down dramatically in their twenties. That's just the way the brain is wired to work.

So if parents expect good, solid judgment and decision making from their adolescent, they may be disappointed. However, if they know that the adolescent's brain is not working at full capacity to regulate his behavior, they will realize they need to step in and serve as the adolescent's training wheels until he is able to function properly by himself.

The teenage years span a total of seven, while true adolescence may be more like thirteen years. I'm sorry to disappoint those of you who might be looking forward to having your almost-eighteen-year-old leave the nest in a few months. Although he might threaten to flee, he probably won't mean it. And if he does opt to spread his wings, there's a good chance he'll be back.

"I feel like I've lost my little girl," one mother said. "She used to love going shopping with me, and we enjoyed walking through the mall and having lunch. Now if I manage to persuade her to join me, she either lags behind or tries to lose me." My advice: Just wait.

SEPARATION AND INDIVIDUATION

The role of the adolescent is to leave behind his childhood identity and develop a new self. This is called separation and individuation. All healthy adults have done this, and it should not be seen as complete rejection of the parents. Instead, it represents the adolescent's attempt to embrace things that define him in new ways.

A young child's identity is clearly an extension of that of his parents. He likes to spend time with them and may even want to grow up to be just like his dad. In childhood, this is fine. No one thinks he is uncool for wanting to mimic his father. In fact, this relationship is laying the foundation for what will happen later on in childhood, adolescence, and finally in adulthood.

In a typical situation, this foundation will be strong enough to withstand the separation and individuation process, and it will serve as a solid base that remains intact throughout the life span of the family. So while it may appear that the adolescent is trying to tear down the foundation, he is actually developing a new self on top of the structure that already exists. In some ways, the adolescent is putting some of his parents' values in storage—we hope for just a short while—while he experiments with the new him.

An adolescent who was adopted will probably have additional components in his separation and individuation process. Unless the child was adopted at birth, he probably has had some level of trauma—either minor or profound—which impacts the quality of the relationships he develops. If his original foundation was laid in a chaotic family, relationships will be somewhat fragmented. If he has a developmental foundation that was created by both a birth family and an adoptive family, the separation process will be more complicated. He may, in fact, be able to separate more effectively from the adoptive family than from the birth family. He may retain the birth family's component because it keeps him connected to their familiarity, and he may even use it as part of his individuation process. If that occurs, the adoptive parents may feel as if they are being replaced by the adolescent's family of origin. In the case of an adolescent identifying with a dysfunctional or criminal birth family, the adoptive parents would have legitimate concerns regarding their child's choices.

Some adolescents engage in the individuation process like a whisper, while others go through it like a shout. Figuring out the difference is simple: Growing extra-long hair is a whisper; dying it bright green and adding multiple facial piercings is a shout.

> Adam had been experimenting with a new image for a couple of years. At the point when he was dressing in all-black skin-tight clothes, complete with chains and flaming-pink hair, he decided to steal some beer from a convenience store late at night. Of course, he got caught. His appearance was a shout, and there wasn't a person in the store who didn't notice him.

Functional individuation involves engaging in productive activities that further one's identity. In situations in which the separation and individuation process occurs in an uncomplicated way, adolescents may involve themselves in sports, the arts, employment, career exploration, service projects, youth groups, and student council. Anything that the adolescent uses to further define himself—for his own sake and for others—could be considered individuation.

Individuation would also include negative behavior, such as drug dealing and using, vandalism, bullying, and fighting. To be a "bad boy" has its benefits within certain social contexts. The problem with becoming your own person in this way is that it has lasting moral and legal consequences. Identities such as these have little utility in the pragmatic world, and parents must actively intervene to correct this kind of identity seeking.

Chad, seventeen, was adopted by a family who lived in close proximity to several of his birth relatives. Because he was an adolescent when he was adopted, he knew where everyone in his birth family lived and he spent time with some of them.

His birth mother was in prison on a variety of criminal charges, including possession of illegal substances, possession of criminal tools, and carrying a concealed weapon without a permit. Chad had no contact with her, but he had clear memories of her and the atrocities she subjected him to. She had allowed him to be sexually abused by many of her male friends, who paid her for access to her son. Chad was angry with her, yet he was trapped into thinking that she might change one day.

He had heard from his relatives that she was scheduled to get out of prison about six months before his eighteenth birthday. When she was released, Chad reconnected with her. He was no longer the little boy she remembered, and she was no longer the mean, abusive person she once was. While this was confusing for Chad, he liked the fact that they had a new kind of relationship. They began to spend time together, more as peers than as mother and son. Chad liked this newfound friend, and the two proceeded to spend most of their time smoking marijuana and drinking beer together. Wow! She was lots of fun!

During this time, Chad began pulling away from his adoptive family. He talked about his birth mom all the time, and his parents suspected that she was exposing him to harmful things. When they attempted to set some boundaries about how much time he could spend with her,

Chad started leaving home without their permission so he could meet up with his "real mom," as he referred to her.

For about five months, Chad's new identity mimicked his mother's. He would say to his parents, "This is who I *really* am. I'm more like her than like you, and she says that when I'm eighteen, I can live with her." His parents were deeply concerned and hurt, and they could only hope he would change his mind and come to his senses before he ended up in trouble or, even worse, became addicted to something.

Chad did leave his home on his eighteenth birthday to move in with his birth mom. Within a very short period of time, she began to expect him to get a job and support her. She also began to demand the respect she felt she deserved as his mother. Their relationship changed dramatically, and they were in constant conflict. When Chad refused to give her his entire paycheck, she kicked him out of her apartment. He was devastated — hurt and rejected once again by the one person he felt should love and protect him.

Chad called his parents and asked if he could move back home. Without hesitation, they said he could. Although he was legally an adult, he felt like the hurt little boy he once was as all of the old memories came back to haunt him. He had been seeking to redefine himself, and now he had lost what he had so desperately latched on to.

However, all was not lost by this experience. Chad realized that the bad memories about his birth mom were accurate, and he understood what his parents meant when they cautioned him about getting so involved with her. The time he spent living with his birth mom allowed him to get a reality check, and although it was hurtful, Chad was able to move on from it. He developed a new appreciation for his adoptive family and felt less intense about having to pull away from them.

DEPENDENCE VERSUS INDEPENDENCE

The individuation process does not happen in a steady forward motion. There are times when the adolescent retreats into a state of dependence and abandons his separating and individuating process. When he takes a break from redefining himself, he is more relaxed around his family. He accepts affection, is cooperative, and acts like he used to. His parents are thrilled! They may even think they are over the hump.

I encourage parents to enjoy these periods of time and take advantage of them (in a positive way). These retreats to dependence are times of receptivity, reciprocity, and emotional neediness. This is not the time to insert remarks along the lines of, "Look at how much fun we're having now that you're acting like a normal kid again." Such a comment is certain to throw the adolescent back into independence mode—precisely what his parents were hoping to avoid or eliminate.

During tranquil periods, parents can begin to enjoy their child in new and different ways. This may be the best time to open discussion on a variety of topics, such as social, political, and spiritual issues. The interaction can become more collegial—the questions open-ended and not instructional or tutorial.

A parent might make a statement such as, "I spoke with Mrs. Stanton today. She's concerned about Phil because she found him smoking pot in his bedroom." If the subject is broached without any editorial comments, the remark might start a conversation that will give the parent some insight into what her child thinks about marijuana. This is not the time to launch into a lecture about drug use.

Actually, most issues that are important to the parent should have been discussed long before adolescence. If they weren't addressed earlier, the message may not be well received at this stage. I often tell parents that if their child has not heard the word *no* prior to adolescence, it may be nearly impossible to start setting limits in the middle of these challenging years.

Because the dance between dependence and independence is guaranteed to occur, the adults in the adolescent's life must be able to determine when to attempt to engage him and when to take pause and wait for an opportune moment. Adolescents like to initiate interactions and quickly respond to them. How they do so is determined by their position in the dependence/independence dichotomy. There will be many times when they will toss out a hook in an effort to see what kind of response they can elicit.

Sometimes this process looks impulsive; other times it seems like a scripted moment. If the parents perceive that the remark is scripted, they may attribute negative intent and respond with defensive fury, particularly if the remark is antagonistic. This kind of response is certain to end in a nonproductive manner for the parent. However, if this response validates the independent status of the adolescent, he may feel that it worked out just fine for him. So while the outcome of the interaction is shared, the meaning is completely disparate.

The issue of intent is one of great importance. It is possible to consciously do something without having the intention that another person attributes to the act. Adolescents often do things simply because they want to, and their goal is not necessarily to bring about discomfort for their parents. I work with many families who demonstrate extreme anger because their adolescent *intentionally* did something to upset them. That is rarely the case, even if the behavior was done "on purpose."

To better understand this concept, let's look at a couple of parallels. A new puppy joins the family. He intentionally grabs the end of a roll of toilet paper and then runs as fast as he can, seemingly having lots of fun in the process. It is the dog's intention to play, but it is not his intention to waste toilet paper or inconvenience the person who has to clean up after him.

Similarly, I recently saw a disciplinary referral from a teacher about a student who was one of my clients. In a large scrawl that reflected her anger, she wrote, "It is his intention to make my life a living hell and keep me from doing my job." Now, this teacher was mad and understandably so, but I sincerely doubt that the adolescent had the specific intent she accused him of. Yes, he probably did everything he did quite deliberately, but it is highly unlikely that his plan was to keep her from doing her job.

When adopted adolescents reject others, their intention is usually not to cause hurt but to avoid being rejected themselves. They have already been cast off by their birth families, and they have no desire to go through that again. When parents and professionals accurately identify the real issue as fear, they can respond differently than they would if they assumed rudeness to be the intention. An empathic response makes the adolescent feel understood, and it might be somewhat constructive in terms of helping him identify his feelings.

About six months after Juan, age seventeen, was placed with his family, his parents began to notice that he frequently attempted to keep his distance from them in public. He tried to avoid them at school-related events, and he would dart behind the bleachers in the gym and remain "missing in action" until the basketball game was over. Initially, his parents thought this was typical adolescent behavior, but Juan's attitude led them to wonder if there might be something more going on.

When they finally discussed their concerns with him, he told them that some other Hispanic kids at school had teased him about having white parents. They wondered aloud why his "real" family didn't want him, and they asked questions about his birth family. "Is your mom a crackhead? Is your dad in prison?" Juan didn't answer their questions, but he developed a heightened sensitivity about being seen with his adoptive parents. Hiding out provided him with a sense of immunity from further harassment.

Juan's parents were glad to know the whys of his avoidance, but they were saddened to hear that he had to deal with such difficult peer issues. Juan was not blowing them off, ignoring them, or rejecting them; he was engaging in a self-protective effort that had nothing to do with his relationship with his parents. They were wise to explore the issue with him instead of making assumptions about his behavior.

Adults should attempt to think about a variety of underlying factors when interpreting adolescent behavior because the factors may be more complex than they appear at face value. I encourage parents to first consider adolescent issues and then combine them with adoption/loss issues.

Of course, some behavior may not have any deep meaning at all and therefore does not require any parental intervention. Parents can't do much to prevent the psychological insults that all adolescents experience, but they can be there to help dust the kids off and send them on their way again.

AUTONOMY SEEKING

Most adolescents believe they can do anything they want. They face the world with unquestioning certainty of what they *know* to be true. Their perceptions equal their reality, and these perceptions guide the decisions they make about what they do. Autonomy is of utmost importance to them, and when they feel they have accomplished something, a true sense of pride sets in.

Troy, age sixteen, wanted golf clubs and golf shoes for his birthday. He had never played golf before, but he had just made a new friend who thought he was the next Tiger Woods. Because Troy knew virtually nothing about golf, his parents decided to include some lessons at the local golf course. When they gave Troy his gifts, he was excited about the clubs, bag, and shoes, but he was less pleased that they had included the lessons.

"I'm not stupid," he said. "I can play golf; everybody knows how to play golf. I don't need lessons." It was his belief that lessons meant he did not know how to do something (which, in this case, he didn't), thereby indicating a weakness and signaling personal inadequacy.

Troy's father said that he had no idea Troy knew how to play golf, but he explained to his son that even professional golfers have coaches to help them improve their game. Once Troy heard that, he decided that the lessons would be okay.

Many times, the things an adolescent does that lead to his sense of industry and success are not appreciated or even apparent to others, particularly those close to him. In some cases, adults outside the immediate family are more aware of, and sensitive to, the adolescent's undertakings and accomplishments.

Parents can help promote the adolescent's developmental process by encouraging and supporting autonomous activities that are safe and age-appropriate. Too often, adults stifle creativity and independence as the result of their fears. *What might go wrong if he does such and such?* Adult brains are frequently primed to worry about the absolute worst thing that can happen, and the adolescent brain is geared toward completion of any task or activity with little or no worry about what could happen. So while parents are worried sick about impending doom, their child is having safe, independent fun.

Tom's parents started worrying when he didn't show up at the appointed hour after a football game. As time went on, their worries increased to wondering if he had been in an accident or even if he had been killed. Finally, Tom returned—about two hours late. He and his friends had gone to a movie, and he had forgotten to call to let his parents know. Although they were relieved to know that he was okay, they wanted to wring his neck when he finally made it home.

Most parents can relate to this scenario. Of course, the kid is thinking that his parents are too worried about everything, and the parents are thinking that their adolescent is an irresponsible, risk-taking kid who is ruining his future. Such exaggerated and polarized beliefs cause much stress for all members of the family. Because the adults are in better positions than the adolescent, psychologically, to be rational, the burden to reduce the disparity between the parent camp and the adolescent falls firmly on them.

Obviously, autonomy needs to be regulated primarily by the parents and, to some extent, by the adolescent himself. When the child does not respect family boundaries, parents must be the ones to address the issue. However, their roles may not end the child's struggle for autonomy because the struggle is a built-in developmental task that may be regulated but not eliminated.

EXPERIMENTATION AND UNIQUENESS

Adolescents want to try the different, the risky, the challenging, the untested. They want to learn something new. Sometimes—okay, most times—they are interested in engaging in things that will contribute to their identity, and parents should not assume that their kids are aware of this. When he wants to take guitar lessons, he's convinced he's on his way to being the next rock star. This kind of experimentation can be supported by parents and other adults without the perennial comment, "You know, few people ever make it big." Let him have his dreams. You did, and odds are it didn't cause anyone any harm.

The exploration into new activities can allow the adolescent to begin to redefine himself, and all of his pro-social efforts to do so should be encouraged. Obviously, parents must decide how far they will go to support the adolescent's interests. If they negatively focus on the kid's stated intention to become a major star, they may miss the opportunity for him to become energized about an activity that will keep him engaged in something positive.

In reality, it's a win-win situation. On one end of the spectrum, he may simply learn to play the guitar and enjoy it. On the other end, he may develop a high skill level that will allow him to achieve long-term success.

As a society, we encourage children to follow their dreams when they are fairly standard—becoming a fireman, a lawyer, a doctor, a teacher, a nurse. However, dreams that seem far-fetched—a rock star, a dancer, an artist, a professional athlete—are frequently squelched. Parents would be better off to support almost *any* adolescent dream, as long as it's legal and safe. The content of the dream is less important than the process of developing the dream and doing what is necessary to reach the ultimate goal. If, by chance, the adolescent develops his basketball skills to a high degree, he may get a scholarship or even get to the NBA. Is there anything to gain by raining on a kid's parade?

Adolescent experimentation comes in many forms and may include such things as hair, makeup, dress, posture, manner of walking, drug and alcohol use, music, selection of peers, nail polish, piercings, sports, and skateboarding. The list goes on and on. Most adolescents will become part of a group that shares similar interests, and such connectivity helps validate their choices. Even though they say they are not influenced by their peers, it has always been my assumption that they know they share a lot with their friends. Peer influence becomes pronounced in adolescence and diminishes with age. However, it seems safe to say that most people are influenced, on some level, by their peers throughout their lives.

Adults typically talk about peer pressure only when discussing negative activities, which causes an automatic defensive response from the accused. It is rare to accuse an honor student of studying so hard just because his friends do.

When adolescents are attempting to fit in, they are simultaneously developing some immunity from teasing. If they dress like their friends, they won't be ridiculed by them. If they are made fun of by people beyond their immediate circle, they can dismiss the comments as worthless since they don't really care about "outsiders" anyway. If adults make negative comments about their appearance, their sense of individuation may be enhanced.

Parents can minimize their worries about how their adolescent looks by reflecting on their own experiences. If you revisit your photo in your high school yearbook, odds are you'll cringe—the hair . . . those glasses . . . that shirt. One of my sons found a photo of me during my college days when I sported a huge afro and asked, "What were you thinking?" I don't remember exactly what I said, but it was close to, "The same thing everyone else was thinking." When adults remember that much of what goes on in adolescence is developmental and transitional, they can tame the occasional panic that occurs as part of parenting an adolescent.

INDIVIDUAL VARIATIONS IN ADOLESCENT DEVELOPMENT

It is important to remember that each adolescent develops at his own pace. If the adoption took place at birth or very early in life, eliminating or diminishing the possibility of trauma, the journey through adolescence may approximate that of a child born into the family. If, on the other hand, the adoption occurred later in childhood or during adolescence, there is a greater likelihood of significant developmental interruption as the result of numerous traumatic experiences. "The term complex trauma describes the dual problem of children's exposure to traumatic events and the impact of this exposure on immediate and long-term outcomes."[1]

Some parents may feel that adoption alone will resolve the damage imposed by traumatic experiences, but that is not the case. "The traumatized child may not be able to blend into the adoptive family. The adoptive family does not have the magic wand that will erase the abuse and neglect suffered by the child. However, the adoptive family can, over time, mitigate the child's traumatic scars."[2]

Developmental interruptions result in delays that leave the individual developmentally immature. If an adolescent doesn't seem to be where he should be on the growing-up spectrum, he probably isn't. Parents may be surprised when their otherwise typical fifteen-year-old begs for action figures when he sees them in a toy store. A week ago he was excited about the prospect of getting his driver's license in the near future, and now he wants action figures! What is *that* all about?

I use the term *bifurcated development* to label this dynamic. *Bifurcated* is defined as "divided into or made up of two parts."[3] Because the adolescent lives in a social world, it is likely that he looks like a fifteen-year-old, dresses like a fifteen-year-old, and sometimes acts like a fifteen-year-old. That is one part of his developed persona. The second component of the bifurcation is the psychologically underdeveloped personality — the piece of the child that has been hurt by the traumatic experiences he endured — and it is this part that usually confuses parents and makes them feel as if they are living with two different kids rolled into one.

External stressors may trigger internal responses to perceived insults, fear of rejection, and activation of loss issues, which may then lead to external responses such as acting out and having tantrums. The adolescent himself probably won't understand this split in his development with any more clarity than his parents do, so treatment is essential. It must also be understood that this is a developmental anomaly, not intentional behavior.

Parents can help the adolescent develop some understanding of this dynamic by putting words to it after an episode occurs, at a time when he is in a receptive mode. He might not even remember the details of what occurred if he was in a heightened state of dysregulation for an extended period of time. Sometimes his dysregulation might seem to sweep him away, almost automatically. When he recalibrates, it would not be unusual for him to lose a sense of what happened during his earlier hissy fit.

It is imperative to help the adolescent gain insight into the feelings he experienced *prior* to anger and rage. When he can sit calmly and reflect on the issue, he will probably get in touch with such emotions as sadness, fear, hurt, or embarrassment. Most people would prefer to experience a sense of power and control rather than feel passive. Therefore, anger is a better "friend" than sadness in some ways.

However, the adolescent will find that his anger does not serve him well, so it is more productive to help him understand that feeling sad or scared will probably not translate into anything negative. For example, if he fears rejection by a peer or his family, it doesn't necessarily follow that he will never have that friend again or that his family will attempt to get rid of him. Feelings of security will bring about a calming over time, and the adoptive parents can expect a settling down and an integration of the disparate developmental components in the adolescent's life.

Two

IDENTITY FORMATION

Creating One Self from Many Pieces

The question that serves to propel most adolescent behavior is *Who am I?* The quest to find an answer leads adolescents down numerous and diverse paths. They must explore many facets of who they were prior to adolescence, who they are now, who they want to be, and where they are going. To do this, they must look into the past.

History helps frame the journey through which the adolescent will reexamine his life, and it provides the answers to the questions he asks. For an adoptee who may have experienced trauma, grief, and loss, the creation of a new identity will be more complex. He is, after all, attempting to build a new person on what may be a fragmented foundation. He will have to pull together all the pieces from the past so he may decide what to keep, what to discard, and what to use to prove to his parents that he is now different than he used to be. He may feel unique in a negative way, feeling that no one understands him. His level of experimentation may be more complex in that it might involve more dimensions than those experienced by other adolescents.

In an effort to symbolically ditch his childhood identity, an adolescent may move in directions frightening to his parents. He may, in fact, choose to identify with elements he associates either with his fantasies or with the realities of his birth parents' lives. If these fantasies or realities include highly dysfunctional behavior such as criminal activity, the adolescent's new journey might lead to the darker sides of life.

These dynamics are not completely within the conscious awareness of many adolescents, but others clearly realize that they are replicating a piece of their birth family's life patterns. Some even feel that they are intrinsically destined to be just like their dysfunctional birth parents, while others fear they will become like the people who hurt them and caused so much despair in their lives.

The adolescent who is born into a family has a built-in, reality-based perspective of who his parents are, what they represent, and what he needs to separate from. In knowing this, he is more easily able to choose the direction in which he wants to gravitate. His journey is not complicated by wondering about who he would have been had he remained in his birth family.

The birth child's process of identity formulation is framed by two major components: his life with his parents and his life in the world separate from his parents. The adolescent whose history includes adoption has at least one additional component: his actual knowledge or perceptions of his birth parents. In situations involving children who have been in multiple foster families, their representations of who they have been will be much more complex. Twenty foster families prior to adolescence will further complicate the delicate process of answering *Who am I?*

It is safe to assume that a child's life mosaic is composed of all of his experiences. If he has been in many families or in an institutional setting with several staff members, his developing identity will have many more primary contributors than a child who was either born into a family or adopted at birth. His composite identity may include influences that he has since forgotten due to time and numerous parent figures. He may not recall who taught him to tie his shoes, ride his bike, or read.

We learn to predict things about the future as a result of our experiences in the past. If we have had an organized and predictable past, it is likely that we will develop an organized and predictable future. Conversely, if the past has been disjointed, unpredictable, disruptive, or even abusive, the transitions from childhood to adolescence and from adolescence to adulthood will be challenging at the very least, if not tumultuous.

Jillian had lived in fifteen foster homes prior to her adoption at age thirteen. Before entering foster care, she had been subjected to sexual abuse by numerous relatives. She had also moved from place to place with her birth parents, as they were constantly getting evicted. She had no sense of continuity in her life, and her capacity to accurately predict the immediate future was seriously impaired.

She was accustomed to randomly moving in the middle of the night and changing schools frequently. There was no consistency or stability in her birth family, and even though her foster homes were adequate, she failed to develop cause-and-effect thinking, the ability to evaluate social situations, awareness of the impact of her behavior on others, and the sense of being able to know how others would relate to her. In addition, she did not have an internalized set of values by which she could judge herself and others. Basically, she was not developmentally an adolescent.

Jillian looked like an adolescent and talked like an adolescent, but she was a little girl internally. As a result, her peer relationships were poor. At first glance, her friends saw an adolescent, but soon afterward, they realized she was different. They shied away from her, and she never quite figured out why she was routinely abandoned by her friends. When her parents realized that she was developmentally delayed, they began to parent her in a more developmentally appropriate manner. By going back in time, so to speak, they helped her pick up the pieces she missed.

When adolescents such as Jillian have deficits in their social perceptions, they are almost always in a state of high alert—what professionals call hypervigilance. *Who's on first? Who's on second? Who's in the outfield?* They are so consumed with attempting to manage their lives that they end up failing to do so. Imagine what would happen if a person riding a bike began to concentrate on exactly what he was doing, detail by detail, every minute of his ride. *Pedal with the left foot. Pedal with the right foot. Here comes a hill. Grab a gear.* He would undoubtedly fall off in an overwhelmed heap.

When you try to micromanage an activity that requires simultane-ously coordinated actions, you will not be successful. Most of us have social interactions that involve a lot of automatic components. In conversations, we don't think about what to say, how to say it, when to say it. Most social interactions are effective when they are integrated, flowing, and uncalculated. Adolescents who cannot manage automatic thinking and performing will have many social challenges, and their identity-seeking activities will probably be convoluted.

The child who is adopted in adolescence has numerous developmental tasks to accomplish. Oddly enough, two of these tasks seem to be polar opposites: attachment and separation.

ATTACHMENT

The adolescent who is moving into a new family must, on some level, enter into an attachment relationship with his parents. If he has had typical attachments in the past, this new bond may simply occur with little fanfare. Once someone has mastered the attachment process at an early age, he duplicates it repeatedly throughout his life. In this case, he should be able to get close to his parents and then begin to separate and individuate at a later time.

If the adolescent has had attachment difficulties, his connection to his new family may involve a lot of work. His parents must be very focused to facilitate the attachment process. (You can read more about this in chapter 4.) Once the connection takes hold, he will likely want to cling to his new family at a time of life when many of his peers are contemplating leaving theirs.

The adolescent's friends may think his level of enjoyment with his family is unusual—and it might be for the typically developing adolescent. But for an adolescent who has never had a family, the adoptive experience signifies something of monumental importance. He finally has what most other kids have had for a long time.

Tim was adopted at fourteen by a single father, and he was quite excited about this because he had never had a dad. He took great pleasure in talking about his new parent—so much so that his high school teacher said she had never heard anyone talk about a parent in such glowing terms.

On the day that Tim was due to leave for a week of basketball camp, his dad drove him to school. As Tim was getting out of the car, he gave his dad a hug and kiss goodbye—in the parking lot, in front of his friends. Another parent jumped out of his truck and asked Tim's father, "How do you get a hug and a kiss when I can't even get a civil handshake?" It was clear that Tim was engaging in the process of building an attachment with his dad.

Parents should be pleased when they see connections being made, even if they consider them unusual for an adolescent. It *is* unusual, but not for a kid who has not had permanent family connections earlier in life. This is where developmental parenting can help. If your adolescent seems to be immature when compared to other kids his age, he probably is, but this should be seen more as a strength than a liability. If he is willing and able to give and receive affection, his overall adjustment will probably be positive. Parents should think of attachment/connection first and other adolescent tasks later.

Some parents are concerned when their adolescent doesn't show interest in doing what other kids are doing, such as driving and dating. If an adolescent doesn't seem to be interested in these things, he probably has a reason for not wanting to do what everyone else is so excited about. He may know, on some level, that he isn't ready to get behind the wheel of a car or to be alone with a date. This kind of adolescent will want to be more involved with family activities than one might expect, and his wishes should be met with a high level of acceptance in an effort to further secure the connection. After all, a solid connection is what the parents were hoping for when they decided to adopt an older child.

Adolescents often seek to attach to people and things, but they're not always looking to attach to their parents. They frequently pursue connections to other adults, new friends, boyfriends, girlfriends, and activities. Attachment and adolescence are compatible, to the point where parents sometimes feel that their kids over-attach to peers and things. Not all attachment behavior is a component of the separation process, but some may well be.

The adolescent adoptee will likely be aware of what he needs to do, but he may not know how to go about it with his new family. If he had adequate attachments early in life, the process with the new family may develop with little difficulty. However, it is unlikely that the adolescent who is available for adoption has had a typical developmental process. We need to remember that almost all of the children and adolescents in the system have had multiple traumas in their lives. If the traumas occurred early on, their development will have been dramatically compromised.

Parents should remember that this fact applies to children and adolescents adopted from other countries, as well. There is a tendency to think that children from other parts of the world do not have the kinds of challenges faced by children in the U.S. foster care system, but that is rarely the case.

SEPARATION

As I mentioned in chapter 1, while the primary task for the child adopted during adolescence is to connect to his new family, he still needs to separate from someone on some level. The "who" may be variable, as his internal sense of who he is may be cloudy— muddied by many placements, complicated by memories or fantasies of his birth family, and confused by mixed loyalties to those caregivers who preceded his adoptive family. If he actively identifies with prior important people in his life, he may feel as if he is being disloyal to his new family. If he does not engage in separation activities, he may feel immature. There is not a clear and simple explanation of how this process occurs since it varies from individual to individual.

Parents should attempt to understand the complex nature of what their adolescent is trying to manage. He doesn't address his developmental processes in a cognitive manner and may, in fact, not even be aware of what is going on. His attempts to integrate the various dimensions of his personality are carried out without much direct thought but rather by behavioral demonstration.

Anthony, adopted at fourteen, knew that his parents placed particular emphasis on the importance of education. One morning during breakfast, he began talking about how much he hated school, how much it sucked, and how he didn't want to go. He had gone through this routine on numerous occasions, but he always made it to school. On this particular morning, his mother had had enough and angrily responded to Anthony, "Just don't go to school then. You'll never get ahead in life, you won't get a job, and you'll probably end up homeless." Anthony then countered, "You never have any confidence in me! You think I'm a loser, just like my birth family is losers!"

His mother suddenly realized what had just transpired. Anthony had ranted about school before because he knew it would push his mother's buttons, but he never managed to get a rise out of her, even though that was precisely what he tried to do. When he made his proclamations about school, he was, in some way, enacting a separation moment. He was well aware of how important education was to his mom, and by dissing it, he demonstrated that he was different from his parents.

When an adolescent talks in extremely negative terms about the things his family values, his parents must consider whether he actually means what he said or if his posturing is simply serving to further his separation process. To determine this, an intense proclamation should be responded to in a way that causes the adolescent to think about what he said and about how his parent reacted.

A better, more thought-provoking reply to Anthony's "School sucks" declaration might have been, "Oh, I didn't know you hated school so much. If it's that horrible, I'll help you get a work permit when you're legally able to quit and get a job. A lot of people don't finish school, and that makes it harder to find decent employment. But you have such a good personality, I'm sure you'll find something to do."

Even if Anthony's mother does not believe such a statement, it just might have some basis in truth. If his personality and work ethic are good, he probably **would** be able to find some sort of job. By joining Anthony's intention, his mother likely causes him to wonder what happened to her education obsession. This, in turn, deflects his need to defend his hatred of school. He is then free to entertain a thought such as, *I don't really want to quit school and leave all my friends and get some dumb job. I want to play basketball, not go to work just yet.* Although he may not say these words to his mother at the time of their altercation, his thought process can flow in a different direction when he no longer feels attacked.

Although easily influenced by others, the adolescent may be more receptive to parental input if he does not feel that his parents are attempting to control him. And let's be realistic here: Most people do not want to feel controlled. Instead, the primary role of parents is to help shape the kind of person their child will become, not try to manipulate him into their vision of who he should be.

Parents who adopt an adolescent may feel they need to play catch-up — essentially trying to go back in time and undo the past. This is not in the best interest of the child, who may feel that everything he has become up to that point is being discounted. Instead, the parents must assess the new family member's developmental process to determine how best to parent him. Is his development delayed? If so, how much so? How much of what has developed in the child is productive? How much is dysfunctional? What information about his progress — or lack thereof — do they think they need to share with him? How receptive is the adolescent of their role as parents? How can they introduce some of their values without seeming to negate his? How does the adolescent see and define himself?

Patience is needed — a lot of patience. Remember, the adolescent is a work in progress, and if he is to accept what his parents have to contribute to his identity, the messages must be sender-genuine and receiver-friendly.

Many individuals who are adopted during adolescence are eager to join the family. They may, in fact, immediately act as if they have been part of the family for a long time — demonstrating an interest in what the family does, embracing what the family values, and trying on new behavior consistent with the family's lifestyle. Conversely, other adolescents decide to remain loyal to their early cultures.

It is safe to say that most of the children available for adoption were born into abusive or neglectful families. If the adopted adolescent chooses to use his birth family's blueprint as his point of reference for identity formation, he and the adoptive family may be in for serious problems. The parents will need to continue their attempts to be included in his life and present their way of living in a nonintrusive manner. Any attempt to force a new life on him will be met with resistance and, perhaps, outright defiance and hostility. In any case, an all-out attack on the birth family will prevent the acceptance and internalization of the new family's values.

That is not to say that parent and child should not engage in frank and open discussions about the realities of the child's birth family, but facts — not emotions — should be the centerpiece of these conversations. When determining how to handle such situations, parents should remind themselves of the forbidden-fruit dynamics. The adolescent will be more likely to accept something new if he doesn't feel that doing so requires him to relinquish everything he feels he has become.

Identities are not static during adolescence; on the contrary, they are dynamic and fluid. Therefore, parents should attempt to encourage the adolescent to integrate the new family's input with his existing personality content. This could be a complex process because it is likely that the child who is adopted in adolescence has identity components from a variety of sources, such as birth family, foster families, social workers, and therapists.

To help meet this challenge, parents must affect a role that is demonstrative as opposed to dictatorial. Instead of berating the adolescent with constant tutorial comments, they should simply let life show him what his new home and family are like. If he likes what he sees, he may be tempted to incorporate these elements as part of himself.

If the adolescent is consumed by loyalty to his birth family or if he assumes his path is destined to mimic the life he was born into, he may attempt to pursue a search for or a reunion with a member of his birth family. Whether or not that is actually possible, his desire to do so may need to be addressed and explored.

SEARCH AND REUNION

Many adoptees think about looking for their birth families or even meeting with them. When dealing with this issue, several factors must be taken into account.

For those adopted in infancy as the result of an adoption plan made by the birth parents, search and reunion may already have been discussed to some degree by all parties involved. This isn't much of an issue in an open adoption, since some contact has probably been made prior to adolescence. If that's the case, the adolescent may already have incorporated birth-family components into his developing identity.

Children and adolescents who were involuntarily removed from their birth families due to abuse or neglect may still want to have contact with them. This may or may not be legally possible, since any contact at all may not be safe. However, this does not negate the fact that the adolescent may want to retain some of what he associates with his birth family.

The adoptive parents should provide all available historical information to help the adolescent remain grounded in reality, even though hope and fantasy may lead him to deny many of the reasons he was removed. It is often helpful for this information to be in written form gleaned from agency records, providing more credibility for the adolescent than simply hearing about it from his adoptive parents.

Adolescents adopted from other countries will most likely have the same kinds of interests in their birth families or in siblings who may have been left behind. Some adoptive families who engage in intercountry adoptions think that birth-family issues will not arise, but even though the likelihood of a resurfacing birth family is remote, the child's fantasies of his birth family or of reunion may still exist. These thoughts and feelings know no geographic boundaries. They are part of identity development and, as such, may increase during adolescence.

Ultimately, identity formation is the compilation of all the individual's life experiences. Adoptive parents must remember that the adoptee's final blueprint of self is probably comprised of multiple layers. In the late stages of identity formation, the individual will integrate all of the blueprints that have been part of his life. Those who have endured a complicated journey marked by a diversity of situations — such as multiple placements or institutional care prior to adoption — will need more time to reach their final definition of self. In fact, they may not accomplish the task of identity formation until they are in their midtwenties. The final blueprint will be the one that defines the individual and answers the question *Who am I?*

THREE

LOSS OF THE BIRTH FAMILY

Exploring Issues of Abandonment and Removal

Adoptees have one essential factor in common: Instead of living with their birth families, they are being raised by parents who adopted them. Some of them might have been adopted in infancy, but these days, the vast majority is adopted well into childhood or adolescence. Nearly all children available for adoption have been exposed to neglect, physical abuse, sexual abuse, or abandonment. Of those adopted from other countries, most have lived in institutions. Sadly, the level of care in such facilities is woefully inadequate at best and abusive or neglectful at worst.

While many people think of adoption as a joyful experience—and it very well may be for all concerned—no adoption can occur without a sense of loss. Every adopted child experiences the loss of his birth relatives, and this emotion often gets pushed aside and overlooked during the adoption process. The adoption agency is delighted to have found a family for a waiting child; the adoptive parents are excited about bringing their child home; other family members are thrilled to have a new grandchild or cousin. Although the adopted child may be happy to be part of this family, the feeling may be bittersweet due to a paradox of emotions: *My new parents are great. Why did my birth mom give me up? I think my new big brother is really cool. What happened to my little sister when social services took her away?* No one can be adopted unless and until he has lost something very important: the family he was born to.

The adopted adolescent is almost psychologically mandated to wonder why his birth parents did not keep him or why they caused him so much harm that he had to be removed. His questions may be endless, yet they may remain unanswered. In fact, there may be no acceptable response for the person who feels rejected.

How would it be possible to come up with even remotely satisfactory answers to such questions as, *Why did they beat me all the time? Why didn't they feed me? Why did my mom choose her loser boyfriend over me? How could my parents just get rid of me? Why did they want drugs and not me? They said they loved me, but is dumping me the way to show it? Why didn't anyone else in the family want me? Why didn't that last foster home keep me?* The list could go on and on, and if by chance there are viable answers that make sense to someone, they may not satisfy the adoptee.

The truth may not provide comfort for the child or adolescent experiencing a sense of loss, even if the quality of the relationship was damaging. Abusive relationships are powerful and energy charged, and the victim may develop a trauma bond with the person who hurt him. As a result, it is not safe to assume that losing a terrible person in one's life is solely a relief.

By the time he reached the age of fifteen, Tyler had been in fourteen foster homes. He was removed from his mother when he was about a year old, placed in foster care for a little more than a year, and then reunited with his mom when she completed her case plan. She had been drug-free for nine months, and she seemed ready for Tyler's return.

Within a few months, however, her former boyfriend reappeared on the scene, and their lifestyle of drug use, chaos, and violence started once again. Tyler was often left alone and locked in his room for hours — sometimes days — at a time. Because so few people in the apartment complex even knew that Tyler had returned, no one suspected that he was being neglected.

For about five months, Tyler's mom kept her appointments with the social worker assigned to the case, and most things appeared to be in order. But when Tyler was seen by a physician for a persistent rash and it was noted that he had lost a lot of weight since his last visit, Tyler was removed once again and placed in a different foster home. In just two and a half years of life, he had experienced four moves.

Fast-forward thirteen years and twelve more foster homes. By the time Tyler was finally placed for adoption, the trauma he had endured had taken its toll.

He felt betrayed by his birth mother, who continued to have visits with him for several years before her parental rights were terminated. He felt sad about losing her, angry that she caused him so much discomfort, ashamed that he had been taken away from her, glad that he was finally adopted and could stop moving around, and confused about why his adoptive parents appeared to love him so much when his birth mom didn't even care enough about him to get her life together. This smorgasbord of feelings left him almost immobilized at times, and at other times he was full of rage and anger. Because his parents had been well prepared for these issues and were able to meet many of his needs, his adjustment improved. He eventually settled in and began to feel like a part of his family.

Adolescents whose lives began in another country have the same kinds of questions as do children who have been in foster care. They wonder, *Why did my parents put me in the orphanage? How could any mother just leave her baby on a train? Why didn't anyone in my country want me? Will I ever see my birth mom again? How can I talk to my sister and grandpa now that I've forgotten how to speak Russian? Does everyone know I'm adopted because I'm brown and my family is white? Why do my parents keep talking about Guatemala? I don't even remember living in that place. Why does everyone think I'm Chinese when I was born in Korea?* Again, the list could go on forever, and it's unlikely that the questions could be answered to the adoptee's satisfaction.

Olga was adopted from Russia when she was eleven years old. She had lived with her dysfunctional alcoholic family until she was four, at which time she was found wandering the streets of Moscow — dirty, hungry, lonely, and scared. The police were able to track down her parents, who were so consumed by their alcoholism that they immediately placed her in an orphanage. She remained there until she was adopted by an American family seven years later.

Four years of maltreatment and seven years of institutional care had created a human disaster, and Olga's adoptive parents were utterly unprepared to deal with a traumatized preadolescent. She was alternately angry and withdrawn. She was furious that her birth parents never came to the orphanage to get her, and she missed her birth siblings, whose whereabouts could never be determined. There was little available information about her life or that of her birth family, and that served to further enrage her.

Olga fantasized about returning to her family in Russia, and she demonstrated little interest in her adoptive family and their other children. She could not — or would not — verbalize any feelings of loss, shame, or rejection. Anger seemed to mask everything, and Olga's parents began to think about having her removed from the family. The negative impact she imposed seemed to create the same kind of trauma she had experienced earlier in life.

Had the family been prepared through pre-adoptive training, they might have been able to weather the torment they were enduring. Instead, they became unreceptive to learning how to live with Olga and help heal the deep psychological wounds that plagued her.

Deborah Silverstein, MSW, and Sharon Kaplan Roszia, MS, have done extensive research in the adoption arena.[1] Their work regarding the seven core issues of adoption offers insight for both parents and professionals about the issues present for most, if not all, adoptees. They offer valuable information on the types of behavior to expect, helping parents better understand the internal dynamics of their adopted child. These experts have generously and enthusiastically given me their permission and blessings to reproduce their crucial work.

ADOPTEES AND THE SEVEN CORE ISSUES
OF ADOPTION®

Suza was four when she was finally adopted, and she had been in and out of foster care for most of those four years. Nathan and Kelly were overjoyed at her arrival, but they couldn't understand her frequent mood shifts and crying jags. Sometimes she just sat and stared into space. Her new parents thought she should be happy, as they were, with their new family.

Adoption can lead to both great joy and tremendous pain. While Suza's adoption and her reaction to it are unique, she and all other adopted persons experience seven core issues related to their adoption. These fundamental issues are loss, rejection, guilt/shame, grief, identity, intimacy/relationships, and control/gains. Regardless of the circumstances of an adoption—infant, older child, international—children are affected by loss, which is the cornerstone of every adoption. Losses related to adoption are lifelong, life-altering, and intergenerational. These losses and how they are handled set the parameters within which an adopted child's life is played out. The losses intermingle with day-to-day attitudes, biases, and perspectives as they unfold alongside the child's development. Adopted children vary in their response to these losses based on temperament, personality style, gender, subsequent experiences, and other factors, such as medical conditions and intellectual functioning.

The presence of these issues does not indicate that the adopted child or the institution of adoption is abnormal; instead, these are the expected issues that evolve logically out of the nature of adoption itself. It is not the authors' intent to question adoption but rather to challenge some adoption-related assumptions, specifically the persistent notion that being adopted is no different than growing up in the family of origin and that children have only happy feelings about their adoption.

Discussions of adoption over the years have overlooked the pain and struggles of adopted persons. Identifying and discussing these core issues and helping adopted children integrate them as they grow universalizes and validates their experiences, decreasing feelings of being different and isolated.

Loss

Loss, the first issue, is like the hub of a large wheel. Without loss, there would be no adoption. All adopted individuals have experienced at least one major, life-altering loss before becoming involved in adoption. In adoption, to gain anything, one must first lose the family of origin. This is true even in the most open of adoptions. Adoption transposes adopted persons from one location in the human mosaic into a totally new configuration. It is these losses and the way they are accepted and eventually resolved that set the tone for the lifelong process of adoption.

Adopted persons suffer their first loss at their initial separation from the birth family, when they are young and most vulnerable. Current research validates what adopted individuals have felt for a long time. Awareness of the adoptive status is inevitable. Even if the loss is beyond conscious awareness, recognition, or vocabulary, it affects the adopted person on a very profound level. Any subsequent loss, or even the perceived threat of separation, becomes more formidable for adopted persons than their non-adopted peers. Clearly, then, children who have had multiple placements, have come from other cultures and countries, and have had a series of "transplantations" have compounded losses. Each loss rests on top of the others, sometimes piling up very high.

For adopted persons, loss in adoption is not a single event but rather a series of ongoing losses. Birthdays, Mother's Day, and Father's Day can be experienced as a reminder of both the original loss and the ongoing nature of that loss. There is no end to the losses, no closure. The initial, identifiable loss rests beneath innumerable secondary or sub-losses. For example, losses in adoption can include culture, religion, ethnic and racial connections, medical information, birth history, siblings, birth order, country, language, family traditions, somebody/anybody with a physical resemblance, foster families, neighborhood friends, pets, teachers, therapists, familiar smells and tastes, social workers, the chance to be normal just like friends who are growing up with the families they were born to, and on and on. As children move repeatedly, the list gets longer. Even after the adoption is completed, there are possible additional losses as adoptive families change: moves, deaths, illnesses, other adoptions, and births.

Adopted children frequently remember best the so-called "little" losses, like the smell of the sheets or the way Grandma smiled. Because loss is always a part of adopted children's lives, it is crucial to support their expression of these losses to begin the healing process. For young children, nonverbal expression through art, music, puppets, or play may be most effective. Older children and adults benefit from being encouraged to write down all the losses, from the big ones to those little ones. Making the losses concrete allows for the grief work to begin.

As the saying goes, an ounce of prevention is worth a pound of cure. Whenever possible, families must work to minimize loss for their children by keeping their connection to important people, places, and events. Parents must be assertive in acquiring information about their children's lives before they came into the family. Pictures, videotapes, shreds of old clothes and blankets—things easily overlooked—can provide a link.

Rejection

The second core issue with which adopted persons must wrestle is rejection. Feelings of loss are heightened by keen feelings of rejection. One way individuals, adopted or not, may seek to cope with a loss is to personalize it. This is the *Why me?* question. Adopted persons attempt to decipher what they did or did not do that led to the losses. Young children, due to egocentric thinking (*I did it*), take responsibility for the things that happen to them, including the negatives, such as abandonment, abuse, and neglect. Adopted individuals may become sensitive to the slightest hint of rejection, disapproval, or dismissal, causing them either to avoid situations where they might be rejected or even to provoke rejection in order to prove their own negative self-perceptions.

Adopted persons are seldom able to view their placement into adoption as anything other than total rejection. *Why did she leave me?* is a frequent question, verbalized or kept deep in their psyches. Adopted persons view the placement by birth family as a personal rejection regardless of the circumstances of the placement. Stories of the birth family relinquishing a child to adoption out of love fall on deaf ears. On the other hand, they separate those events from how they feel about their adoptive family. But loving an adoptive family does not take away the pain of those feelings of rejection. Adopted children, even at young ages, grasp the concept that to be "chosen" into an adoptive family, as the story is often told, means first that one had to be "unchosen."

Adopted persons who come from other countries, for example, often ask why an entire country let them go. *Wasn't there anybody in the whole place who wanted me?* is a basic question. Children adopted in the United States wonder why other birth family members didn't come forward to take care of them. Adopted children witness poor families, single parents, young parents, and even ill parents keeping and raising their children. As a result, their con-clusion is often that something about them *personally* caused the adoptive placement. The language of adoption reinforces notions of rejection, such as "an unplanned pregnancy," "a mistake," or "a special-needs child," as do the explanations well-meaning adults give adoptees about why they were placed for adoption. They feel they were unlovable, unwanted, unworthy, or defec-tive. They wonder if they would have been kept if they were better, taller, blonder, less demanding, cuter, and so on. The sealing of records, even for adult adoptees, further perpetuates the feeling of not being worthy, not ever being entitled to receive one's fundamental information. Even if the adoption is open and the child has access to the birth family, the same kind of ques-tions can arise when the birth parents go on to have other children: *Why can they raise that child and not me?*

One way to help adopted children deal with feelings of rejection is to help them sort out the facts about their adoption from their feelings about adoption. Children need support and validation when they express feelings of rejection. For example, when adopted children wonder aloud about not being allowed to stay in the birth family, adoptive parents can say, "I can understand why you might feel that way," instead of yielding to the urge to deny those feelings with the happy adoption story. Parents need to be open and honest in giving age-appropriate information and avoid taking children's comments or questions personally as if the child were rejecting them. This stance gives parents the ability to better support the child's emotional work.

Feelings of fear of rejection can chip away at a person's self-esteem. Good self-esteem is built on having (1) positive role models; (2) a sense of belonging (being in the right place); (3) an awareness of one's unique role in a family, a community, and the world; and (4) a sense of power and control in one's life. Positive role models come from the child's birth family, the adoptive family, and adult adopted persons who have already successfully met the challenges of adoption. A true sense of belonging comes from the adoptive family claiming the child and feeling entitled to parent without dismissing or being in competition with the birth family. Families can help children develop their sense of uniqueness by recognizing, exploring, and encouraging the child's abilities, looks, and special talents, even if they differ greatly from those of the adoptive family. Children feel powerful when they are given real, age-appropriate choices—from what they want to eat to what they wear to who their friends are. Good self-esteem supports the child's progress through the seven lifelong issues.

Many adopted persons, even those adopted as young children, struggle with attachment difficulties. An awareness of loss and rejection may reinforce an adopted person's wariness of close, intimate relationships. Children suffering from various attachment difficulties—due to these previous unresolved losses, experiences, or feelings of rejection—often create further rejection in their adoptive placements. They tend to feel or believe they will be "safer" if they create a distance in their connections to others. Much of their so-called acting-out behavior is aimed at keeping distance. Other adopted children are actually struggling to overcome these tendencies, but the behavior, which once worked in their dysfunctional birth families, is not appropriate in their new families. This, then, is maladaptive attachment behavior. Parental commitment, different from attachment or even love before the attachment becomes secure, is what holds these adoptions together.

Guilt and Shame

A sense of deserving loss and rejection may lead adopted persons to experience accompanying feelings of guilt and shame. They might believe there is something intrinsically wrong with them or their actions that caused the losses to occur. Guilt, the feeling of having committed an offense or of being responsible for some offense, refers to actions or behavior; adopted persons feel guilty for what they did (or didn't do) that caused the adoption. Shame is a painful emotion resulting from an awareness of personal inadequacy, deficiency, or deficit.

For example, children placed as infants might feel that they kicked too much *in utero* or cried too much in the nursery. Children adopted at an older age feel that it was their behavior or misbehavior that caused the previous disruptions and familial loss. They report knowing that they caused the beatings or the sexual abuse. It is often very difficult to dissuade them from these beliefs, in part because of their egocentric thinking and in part because of the message they may have been given by abusive or drug-involved birth parents. In addition, because of the way adoption is often presented to children, especially those who come from the foster-care system, they may feel ashamed of their origins. They come to sense that their parents are "bad" and that, therefore, so are they. They are embarrassed by their adoptive status, often concealing it from peers.

Adoptive families must be sensitive to their children's feelings of guilt and shame. Children need to understand that adults are responsible for what happens, not children. Adults also need to correct messages and misperceptions that children maintain about having caused bad things to happen. Sometimes children believe they have caused events purely by wishing or imagining them. These impressions, too, need to be corrected. Adoptive families must find individuals or information that can portray the birth family as real people—a mixture of good and bad. Children need a full picture of their families of origin so they can identify with more positives than negatives. This is where extended birth-family members can prove to be an invaluable resource.

Grief

Every loss must be grieved. Adoption-related losses are no different. The losses in adoption, however, are sometimes difficult to mourn in a society where adoption is seen as a problem-solving event filled with joy. There are few rites to mark the loss of caretaking parents, lost dreams, or unknown family members. Grief washes over adopted persons in stages or waves, particularly at times of other loss or developmental transitions. It is important that adopted persons understand and can accurately label the feelings of loss, including numbness, sadness, anger, depression, emptiness, or anxiety.

Children frequently do not understand that feelings always change. They fear that they will always feel sad or mad rather than grasping the notion of "grief work." Adoptees in their youth find it difficult to grieve their losses although they are, in many instances, aware of them, even as very young children. Infants can and do grieve. Children, however, often look very different from adults when they grieve, so adults may miss the cues. Children might not visibly demonstrate their feelings; might numb out; might have physical symptoms, such as stomachaches, headaches, or frequent colds; might regress; might have explosive or acting-out behavior; or might isolate and withdraw. Youngsters removed from abusive homes might be expected to feel only relief and gratitude, not grief. Children arriving from other countries might be expected to be excited and happy, not suffering from culture shock and grief. Children who are living in survival mode cannot take the time or energy to work through these losses. Grief can be, at times, a luxury.

Adults frequently block children's expressions of pain or attempt to divert them. Sometimes adults misinterpret an apparent lack of reaction as a lack of true feelings about the loss. In addition, due to the developmental unfolding of cognitive processes, adopted children do not fully appreciate the total impact of their losses until they become old enough to understand what really happened to them. This could take into mid-adolescence or even adulthood. This delayed grief drains resources from the child and might lead to uneven learning, depression, acting out through substance abuse, or aggressive behavior.

Adoptive parents help their children best by allowing them to express their grief openly and by listening carefully and offering comfort and hope. Parents need to create a safe environment for the child to express his whole range of feelings. Parents must use simple, clear language to explain to the child what has happened to him, avoid rushing the grief process, and anticipate that the grief will surface and resurface as the child grows, especially at times of other loss or at anniversaries of various losses. Parents must address the past and give realistic hope for the future.

Identity

Adoption might also threaten an adopted person's sense of identity. Identity is defined by both what one is and is not. Adoptees, born into one family, lose an identity and then "borrow" one from the adopting family. Adopted children frequently wonder who they really are and where they belong. Are they more like their birth family or more like their adoptive family? What have they inherited and what have they acquired? Are they a "bad seed," destined to become just like their birth parents?

Adoption, for some, complicates the development of a complete or integrated sense of self. Adopted persons might experience themselves as incomplete, deficient, or unfinished. Sometimes they state that they lack feelings of well-being, integration, or solidness associated with a fully developed identity. Adopted persons lacking medical, genetic, religious, and historical in: Were they, in fact, merely a mistake, not meant to have been born, an accident? For male adoptees, the problem associated with the development of a full identity might be compounded by the lack of attention from and information about birth fathers. A lack of identity might lead adoptees, particularly in the adolescent years, to seek out ways to create a feeling of belonging. Sometimes they devise extreme measures, joining radical subcultures, running away, becoming pregnant, or totally rejecting the adoptive family.

The task for adoptive parents, then, is to support their children in developing a sense of where they came from and who they are. Here again, accurate and positive information about birth-family history that provides role models and options for the child is crucial. Children need to understand the roles of inheritance, nurturance, and learning in the formation of the self. An awareness of choice is a key ingredient. Adopted children might need additional support and acceptance to explore possibilities in their makeup that might fall outside the makeup of their adoptive parents. For example, a tone-deaf child in a musical adoptive family might have skills as a basketball player that should be encouraged.

Intimacy and Relationships

The multiple ongoing losses in adoption — coupled with feelings of rejection, shame, grief, and confusion regarding identity — may well affect the development and quality of interpersonal relationships and intimacy for adopted persons. Many have reported that they are aware of holding back part of themselves in relationships, always cautious and watchful. Some state that they have never truly felt close to anyone; others report a lifetime of feelings of emptiness that they relate to a longing for the birth mother they might have never seen.

For some adopted children, the placement and subsequent losses may have disrupted early bonding and attachment. In addition, the associated anxiety may have interfered with relationships in the adoptive family, as well. For example, children coming from orphanages and institutions where they have had multiple caretakers and no clear attachment figure may have great difficulty relaxing into their family. They may remain continually anxious and clingy or ambivalent and avoidant. Adoptees' intimacy issues are particularly evident in relationships with the opposite sex and might revolve around questions about conception, biological and genetic concerns, and sexuality. Adoptees, as adults, might find themselves staying in unhealthy relationships or avoiding intimate relationships altogether to avoid potential loss.

It is crucial that adoptive parents move past their children's barriers and create close, secure attachments and relationships with them. These processes may take years and may have to be reworked again and again as children grow, change, and struggle to incorporate the adoption experience into who they are and who they will become.

Control Issues

Adopted persons must come to terms with issues of mastery and control and own the gains they have made through adoption. Adoption alters the course of an adopted person's life. This shift presents additional hurdles in development and may impede emotional growth, feelings of responsibility, and a sense of self-control. Adopted persons are keenly aware that they were not party to the actions and decisions that led up to the adoption. For many, adoption would have been their second choice. They had no control over the loss of their birth family or even in the choice of the adoptive family. The adoption plan proceeded with adults making life-altering choices for them. This unnatural change of course may impinge on the development of their feelings of mastery, accomplishment, achievement, fulfillment, competence, and completion. Adoptees might also lack internalized self-control, leading to a lowered sense of self-responsibility. Adopted persons, then, might view themselves as the "victims" in the adoption process and may seek to perpetuate that unfortunate role.

Adoptive parents must give children age-appropriate choices and responsibilities throughout their development, avoiding power struggles and control battles. It is also important to acknowledge children's feelings about their lack of control over their lives today.

Rituals and ceremonies can help children work through the seven core issues. Rituals can be as simple as lighting a candle to mark an anniversary or as detailed as having an elaborate ceremony to facilitate the letting go of painful memories.

There are many gains to be won as adopted persons work their way through these issues. People who have faced and struggled with difficult issues seem to develop inner resources and become deeper human beings. Adoptees can gain a broader perspective and different outlooks on life and come to know that they can and will survive and even grow from the loss experience.

The experience of adoption can be one of loss, rejection, guilt/shame, grief, diminished identity, thwarted intimacy, and threats to self-control. These seven core issues permeate the lives of adoptees regardless of the circumstances of the adoption. Adoptees may repeatedly do and undo their adoption experiences in both their unconscious minds and their daily lives. Identifying these basic issues can assist them in doing the necessary work to move into the promise and joy of adoption.

It seems to me that if adoptive parents can keep these core issues in mind when they are struggling with the problems of day-to-day living, they may find they have a new perspective—an understanding of the context of what seems like crazy, disconnected behavior. An old adage in the mental-health arena is "All behavior is purposeful and has meaning." This may be difficult for parents to swallow when faced with extremely difficult challenges.

Parenting an adolescent who has had turbulence in his life prior to adoption may require the ability to speak two languages: the adolescent's spoken word and the deeper meaning behind it. I have put together a list of twenty statements that your adolescent might say. Try to match the statement with one or more of the seven core issues we've discussed:

- I didn't make the team.
- I didn't get asked to the dance.
- I didn't get invited to the sleepover.
- She didn't want to go out with me.
- I guess they didn't want me to come to the party.

- I didn't pass my driver's test the first time.
- I didn't wrestle very well at the tournament.
- I didn't make the show choir.
- I didn't get a part in the play.
- The kids thought my outfit was ugly.
- My cell phone is so generic.
- Everyone knows I'm adopted.
- People think that my birth parents didn't want me.
- I don't look like my family.
- Why was I such a bad kid?
- No wonder they got rid of me!
- Even my favorite teams always lose.
- Maybe I'm a loser like some kids say.
- I can't figure out my life like other kids.
- I have a hard time finding a girlfriend.

Many of these statements are typical for adolescents, but for the adopted individual, they are usually compounded by greater intensity and past history. Many circumstances trigger old memories for adolescents, but, as time goes by, the memories may be altered by new experiences. This is a process that happens with all of us, but at least we have the continuity of people in our lives who were there when the event occurred, serving as a reliable source to confirm or correct the memory. The adopted person typically does not have anyone to validate what he thinks he remembers. Consequently, he might frequently feel confused about events he recalls regarding his birth family, the Smith foster home, second grade, the orphanage, and so on. This phenomenon of not having certainty about what happened, about where it happened, and about whether it really happened at all might contribute to the pattern of lying or inventing truth that so many adoptive parents observe.

As my understanding of what is referred to as "primary process lying" has deepened, I have come to believe that such behavior is often due to the losses the adoptee has experienced. Because many adopted adolescents who have experienced trauma are hypervigilant, they are always poised to respond to any question that may be asked of them. Of course, they cannot predict the specific queries that will be posed, so they ready themselves with a mental bank of responses. They grab one almost arbitrarily in reply, which might explain why their answers often do not seem to fit the questions.

Adopted adolescents who have endured early trauma lie differently than typically developing adolescents. The traumatized adolescent lies in an effort to cope with his inner pain, while his less-disturbed peers might use lying as a component of their separation and individuation process.[2]

In their view, any answer is better than "I don't know," especially if it is related to something they *should* know, such as, "Where did you live when you were in fifth grade?" Most people can answer such a question with ease, but many children who have been in foster care do not organize their lives chronologically and may not be clear about specific details. An adolescent who has spent time in an orphanage until the age of ten or eleven may not even have been in a school setting with grades comparable to those in the United States. They may not want to say, "I was in an orphanage," because such an answer opens up a Pandora's box of unpleasant memories, embarrassment, or one or more of the seven core issues discussed.

People often give themselves free rein to ask adoptees and their families questions they wouldn't dream of asking non-adopted persons. In the "normal" arena, they would consider such behavior to be inappropriate and intrusive, yet those rules of courtesy and civility seem to be tossed aside in the case of adoption. Even some professionals do not manage themselves very well when working with adoptive families. It is almost as if the mere fact of adoption makes some people assume they have the right to explore all areas of the adopted individual's life.

Adoptive families may need to intervene to protect their child from rude, interrogating outsiders—whether teachers, counselors, doctors, or the folks next door. Given the losses associated with most adoptions, adoptees should not lose their privacy due to the thoughtlessness of people who have no right to the information they're seeking.

Families need to be prepared to deal with unexpected intrusions into their lives; many families come up with funny and creative responses to ridiculous inquiries.

FOUR

FACING FRUSTRATION

Dealing with Your Child's Challenges

Parents whose adolescents are experiencing difficulties seem to be in perpetual pursuit of a definitive answer to the question *What can I do about this?* Professionals feel they need to respond with cut-and-dried, guaranteed-to-work solutions, but the problem is that they don't exist.

In most cases, there are no absolute fixes for each and every issue that an adolescent presents. When parents believe that a single magical strategy will resolve all psychological or behavioral problems, they tend to rely on that strategy as opposed to relying on the relationship with their child. In my practice, I find that not offering parents a specific solution opens up the door for working together to think of things that might help remedy the difficulty.

Most behavior will not change simply because some sort of intervention takes place. Teachers often direct parents to "make Jimmy do his homework." The parents then ask me how to accomplish this, and I always reply, "I wish I knew!" The truth is that this particular problem is not one that parents can control. As mentioned earlier in this book, parents can do very few things to regulate their adolescent's behavior. They can influence, guide, and model, but they probably cannot make the child do his homework. Perhaps some sort of cooperative effort might address specific difficulties, but attempts at *making* another person do just about anything— particularly in adolescence—are bound to fail.

Todd hated school and just about everything else in life except video games. When his parents dragged him in to see me, he was already well into his second year of seventh grade and failing yet again. His terrible grades were not due to a lack of understanding of the subject matter of his classes — he simply didn't engage at all. He'd put forth a little effort in gym, but that was about it. His parents were furious with him, and he had little or nothing to say to them. They had exhausted themselves.

When they told me that Todd was grounded and had been since the beginning of his first round of seventh grade, I was unconvinced. That meant a total of sixteen months! Amazed that a kid could go that long under "lockup," I asked Todd's parents what it meant to be grounded in their family. They replied that it included no television, no phone calls, and no visiting friends or having them over. If he completed his chores, he was allowed to play video games once a week. During the week, he had to spend at least one hour at the kitchen table doing — which translated to staring at — his homework. He always cooperated by sitting down at the table, but he never did a single bit of schoolwork. Occasionally, he would scribble a few words on a page, but it never had anything to do with the tasks at hand. His grades remained consistent — all Fs. Oh, that's not quite right — he did get a C in gym.

Todd's parents focused all their energy on their son and his education. Over time, it became the driving force in their lives. They were highly committed to "breaking" Todd, and he seemed just as passionate about watching his parents drive themselves crazy as a result of their singular obsession with school.

I decided to meet with Todd's parents privately in an effort to get them to think about other approaches to this problem. They immediately told me that they had seen several other therapists who also suggested that they give up on the grounding and try something else. They then assured me that they were not going to make any changes until Todd became productive in school. They firmly believed that eliminating the grounding meant that Todd had won, and they were not about to let that happen.

When I asked them whether or not they thought their method was working, they became extremely angry with me. I rarely get involved in micromanaging what parents do to handle their adolescent's difficulties, but this situation seemed to require a more direct intervention by me.

I reviewed Todd's pre-adoptive history and discovered that he had been subjected to profound neglect. His birth mother kept him locked in a closet for up to ten hours a day. When she brought him food, he was forced to eat it on the closet floor. He was not allowed to use the bathroom, so the floor served that purpose as well.

To make matters even worse, Todd was not alone in the closet. He was usually with his siblings — sometimes two, sometimes three other children shared the tiny space — all of whom ate off the floor, eliminated on the floor, and otherwise just sat there. Sadly, this afforded Todd the ideal opportunity to perfect his sit-and-do-nothing skills, which he put into play so patiently at his homework table.

Once I knew more about Todd's background, I had new ammo for his parents. I reviewed his history with them and asked a few pertinent questions. "Do you think that after staying in a closet for most of his first five years of life that Todd considered it a horrible experience to sit in his comfortable house for sixteen months? Do you think that being grounded is something new and corrective for him?"

While there were no signs of their mellowing, I began to see that they were starting to reframe their perceptions. I pointed out that grounding Todd and having him sit at the table night after night was similar to what he had experienced in his birth home. Although his parents' mandates were not cruel or abusive, they were essentially useless. Todd had learned to adapt to the limits of a closet, and he could simply go on automatic pilot while he faced his new restrictions. No wonder none of it seemed to bother him. It was, in fact, so much easier to tolerate than the closet in which he'd resided, so he perceived it as underkill.

I'm not sure what it was that finally made sense for Todd's parents, but they decided to let go — or at least pretend to. They told their son, "We're tired of watching you do nothing, so we're giving up. If you want to be in seventh grade for a third time, or even a fourth or fifth time, go ahead and keep vegging out."

They gradually lifted the grounding, but since Todd had been out of circulation for so long, it took forever for him to reconnect with friends and social activities. Even though I'd love to say he changed his ways and became an excellent scholar, that wasn't the case. He did, however, try to do more in school. Unfortunately, he was so far behind that the school had to modify the curriculum for him, provide some academic accommodations, and push him along a bit. He did not actually pass seventh grade, but the school administrators made the decision to assign him to eighth grade anyway. No one had ever failed seventh grade *twice*, and they had no desire to establish a precedent.

As parents watch their adolescent struggle with his journey into adulthood, they often feel helpless, frustrated, excited, powerless, impotent, furious, hopeful, sad, lonely, isolated, encouraged, depressed, and distraught — and that's merely a sampling of their emotions. Just reading through the list can be overwhelming! Many of these negative feelings contribute to the end-of-my-rope syndrome, while positive ones may lead to a high that can easily be dashed by the adolescent's next move. In many ways, the parents are experiencing feelings parallel to those of the adolescent: the ups and downs of mood changes. No wonder so many parents and adolescents seem to be in a perpetual control battle — they're both facing what appears to be a no-win situation.

Issues of control are common in adolescence. When someone feels as if he is losing control, he experiences an automatic surge to grasp at anything that may reestablish equilibrium because this is a condition that provides a sense of well-being. The problem with unilateral equilibrium is that the other side is not sharing the balance; in fact, the parents' comfort may be aggravating to the adolescent. This aggravation may lead to yet another adolescent-initiated attempt at reestablishing his own equilibrium at the expense of the parents' comfort.

Adolescents feel that they have either everything to lose or nothing to lose. The brain at this stage of life seems to operate in polarities, and parents are often faced with issues that are blown completely out of proportion. For example, a lost cell phone translates to, "My life is over because no one will be able to talk to me and I'll lose all of my friends!" Conversely, important things—such as failing a class when only three weeks are left to pull the grade up—aren't even considered by the adolescent. Parents frequently feel that they either are extinguishing a fire, as with the cell-phone loss, or need an incendiary device to get the kid to talk with his teachers to find out what he can do to pass.

Kenyon had been texting for hours. His parents grew increasingly frustrated because they knew he had a lot of homework to do. The longer he sat in the living room with his ever-present companion, his cell phone, the angrier his parents became. They began threatening to turn his phone off or take it away completely.

Because Kenyon's phone represented his connection to all of his friends—his lifeline, so to speak—the loss of it represented the loss of friends, a social network, and his life as he had grown to know it. Because he had joined his family only a year earlier, his friendships were new. He was terrified that he might lose them, just as he had lost so many other connections due to his journey through several foster placements.

His parents feared that he would win this battle if they didn't take his phone away. Kenyon believed that if they did take the phone, he had nothing else to lose. In his mind, going off on them couldn't possibly make the situation any worse. I'm sure you can write the rest of the story with a variety of endings, all of them marked by negative outcomes.

This kind of escalating situation is not productive for anyone. If Kenyon's parents take the phone, what have they won? Do they really expect him to retreat quietly to his room and complete his homework? If he continues communicating with his friends and neglecting his assignments, what have his parents lost? In this situation, Kenyon's schoolwork is *his* to do or not do. The consequences of his behavior are his alone, and his parents' inflamed interaction does nothing to strengthen family relationships or get the homework done.

Parents must think about how they can build and maintain connections with their child. If the adoption took place during adolescence, it is even more important to work on the *building*. If the adoption took place earlier, the focus must be on the *maintaining*.

Kenyon's parents might have had a more productive evening with him had they asked him to stop texting for a while so that they could do something together as a family. They might even have asked him to be ready to go with them to the mall within half an hour. When stuck in a no-win situation, parents will feel better if they do something with the adolescent that brings about a meaningful, connective interaction instead of creating a disconnection that leaves everyone involved feeling angry.

Dr. Foster Cline and Jim Fay, authors of *Parenting with Love and Logic*,[1] offer three basic, valuable concepts. I often say that if parents could do these three things with regularity, they would find greater satisfaction and success in their efforts to parent and bring about the results they desire. Those concepts are:

- Avoid control battles at all costs.
- Win the ones you take on.
- Pick and choose your battles carefully.

Most control battles are just that—battles for control and control alone. In most instances, the issues that appear to cause angst for parents and adolescents are nothing more than surface triggers. The *real* issue in the argument between Kenyon and his parents was the fact that his mom and dad were afraid he was going to fail a class. When people fear something, they tend to exaggerate the answer to the question "What is the worst thing that will happen in this situation?" Instead of thinking that he might fail one class, they were probably thinking of infinitely worse outcomes, such as:

- *You'll never graduate from high school.*
- *You'll never get into college.*
- *You'll never be able to get a decent job.*
- *What will Grandma think about us if you fail?*
- *You'll probably get fired from your first job because you won't listen to what your boss says.*

- *You might end up in jail for not obeying the law.*
- *I don't want to have to support you forever.*

These thoughts all represent the worst scenarios that, in all likelihood, would *not* happen. In reality, the most negative result of a single failed high school class would be the need to retake it or get an F, which wouldn't have much bearing on the future. When parents shift into panic mode, it parallels adolescent apathy and almost always causes a *decrease* in the adolescent's interest in doing what the parents want. The parents end up initiating the response they want the least because their alarm enhances adolescent denial. Let's see what this process looks like.

> Dad: "Kenyon, I think you should stop texting so you can get your homework done. You're going to fail if you don't do the makeup work."
>
> Kenyon: "Don't worry about it. I'll do it later tonight or in study hall tomorrow."
>
> Mom: "You always put everything off until the last minute. Why don't you get it done and then talk to your friends?"
>
> Kenyon: "I'm talking to them now, and I don't want to stop."
>
> Mom: "If you don't stop right now, I'm going to take your phone away for a week."
>
> Kenyon: "If you do that, I won't do any work at all. My friends are all I care about. School is stupid, and I hate my teacher. She's an idiot."
>
> Dad: "You need to respect your teachers, and you need to respect us. As parents, your mom and I want you to listen to us."
>
> Kenyon: "You're not my real parents anyway! I'll do what I want; it's my life."
>
> Dad: "We're the only parents you have, Kenyon! And it's not your life—yet. When you're eighteen, you can do what you want."
>
> Kenyon: "I'm not gonna fail—just wait and see. And if I do fail, it doesn't even matter. Who needs algebra, anyway?"
>
> Mom: "You might not even graduate. Then what will you do?"
>
> Kenyon: "I'll be fine. Don't worry about me. If I don't graduate, so what? I can always get my GED."

As the parents increase the severity of what they say might happen, Kenyon increases his minimizing statements. It is counterproductive to continue to dramatize what *could* happen because it almost forces the other person to point out why those things *won't* happen. This kind of dance will almost always end with the partners further apart than they were at the beginning of the interaction.

The texting battle probably could have been avoided if Kenyon's parents remembered that they cannot win any battles that have to do with education. School is clearly the student's job, and he is ultimately the only person who can control how much studying he does, what assignments he completes, and when he turns them in — if at all. The third point made by Cline and Fay is to pick and choose battles carefully. This means that parents must not engage in battles they cannot win and must therefore be very selective about the confrontations they opt to take on.

It is important for parents to communicate with their adolescents — a lot. The more active the communication, the greater the likelihood that it will be well received. They must also learn to recognize when the adolescent is in receptive mode. If he's not, there is probably no point in saying anything.

Varying the message helps to ensure that it will be received as it was intended. Too often, parents repeat again and again the point they're trying to make. After an adolescent has heard the same message in the same way — maybe even in precisely the same words — his ears close and his brain shuts down.

Sometimes parents are afraid to voice their thoughts and opinions for fear of rejection or a highly fueled response from their child. Adolescents know when their parents are walking on eggshells, and they typically don't respect it. On one hand, they are glad they are not being confronted, but at the same time, they perceive weakness. If the parent is seen as weak, trust is diminished, and because trust is a critical component of any relationship, parents absolutely must keep it at the center of their interactions with the adolescent.

Most parents know when they are blocking effective communication with their child. In fact, many of them have vowed not to say the kinds of things their parents said to them when they were the same age. However, when faced with feeling that they are on the losing side of an argument, inflammatory words fly right out of their mouths with little thought.

Things that parents say prompt a variety of responses and thoughts in the adolescent. Parental pronouncements are also indicative of what they are actually feeling. Much of what is said by both parents and adolescents looks and sounds like anger, but anger is most often *not* a primary feeling. It typically masks fear, sadness, or other feelings of vulnerability. People avoid emotions that leave them feeling vulnerable, preferring instead to have some sort of strength or power. This is true for adolescents and parents alike, so it is understandable that, in the face of frustration and powerlessness, most people resort to language and posturing reflective of their attempts to establish a sense of control.

When a kid says outrageous things, parents must be able to decipher the meaning behind the language. Conversely, it is unlikely the adolescent will have the capacity to think about what his parents are actually feeling when they make angry statements: "You've made our lives miserable." "I don't know what we were thinking when we decided to adopt an older child." He may believe that the adults truly mean what they say, and he may hang on to the words long after the skirmish is over. It is important for the parent to address an angry exchange in an effort to correct any misperceptions that the adolescent may have and to model how to make amends. Most things can be corrected retroactively, but the parent will undoubtedly have to take the lead. Decoding what both parties have said in the heat of the moment will help the adolescent process the interaction and understand what actually transpired.

Marcus had become very hostile and began to exhibit what looked like anger. He was constantly mad at everyone in his family. At the age of seventeen, he had been with his family for about seven years. For the most part, he had forged solid connections with his parents and siblings.

His parents could not identify what triggered his episodes of anger, but they were fairly certain that another feeling preceded the explosions they saw. They had brought Marcus to therapy, and even though he protested participating, he ultimately engaged rather comfortably. His original protests allowed him to appear disagreeable since going to therapy just didn't seem like something any honorable adolescent should do.

Early in treatment, Marcus seemed to be open. When asked what feelings come before anger, he quickly answered, "Embarrassment and fear." It is my guess that this response was accurate. This revelation helped his parents understand what kinds of situations might be problematic for their son, and after he was able to accurately define what prompted him to demonstrate anger, he was more able to engage in self-regulation when embarrassed or scared.

When parents understand the underlying issues, they are better able to put some words on the adolescent's behavior that may help prevent an explosive episode, or at least clean it up down the road.

Parents, too, mask their vulnerable feelings with anger, particularly when they feel as if the adolescent is attacking them. We often tell parents that their anger is like vitamins for the adolescent's expression of anger. In other words, the parents' anger is bound to bring about an angry response from the adolescent. On the other hand, parental calmness is likely to result in a more regulated response from the adolescent.

Certainly, angry encounters will exist in any intimate relationship system. Minimizing their numbers and their intensity is desirable, and that should be the goal of parents whose adolescents frequently challenge them.

An agitated individual often sets the tone for the overall social environment, feeling somewhat satisfied when others become as out of sorts as he is. Some parents attribute much intentionality to their adolescent's process of transferring his anger and tension to them. Although some of the behavior is done on purpose, as mentioned earlier, it is unlikely the adolescent is aware of his internal need to have others as upset as he is.

Parents can get an idea of how their adolescent feels much of the time by monitoring their own feelings. How they feel when they are highly agitated is probably how their child feels most of the time. This insight might allow them to be calmer when facing issues that seem to be emotionally overwhelming. When parents set a placid tone in the family, everyone involved may reach a level of emotional attunement that is more regulated and less reactive. When this occurs, even the adolescent may come to appreciate the levelness of his emotional state.

TRANSFER OF FEELINGS

The transfer of feelings from one person to another is common in almost all social situations. At one time or another, you've probably been in the presence of a couple having a heated disagreement in public. If they're in close prox-imity to others — even strangers — their hostile feelings impact the sense of well-being of the people around them. If they're part of a small group, every-one may get quiet or begin to have animated, invented conversations, trying anything to diffuse the tension. In any case, emotional pollution occurs, and it is doubtful that an amiable balance will be reestablished.

It is not likely that the arguing couple had the intention of ruining the social atmosphere, even though they probably succeeded in doing so. Similarly, when adolescents negatively impact the family's sense of balance, they probably do not do so with the intention of causing everyone else to be as uncomfortable as they are. It just happens.

Dysregulated feelings — such as agitation, anger, terror, fear, and intense sadness — are more effectively transferred to another than are regulated feel-ings, such as calmness and reflectivity. High-intensity feelings are more con-tagious, more explosive, and more arousing than low-intensity feelings, which means that an angry individual has more impact on his social situation than the situation has on him.

Parents often feel the need to be calm in an effort to remain in control, but their serenity can sometimes drive the dysregulated person into an even higher level of arousal. Conversely, if the parents' arousal level is as intense as that of the adolescent, it's also likely that the situation will escalate. This sounds like a no-win situation, since any engagement from the parent may result in a continuation of the acting-out episode. On some level, conscious or unconscious, the adolescent seems to have a need for everyone to be as emotionally aroused as he is. This need drives his behavior toward attaining that goal.

Adolescents are not alone in their need for affect — or social — synchronicity. It is, in fact, something most people seek. When a person tells a joke, he wants others to find it as funny as he thinks it is. When someone dislikes another person, he seeks support for his perspective and does not want to hear, "Oh, really? I've always liked her and never thought of her as bossy." When someone loves the food at a particular restaurant, he would like those around him to agree that the place serves the best pizza in town.

With this dynamic in mind, a parent on the verge of a negative interaction with an adolescent should seek to avoid engagement because withdrawing from the encounter might be the only response that de-escalates it. The mom or dad might make a clear and firm statement such as, "I really don't want to fight with you right now, Justin. I'm going to the kitchen so I won't bother you." These words aren't maddeningly calm, nor are they charged with fury. They simply and neutrally state what the parent intends to do. There's no threat, no reminder, no backing down. And it's virtually impossible to argue with such benign words.

Attempts to change the adolescent's behavior — telling him to settle down or tossing out threats — will probably be fruitless and counterproductive. The middle of your adolescent's rampage is not the best time to interject something like, "If you can't control yourself any better than this, I can't trust you with the car tonight! You'll probably kill yourself or someone else!" Going to such extremes is not usually helpful, and it will not be well received by the adolescent. I just can't imagine any seventeen-year-old responding to that kind of threat by saying, "Gee, Mom, I'm really glad you're concerned about me, so I'll drive extra carefully. Thanks."

When the transfer of negative feelings occurs frequently, parents see themselves as ineffective. Their mission is to have more impact on the adolescent than he has on them, but if they end up sharing his negative feelings, they will feel powerless. When this occurs, they are rendered impotent. They may continue to over-parent or to withdraw for long periods of time, neither of which is helpful.

Parents must be aware of the dynamics of transferred feelings so they can decide how to avoid or minimize the repercussions of their adolescent's contagious emotions.

TOO MUCH TALKING CAUSES TOO LITTLE LISTENING

Parents who feel as if they have lost their bearings may find that they rely on oft-repeated clichés, which do not facilitate reciprocal communication. I've thought of some of the more common statements that parents use when they are about to unravel. I've made comments about each of them in an effort to add some humor to what often doesn't feel very funny. Laughing at yourself can help maintain equilibrium when you are feeling rudderless in a storm. Perhaps when the adolescent is in a mood to talk, you can ask him what he thinks when you fall back on any of these statements.

"That's it! I won't live like this anymore!" Comment: Just what do you plan to do? Is this a suicide threat? The adolescent may be thinking, *Great, I'm sick of you living like this too.*

"I will not put up with this!" Comment: Again, what are you going to do? Pack your bags? Toss him out on the street? Swallow a couple of sedatives and hope tomorrow will be a better day?

"I'm the parent!" Comment: Odds are the adolescent knows this. Take a closer look at your motivation, and you might realize that this is simply your attempt to remind yourself that you should be in control of *something.*

"Who's the adult here?" Comment: This is probably a way of telling yourself that you're the one who's supposed to be acting like a grown-up.

"It may be your life, but if you get sick from not wearing your coat, I'm the one who will have to pay the doctor's bill!" Comment: Once you start talking about money, you've probably run out of legitimate concerns and have nothing useful to say.

"If I've told you once, I've told you a thousand times . . ." Comment: What makes you think that one more time will do the trick? If you're sick of saying it, your kid is probably sick of hearing it.

"If I had talked to my mother the way you talk to me, my father would have killed me!" Comment: Just what are you suggesting? It's probably not a good idea.

"When I was your age . . ." Comment: You lost his attention after those five words.

"If you're late tonight, you're not going out for the rest of the weekend!" Comment: If *the* place to be is at tonight's party, he may not care about being grounded for the rest of the weekend. Therefore, this proclamation may actually suggest that he stay out until the sun comes up since the proposed consequence is of no relevance to him.

Many of you are probably wondering, *What can I say that* will *be helpful?* Good question. Try something new that you haven't said day after day. Adolescents are more likely to pay attention to something they haven't heard a hundred times before. It doesn't help to talk about another point in time — such as when you were his age — because he lives in the moment. Telling him that you didn't have a cell phone and your life was just fine does not register with today's adolescent. My grandmother, who died at 107 years of age, never told me I didn't need a car because she rode to high school by horse and buggy. Times change. Live in the present with your child.

If you don't want your adolescent to have a cell phone, talk to him about the actual reason why, and don't dilute your message by adding something from a historical perspective. He may not agree with your reason — he may not like it at all — but he may get it more clearly when you leave out the reference to something from forty years ago. In fact, he may actually think about the reason as opposed to automatically dismissing it.

It might be an interesting experiment to talk to your adolescent in the same way you talk to his friends or to other people who are not part of your family. Sometimes we are so much nicer to people on the outside, and those interactions do not typically result in arguments or control battles. Parents are usually not critical of an unrelated adolescent's hair, makeup, or clothes. In fact, they probably have congenial conversations with other people's kids regardless of how strange they might look. They're not going to get judgmental because, after all, this isn't their kid. I'm quick to comment on the creativity of an elaborate tattoo when I see one on my young clients, although I don't think I would find it quite so interesting if it were permanently etched into the arm of one of my sons.

CONTROL, CONTROL, CONTROL

If "Location, location, location" is the mantra of real estate, then "Control, control, control" is the mantra of adolescence. Issues of control often frame the adolescent's journey to find the elusive sense of self. While he's engaged in this pursuit, his mom and dad — who are having a hard time controlling him — are busy trying to control *everything*. When parents attempt to control too much, they fuel the adolescent's search for autonomy and strengthen his need to prove that his parents can't control him at all.

One of the more difficult areas that we deal with in our practice is helping parents recognize the matters over which they actually do have control. It is amazing how many reasonable people become unreasonable when facing control issues. When we point out that they have absolutely no influence over a specific issue, many of them immediately jump to ten more things they want to control. It's almost as if they're driven by a universal parental mandate that says, "You must control something! If you don't, you are not a good parent and your child is getting away with [fill in the blank]."

As I've said before, sometimes there is nothing a parent can do to prevent a situation from occurring. Sometimes there is nothing a parent can do to protect an adolescent from his poor choices. And with this knowledge comes a strong sense of powerlessness. I am not suggesting that parents throw up their hands and withdraw from parenting, but I am suggesting that they realistically assess just what they can do and then decide how to do it.

Every parent shudders as the newly licensed adolescent pulls out of the driveway for the first time on his own. When my sons began to drive, I recall talking to myself a great deal. Looking back, I realize that this solution was probably more effective than trying to explain to the boys what was going through my head. My favorite calming self-talk was, *Most of them make it back home in one piece. They usually don't kill themselves or anyone else when they're behind the wheel.* I think I must have mentally recited those words tens of thousands of times, and although they may not offer much immediate consolation, they *are* true. Parents often automatically fear the worst possible consequences, and I am not sure that such thoughts can be avoided. But Mom and Dad need to maintain sight of the fact that once the car is in motion, they are not in control of *anything* related to safety.

Parenting adolescents is frequently a balancing act involving:

- What you want to control
- What you need to control
- What you can control
- What you should not control
- What you cannot control

If you make the necessary determination with careful and realistic thoughtfulness, you might feel balanced and consequently in control of your own feelings and responses.

Jerome, age fourteen, came to my office with his mother for their scheduled appointment, and it was clear they had been engaged in some sort of conflict. Jerome's mother was furious, and Jerome was smirking, which, of course, added to his mother's distress. As we began to talk, I learned what the problem was: Jerome was wearing flannel boxers — and it was July. His mother was convinced that Jerome was wearing them just to make her mad. "It's ninety degrees outside," she stated emphatically. "Why would anyone wear flannel anything?"

I have to admit I wondered why anyone would care what kind of boxers someone else was wearing. As his mother went into great, and ridiculous, detail in an effort to defend her position, Jerome took the typical adolescent position by saying, "It's my butt. It's my life."

His mom continued her rant, stressing the importance of his not wearing flannel in the middle of summer. She addressed possible health risks. She complained about the expense of a doctor's visit. She concluded with, "If he wore his pants up where they belong instead of letting them sag, I wouldn't even have seen those boxers." Her last statement seemed closer to the truth than anything else she'd said up to that point, and although it shed a bit of light on the situation, it was still an issue that was out of her hands.

I decided to interrupt the arguing, so I simply asked Jerome's mother, "Why do you care if he sweats?" At that point, the three of us started to laugh at the absurdity and unimportance of the argument.

Clearly, Jerome's mother had managed to get caught up in something that (1) she did not need to control; (2) she should not control; and (3) she could not control. For obvious reasons, it makes sense to ignore or avoid matters such as this. The habit of unnecessarily controlling something is usually a sign of a parent who either is a control freak or is exhausted from all the control battles that have been sent her way by the autonomy-seeking adolescent.

An adolescent's quest for autonomy is developmentally appropriate, so parents should expect it and accept it. If a person had significant developmental interruptions in his life before adoption, he may be somewhat delayed, and issues associated with adolescence may not emerge as early as expected. Those with serious attachment difficulties will probably have exaggerated issues regarding autonomy and control, and even micromanaging adults cannot counteract them. The most important issue for parents to focus on is safety, which must always have a high priority. If your adolescent seems immature, be glad as you may get a reprieve for a period of time.

As the adolescent matures, parental control of many issues can, and should, relax. If your child will be going to college, joining the military, or living on his own, he needs to be prepared for the kinds of day-to-day decisions he will need to make. Increasingly shared control throughout high school will help him prepare for this "real world" we keep talking about. When given choices, many adolescents surprise their parents with their good decisions.

> When seventeen-year-old Tom's parents asked him what time he would be home from the movies, he said between ten and ten thirty. They had been prepared to give him an eleven o'clock curfew, so they were happy when he opted for an earlier time.

It makes sense to factor in some flexibility when discussing curfews because a span of time is more reasonable than a fixed hour. I have found that when people are bound by a specific time, they get into conflicts about what is considered late. I've seen families who determine lateness by mere minutes — "Your curfew was ten o'clock, and it's now five after ten. If you can be five minutes late, you could have been five minutes early." Does it really make that big of a difference?

To get a better perspective, think about early versus late in the adult world. Most people who show up ten to fifteen minutes late for a social encounter are close enough to be considered on time. However, if your plane is due to depart at eight fifteen and you get to the gate at eight thirty, you're out of luck. It depends on the situation.

To avoid any unnecessary conflicts, give your child a reasonable window for his return home and make his curfew dependent upon the particular activity in which he's involved.

Let's take the example of a sixteen-year-old who plans to attend a Friday night football game. The game might end around nine thirty, followed by a stop at the local pizza place. Eleven to eleven fifteen might be an acceptable curfew. If he's going to a Saturday afternoon movie that ends at three, then stopping for a quick snack, being home between four fifteen and four thirty is reasonable.

Keep in mind that a curfew for an adolescent is a dictum to stay out as late as the curfew allows. When a parent tells an adolescent that he has to be home by eleven, the adolescent thinks, *I must stay out until eleven.* It is the rare adolescent who returns home earlier than expected. After all, what would his friends think of him if he didn't squeak in at the final hour?

DATING (NEVER MIND IF *YOU'RE* READY — IS YOUR *ADOLESCENT* READY?)

Absolute rules about dating are not always helpful to parents. Some families have a rule about how old an adolescent must be before he can date. It might be more beneficial to make those kinds of decisions based on the adolescent's developmental preparedness.

Parents need to think about several issues relative to the dating situation. *Is my daughter developmentally delayed? What kinds of decision-making skills does she have? Is my son trustworthy and reliable? Did he experience sexual abuse? Does he have sexualized behavior? What are his peer relationships like, in general? More specifically, how does he relate to girls? How does my daughter relate to boys? Has she had developmentally appropriate relationships? Have we had sufficient discussions about sex, morals, and related issues?* Adolescence is not the time to begin talking about these things; rather it is the time to *continue* talking about them.

As children develop into adolescence and adolescents develop into adulthood, they go through varying patterns of peer relationships. Those patterns look like this:

CHILDHOOD

- Same-gender playmates—one-on-one
- Same-gender group play

EARLY ADOLESCENCE

- Same-gender friends—one-on-one
- Same-gender group affiliations
- Mixed-gender friends—one-on-one
- Mixed-gender group affiliations

LATER ADOLESCENCE

- All of the above
- Dating relationships

As an individual matures, he expands the configurations of his relationships. By late adolescence and early adulthood, he is more diverse than earlier in life. If the adolescent was adopted at a young age, his parents probably know his patterns of thinking and behaving, so their comfort level with his embarking on new things will be greater than if the adoption occurred in adolescence. If there was significant trauma in the adolescent's life, it is likely that at the age of sixteen, he is not quite sixteen. If his behavior is more like that of a thirteen-year-old, his parents' response to the dating question should be obvious.

Parents are wise to establish boundaries for their adolescent's dating activities. Group activities offer safety for everyone involved, and most adolescents feel more comfortable when they can avoid situations in which they may feel pressured into using drugs or alcohol or engaging sexually. (Chapter 6 addresses sexual issues in greater depth.) Many adolescents want to make the right decisions about their moral dilemmas, but there are times when good thinking transforms into bad behavioral choices. Parental involvement offers limits and comfort for the adolescent who may want to say no to something but feels excessive pressure to do otherwise. Parents frequently tell me about adolescents who plead, "Tell them I can't go," when friends call with an invitation to an event they would rather not attend.

Each time the phone rang, Kevin would run to tell his mother or father to answer it. He seemed terrified about who might possibly be calling. Sometimes it was a friend calling for his mom, sometimes an associate from his dad's office, sometimes a neighbor, sometimes one of Kevin's classmates.

After a week of Kevin's fear, his dad begrudgingly picked up the phone one evening at Kevin's usual insistence. "It's for you, Kevin," he said, extending the phone in his son's direction. "It's someone named Heather."

"No-o-o!" Kevin pleaded. "Tell her I'm grounded until further notice! She's been following me around school for weeks, and she keeps trying to get me to go to the movies with her. She scares the heck outa me!"

This was the call Kevin had been dreading. Because of his complete discomfort about Heather, he didn't want to socialize with her, yet he didn't know how to say no. By getting his father involved, Kevin didn't have to be the one to refuse the unwanted invitation.

His dad did, in fact, say that Kevin was grounded indefinitely. While he didn't like the idea of lying, his son's feelings were his top priority. He also knew that Kevin's emotional immaturity indicated that he wasn't ready for even the most casual dating, and it was his preference, too, to push the timing back until his son was better prepared for the experience.

Adults often make the mistake of asking an adolescent about his dating status. In turn, these questions make him feel as if he *should* be in a relationship. One fourteen-year-old told me that every adult in his life—even his dental hygienist—asked him about his girlfriend situation. When he said he didn't have one, they never knew quite how to respond.

The constant queries about his love life made him feel as if he were doing something wrong by not having a girlfriend. But he was confident enough to explain to the inquiring adults that he had just been adopted and thought he should spend his time with his family. Clearly, this young man's judgment was better than that of the grown-ups asking the intrusive questions.

A couple of years ago, I had a client who was in sixth grade. He was exhibiting a lot of anxiety, and it eventually came to light that his concerns were about his school's upcoming Valentine's Day dance and flower sale. The students were supposed to buy a flower and have it secretly sent to someone. He was very worried because he didn't have anyone to send a flower to, and he was even more worried that he wouldn't receive one and his friends would make fun of him.

After talking about the flower issue, we came up with a plan. Because it was a secret process, we decided that he could send a flower to himself and no one would ever know. He thought it was a funny idea and followed through with it. When he received a flower from a "secret girl," his friends were extremely impressed.

If an adolescent isn't ready for dating or driving or any other adolescent task, parents should probably support the kid's choice. He may know something that makes him think he's not ready for whatever the issue is. When in doubt, parents and other adults should forget about chronological age and assess developmental issues.

LOSS AND LOVE

Parents must remember that adopted adolescents have experienced losses, and these are reactivated by new losses. Therefore, when an adopted adolescent falls in love, spends fun time with a girlfriend or boyfriend, and then shifts into a tumultuous relationship and an eventual breakup, there may be a wildly overreactive response. The loss may represent many of the seven core issues of adoption discussed in chapter 3, and the adolescent may feel that this is the end of his life as he has known it. *I will never have another girlfriend — that's it.*

I have worked with many adolescent clients who describe the end of a relationship with statements such as, "We were so close. She's the only one who understands me, who knows me. I've told her things I've never told anyone before. We are so much alike. I have no idea what I'll do without her. Maybe I should just kill myself."

Issues of rejection, loss, and shame rear their ugly heads throughout the life of an adopted individual, and they may be at their all-time high during adolescence. Adolescence is a time of drama—individual, collective, and contagious. When an adolescent commits suicide or dies in a tragic car accident, everyone seems to have been connected to him. "He rode my bus." "He sat next to me in English." "He had the locker next to mine." "His girlfriend was my best friend's cousin." The relationships, real or perceived, constitute the adolescent's reality. Parental admonitions of "You didn't even know him!" are neither constructive nor helpful. The adolescent feels as if he's lost everything, and this is particularly true if he was adopted.

Parents must be concerned about the impact of loss, especially when there is a history of loss. Any talk about suicide should always be taken seriously and never minimized. Parents should make it a point to find out:

- Has the adolescent thought about hurting or killing himself?
- Does he have a plan? What does it entail?
- Does he have access to his plan? Can he actually implement the plan?

If a person has thoughts of suicide, has devised a plan, and realistically has the potential to carry out that plan, he must have an emergency assessment by a mental-health professional. If, on the other hand, the kid says, "I'm going to hold my breath until I die," it might just mean a call to a professional to get an appointment for outpatient therapy. Why? You can't kill yourself by holding your breath.

All talk about hurting oneself or suicide demands a parental response of some sort. And if an adolescent has a history that includes loss, parents must be particularly sensitive to the new losses in his life.

PLAYING BY THE RULES

It is important to remember that whatever configuration the family rules take on, they must coincide with reality. Relationship expectations, rather than a list of rules, are probably more effective strategies for parenting. We often ask adolescents to "do this for yourself—not for me." In truth, I think it's perfectly fine to ask our kids to do things for us. Do we really think they'll call home to check in because they want to do it? Will they drive extra cautiously for themselves, these kids who believe they're invincible? Probably not, but they just might be willing to do it for Mom and Dad. Consider the following exchange:

Parent: "Please call me when you get to the game so I know you arrived safely."

Adolescent: "Oh, I'll be fine, Dad. Don't worry. It's stupid to have to call you. I'm not a baby."

Parent: "I know you're not a baby. It may be stupid, but I'd just feel better if I heard from you. If you're too embarrassed to call, just text me—that'd be fine."

Adolescent: "Okay, Dad, I'll do that."

Parent: "Thanks a lot. I'll wait to hear from you."

The text arrives:

Adolescent: "Made it OK. C U L8R."

Parent: "Thx. Have fun."

Painless, right? Dad's relaxed, and all it took was a bit of thumb work on his son's part.

In *7 Things Your Teenager Won't Tell You: And How to Talk About Them Anyway*,[2] Jenifer Lippincott and Robin M. Deutsch, PhD, discuss three rules of play that make complete sense to me—and I think they will to you, too. Almost everything of importance falls under these rules, and it is unlikely that too much chaos will result from applying them in your family. They are reasonable and probably acceptable to most adolescents:

- Stay safe.
- Show respect.
- Keep in touch.

If most of what you do as the parent of an adolescent is related to these three simple maxims, you will have an easier time than if you attempt to micromanage his life. Along similar lines, Cline and Fay, in *Parenting with Love and Logic,* say that children and adolescents should make their best effort to be:

- Responsible
- Respectful
- Fun to be with[3]

If you look at the big picture, assess the realities of what you worry about, and pay good attention to the quality of your relationship with your adolescent, you will, without a doubt, help facilitate his journey into young adulthood.

FIVE

ADOPTING AN ADOLESCENT

Why It's a Viable Option

When prospective parents tell their friends they are planning to adopt an adolescent, they are frequently met with reactions that include surprise, skepticism, shock, dismay, and the occasional suggestion of medical intervention until the moment of insanity passes. People wonder why anyone would even dream of taking on that kind of challenge, why an intelligent couple can't see how crazy their decision is, why they can't be content to simply enjoy the life they have. Negative thoughts about adolescents, in general, seem to flow through adult minds at rapid speed. Adolescents who have grown up in the child-welfare system may present an even more disturbing picture since they usually have a range of difficulties related to trauma, multiple placements, and countless losses.

The collective assumption seems to be that all adolescents are rebellious, hormonally driven creatures who terrorize their families and schools and are prone to having strange clothes, bizarre hair, and outrageous beliefs. While some of them fit this stereotype, most of them do not.

As of September 30, 2006, there were approximately 49,602 adolescents (ages ten to seventeen) in foster care in this country who were available for adoption. This represents 38 percent of all waiting children.[1] A significant number of them will age out of the system and become floating members of society, untethered to anything or anyone. Sufficient evidence suggests that individuals who have spent time in foster care move into another "system" upon reaching adulthood, overrepresented in mental-health institutions, correctional facilities, and the homeless population. Even when foster families allow an adolescent to stay with them after the state terminates funding, such commitment does not usually rise to the level of adoptive status, which would afford more assurance that the family will remain connected and supportive throughout the adoptee's life. If the data about those who age out of foster care is accurate, it seems that it is incumbent on our society to encourage families to consider adopting those who some think are "too old."

How old is too old? As people get older, they often develop a greater appreciation for their parents and siblings than they had during childhood and adolescence. Families help and support each other throughout the lives of all family members. Conversely, when a young person enters adult life unsupported by a family system, he is at high risk for just about every negative thing that could possibly happen.

When people consider adoption, they often think that younger is better, but little data exists to support that assumption. I think many prospective parents feel that they will stand a better chance of impacting development if they adopt an infant or a very young child. Even though such a belief seems to make sense at first glance, it doesn't take into account risk factors such as drug and alcohol exposure *in utero*, early abuse and neglect that resulted in the child's removal from his birth home, or orphanage care in another country. Most children available for adoption today — wherever in the world their origins are — share many of the same factors that may impair their development, health, behavior, and overall adjustment. A single factor such as age is not sufficient to use as a predictor of success, or lack thereof, in adoption.

Adolescents can be fun and fascinating works in progress. They change a lot — sometimes very quickly. They have new friends, new career goals, new girlfriends or boyfriends on a constantly revolving basis. They're passionate about their martial arts class for three years running, and then suddenly they're bored with it. One week they're addicted to burgers and fries, and the next week they're strict vegetarians. They love to cuddle with their parents in

May and then don't want to be seen with them in June. By August, cuddling is good again.

So many adolescents who are in foster care are waiting for families. The ones with whom I have spoken are eager to settle in so their lives can finally be lived without wondering when the next move will come. They want to be a part of a family just like their friends are.

It's difficult to be a foster child, particularly in adolescence. As foster kids grow into their late teens and their peers start talking about future plans, they feel left out of the conversational loop. *What are my plans? Where will I be living? How will I survive? Will I even be alive?* They have no answers to these pressing questions.

Sixteen- and seventeen-year-olds in foster care must be terrified to think about the emancipation they will be facing in a very short time. People are constantly telling most adolescents, "When you're eighteen, you can do what you want."

For adolescents who are in their birth families or who were adopted earlier in life, this phrase may not trigger anxiety. However, foster kids often hear these words without any meaningful context. They're typically given the "When you're eighteen . . ." speech when they complain about a foster home or object to an agency rule they feel complicates their lives. When they are younger, they might think, *I can't wait until I don't have any more social workers or foster parents!* But they probably don't think, *Where will I be?* As the reality of being set free looms closer, the adolescent in foster care is bound to be paralyzed by fear and trepidation.

Being adopted, undoubtedly, provides a sense of continuity—of permanency. The adolescent who is adopted can more comfortably look to the future with a sense of predictability and security. He can make plans that won't be derailed by emancipation from foster care and total immersion into society with little preparation and few skills to ensure success.

WHO ADOPTS ADOLESCENTS?

People who consider adopting an adolescent are probably not thinking about raising a child or parenting for a long period of time. They are well aware that they won't be dealing with childhood issues, although many adolescents who have been in foster care or an orphanage are developmentally more immature than their chronological age suggests. The adopting parents may be looking forward to someone joining the family who is up and running and ready to go. They won't have to worry about bedtimes, changing diapers, or teaching someone how to tie his shoes. They may think they will enjoy being part of an adolescent's life.

Adopting and parenting adolescents require a different mindset than adopting and parenting younger children. Parents can solicit meaningful input from the adolescent relative to what he needs, wants, and expects. When a six-year-old joins a family, parents can be more overtly directive than they can be with a fifteen-year-old. The fifteen-year-old, on the other hand, can have a greater say and more active involvement in the family's activities, offering suggestions on plans for the weekend or helping to organize a backyard barbecue.

As I mentioned in the introduction, parents who adopt an adolescent must be friendly, engaging, and magnet-like—serving as a draw, not a repellant. During initial visits prior to adoption, both the adults and the adolescent will be making judgments about each other. A younger child won't have the capacity to evaluate what kind of parents these new folks will be, but the adolescent is bound to have his radar finely tuned in an effort to determine if this prospective new home and family seem right for him.

I encourage parents to have visits that reflect what the family actually does on a weekend. For example, if the family does chores on Saturday mornings and they expect the new kid to help out, that should probably happen on a visit. Some families make visits all fun and games, and then once the final placement is made, they get real. Start out real, and the adolescent won't feel as if he was subjected to a bait-and-switch deal.

These visits do not have to be undertaken over a lengthy period of time. Once a final decision has been made about the placement, both the family and the adolescent should provide input regarding when the move should occur.

Sometimes a blind meeting—a casual encounter arranged prior to the adolescent's knowing that the adult may be his prospective parent—can be helpful. Many adoption professionals don't like this kind of visit, but I personally think it has value. Both of my sons and I had blind meetings that went well and resulted in their being adopted. These visits are easy to arrange, nonthreatening, and can have a very positive outcome.

Jennifer, age sixteen, was excited about her upcoming trip to see a performance by a local dance troupe. The outing had been arranged by the adoption agency handling her case, and Jennifer's love of ballet fired her enthusiasm.

Without Jennifer's knowledge, her social worker, Monica, had invited a couple who was considering adopting the girl. They had heard a lot about her and were anxious to get to know her better. When the three of them met, Monica simply introduced the couple as friends of hers.

After the dance performance, Monica asked the couple if they would mind driving Jennifer back to her group home since they were going in the same direction. They agreed, which gave Jennifer and her possible family-to-be the opportunity to talk during the rather lengthy car ride. The three chatted comfortably and amiably, talking a lot about their shared interest in all types of dance. They were able to get acquainted in an easy and relaxed environment, without the pressure of "to adopt or not to adopt."

The following week, Monica and the family attended a holiday performance at Jennifer's school, where she danced the part of Clara in *The Nutcracker*. Afterward, they all went out for Chinese food. At the restaurant, Jennifer's worker told her that she thought she had found a family she would like. Jennifer began asking questions, and after a while, the couple, who had decided to go forward with the placement, identified themselves. Jennifer was thrilled, as she really liked these people. She was eventually placed with them and adopted.

Some professionals feel that this process is somewhat of a betrayal, but I fail to see it that way. I think it reduces the stress the adolescent would feel if he knew that a family was considering adopting him. It also reduces the pressure on the parents because their decision whether or not to move forward is not influenced by their concern about possibly rejecting the adolescent if they felt that the match wasn't a good one.

Robert, age thirteen, was having a casual lunch at a local deli with his social worker. He was not aware that his prospective adoptive father would be stopping by and posing as the worker's friend. The placement worker invited his "friend" to join him and Robert, and the three spent the next half hour eating and talking. This blind meeting was easy and friendly. Subsequent visits began soon afterward, and they were equally positive.

Neither Jennifer nor Robert felt betrayed because they both ended up in adoptive families where they felt like they belonged. Think about it for a minute: Feeling betrayed in this situation would be akin to a child feeling betrayed when he eventually finds out that Santa Claus is fictional. I've never known anyone who grew up distrusting his parents because they encouraged him to believe in Saint Nick. In fact, most people who thought Santa Claus was real when they were young go on to share the delightful myth with their own children.

GETTING TO KNOW YOU . . . GETTING TO KNOW ALL ABOUT YOU

Adolescents are very judgmental—quick to decide who's okay and who's the enemy. During the preliminary stages of placement, all parties might act differently than they normally do, and this dynamic—a basic part of human nature—simply cannot be avoided.

Take the example of a new employee, whose performance and attitude are different at first than they will be in three months. This is sometimes referred to as the "honeymoon period"—the time in which someone is on his best behavior. It is important to keep in mind that this is not usually a purposeful attempt to disguise oneself or hide a terrible flaw. In most cases, it is nothing more than a desire to be liked by others, and it's perfectly normal. What worries me is when this eager-to-please behavior does not occur. If someone—your adopted adolescent, a coworker, or the guy next door—is completely rude at your initial encounter, odds are your relationship will go downhill at a rapid pace.

I'm not quite sure why people are surprised when their negative attitudes don't produce positive responses. When people feel scolded, lectured, or put down, they typically don't respond with a great attitude. And why should they?

On the other hand, treating someone respectfully by initiating an open, friendly exchange can be contagious. Parents would do well to ask themselves, *If I talked to my friends the way I talk to my kids, would I have many friends left?* If the answer is affirmative, then you're on the right road. If not, try making some changes.

Jacob, age thirteen, was tired of the incessant arguments he had with his parents, even though much of the chaos was created by his behavior. He decided to tape-record the three of them in the middle of one of their tirades. When he played it at his next therapy appointment, his parents were surprised and embarrassed to hear themselves. They had no idea how far out of whack their altercations had become.

A lot can be gained by keeping family relationships open and friendly. It's a great way to learn about your adolescent, his friends, and what is going on in his life. In fact, you may end up hearing more than you really want to know.

Ty, age sixteen, has a very upfront relationship with his adoptive mother. One day he announced to her that he thought everyone should have one person in his life with whom he could safely share everything, and he decided that his mom should be that person. Feeling honored that he trusted her with his deepest secrets, she readily agreed with him. At that point, he proceeded to tell her that he was no longer a virgin and went on to share details of his latest relationship. *Too much information! Too much information!* were the words than ran through her head, but the connection she was forging with her son was stronger than her desire to remain in the dark about his sexual activity.

When you adopt an adolescent, you can expect to have a unique relationship, much different than if you had adopted him earlier in life. He doesn't have to act as if he hates you because he hasn't lived with you long enough to feel the need to prove that he is separate from you. He wants to get close to the family, and you can help him do that if you avoid pointing out the things he should change. He has a very real history, some sense of self, ideas about how he looks and wants to look, and what he likes to eat and wear. He also has memories that do not include his new family, and all of these things must be respected.

Tamika, age thirteen, joined her adoptive family in August, just in time to start the school year while getting to know her new parents. She had been in one foster home for about seven years prior to being placed for adoption. Her relationship with the family was a positive one, and she had thought they would adopt her. However, several issues arose that ultimately necessitated her placement elsewhere. She was sad and lonely, and although she seemed to like her new family, she struggled with both the loss of her former family and the process of joining her new one.

As late summer led into fall, Tamika began talking about how much she missed the other family. She shared numerous memories of Christmastime, reminiscing about the traditions they had, what they ate, and how much she liked to decorate the house for the holidays. Tamika's adoptive mother began to feel threatened and somewhat sad that her daughter didn't seem interested in planning Christmas with her new family. When I spoke with the mom, it was clear that she felt left out and a bit jealous.

I explained to her that Tamika could only relate to past Christmases because future Christmases were an unknown entity to her. I suggested she begin to talk about the coming holiday, incorporating some of Tamika's fond experiences with the adoptive family's customs. By blending the old and the new, Tamika's comfort level might very well increase.

People sometimes forget that positives from the past make it more likely that the present and future will hold positives, as well. The quality of past relationships is somewhat indicative of the shape that new relationships will take. In fact, the past is the best predictor of the future in almost all situations. Tamika's new family should have been happy that she'd had such a good connection with her foster family because that kind of harmony could easily translate into her relationships with her new family.

In addition to memories, a personal fashion statement is something that an adolescent will want to cling to. If your adopted son has been wearing baggy clothes for years, it is safe to assume that he'll want to continue to do so after he joins your family. His arrival in his new home shouldn't require him to check his ego at the door. It is with him, it defines him, and it is a fact of life that adopting families must accept. If he's used to oversized jeans and hoodies, he's not suddenly going to beg you to buy him khakis and button-downs so he can alter his style to match that of your family. In fact, when people move from one place to another, they are more likely to seek out what is familiar rather than to initiate any more changes.

When James, my youngest son, came home at thirteen, he was in love with baggy clothes. Some of the items he brought with him were not exactly what I would have chosen for my son, but I knew better than to try to convince him otherwise.

On one of our trips to the mall, he desperately wanted a coat that looked large enough for a few people to wear simultaneously. It happened to be marked down 75 percent (and no wonder, because the size was virtually inhuman), which made the purchase less painful for me.

James was thrilled when I agreed to buy the coat. When we returned home, we tried it on *together* and successfully zipped it up, at which point he realized just how big it was. I don't recall how long his wearing the coat lasted, but after a relatively short period of time, he began to develop friendships with kids who were not part of the baggy crowd. That alone brought about a natural change of clothing tastes. His new preferences were more expensive but easier for me to look at and be around.

Food is another hot-button area for a new family. To avoid unnecessary battles, parents should probably just accept the fact that adolescents are not going to change what they like to eat, how they eat, when they want to snack, or any other habit related to food. For most people, food preferences change very little over time, and this holds especially true for adolescents.

Some kids who have been in foster care will eat only a limited selection of foods, and I believe this pattern is yet another side effect of multiple placements. Most people, even those who like to try new dishes, often find comfort in familiar foods. Because foster kids move so much and every family's food is different, they limit their choices to the few things that will taste virtually the same no matter whose table they are on. Packaged macaroni and cheese, pizza, hot dogs, and hamburgers are usually safe. One thing is clear: If there's a new adolescent in the family, his preferred foods must be added to the menu.

Early in my career, when I was working as a juvenile parole officer, I had to move Trevor, one of the adolescents in my charge, to a temporary foster home. He had grown up on the rough-and-tumble streets of Cleveland, and I was taking him to the only home available on an emergency basis. The family was upper class and very worldly in terms of the arts, travel, and — you guessed it — food. When we arrived, they were just about to have dinner. I had not planned on staying to eat, but at their insistence, I agreed to do so.

Trevor and I sat down at the dining table, and when the food was served, I had no idea what it was. It looked brown, lumpy, and alien — and not very appetizing. I couldn't help but wonder, *What must Trevor be thinking?* The father of the family noticed we were less than enthusiastic about the meal, and he asked us if we liked steak-and-kidney pie. I had never even heard of it, so it was a pretty safe bet that it was foreign to Trevor, as well. I mumbled a response about not having a very imaginative palate. I pushed my food around a lot, ate a little, and silently vowed never to try anything that involved meat in a pie shell ever again. Fortunately, Trevor stayed with the family for only a few days, and I'm sure his first stop upon leaving was the nearest burger joint.

Food definitely falls into the category of "power struggles to avoid like the plague." Parents continue to tell me the value of introducing new foods and getting the adolescent to eat in a healthier way. If that's the family's main goal, I can guarantee they will probably be fighting through most meals. Working on the relationship is of primary importance, and any changes the adolescent makes will happen within the context of that bigger picture.

TEMPERAMENT

Temperament, which is present at birth, is a major concern when adopting an adolescent. We once embraced the concept of *tabula rasa* (Latin for "blank slate"), which means that the kind of person an individual becomes is solely dependent on his experiences and sensory perceptions of the outside world — "nurture" as opposed to "nature." We now know that personality is part of a more complex mix, incorporating such components as genetics, temperament, psychosocial issues, and environment.

For an adoption to have the greatest chance of success, it is important for parents and their new adolescent to be at least somewhat matched in temperament. Sadly, I've seen online dating services and computer matches of dog breeds to pet owners that generate more appropriate pairings than do some adoption agencies.

Mark, age sixteen, was placed with a family whose birth children were grown and out of the home. Both parents and all of their offspring were academic scholars with advanced degrees in a variety of fields. The parents lived in a wealthy neighborhood and frequented the opera, the ballet, the symphony, live theater, and art museums. Their favorite way to relax was to curl up with a good book.

Of course, there is absolutely nothing wrong with any of these pastimes. However, Mark had grown up living in cars, being evicted from apartment after apartment, being abused by his mother's multiple boyfriends, and having erratic school attendance. Can you see where this is going?

When Mark received his first report card after moving in with his new family, his parents were distraught. They could not believe that he was happy with Cs. No one in their family had ever gotten Cs, much less Ds or Fs. They complained to me, "Mark just doesn't have a lust for learning. This is not acceptable."

It became clear we needed to have a serious discussion about parental expectations. Sadly, I could never get Mark's parents to understand that Cs were great grades for Mark. He had missed so much school over the years that it was amazing to me that he even went to class or cracked a book at all! They never should have compared him to their birth children, who had good early lives, solid relationships, no trauma, extensive exposure to cultural activities, and constant immersion in an environment in which sociopolitical and academic discussions occurred at dinnertime. Dinnertime? Mark never had *any* time—no bedtime, no mealtime, no getting-up time, and definitely no reading time.

If the placing agency provides information that reveals the adolescent's interests, temperament, attitudes, and activity levels, parents should compare these details to their own personalities, likes, and dislikes. For example, if their prospective fourteen-year-old son lives to play sports, this means they'll be sitting through games, matches, and meets every season of the year. If, by chance, they don't like athletic events or competition in general, they should give careful thought to whether or not they can genuinely adjust to taking on the sports dimension. If they do not want to get involved in this important aspect of the adolescent's life, they should probably consider adopting a child whose interests are more compatible with their own. Most adolescents who fiercely love to compete are not going to surrender to a lifestyle of reading just because that's how the new family spends their leisure time.

If the adolescent is described as being quiet with an interest in art and music, the family who is considering adopting him should be comfortable with such pursuits. This means being prepared to support his involvement in classes to further develop his talents and a willingness to spend time at art galleries and concerts. Again, if this doesn't sound interesting or possible, the match should be reconsidered. Expecting a budding Picasso to make the switch to football is illogical as well as unfair. It is critical to recognize who the adolescent truly is—what he likes to do and what he's good at—if the relationship is to flourish and grow.

Never underestimate the importance of interest and temperament compatibility. Prospective adoptive parents must respect their own preferences as well as those of the adolescent. Adopting someone with whom they share very little will make the process more arduous than necessary. Essentially, people are who they are, and some aspects of personality will not—and should not have to—change.

Think about the dog world for a minute. A border collie is mandated to herd and work; a Labrador retriever gets excited just seeing a body of water; a Jack Russell terrier is constantly busy, not unlike a child with ADHD. These personality traits are primarily fixed, making it unlikely the border collie would be a good companion for a sedentary apartment dweller, the Lab would stay out of the neighbor's pool, or the terrier would be a suitable guide dog. And so it would be just as challenging to try to create harmony between an adolescent and parents who live their lives in disparate worlds.

Some adults might feel they should be able to adjust to having a child who is different from them, but this isn't really a fair "should." Instead, they would be better served if they asked themselves a few key questions: *Can I develop an interest in what the child is passionate about? Can I do this without seeming to be going through the motions? Can I support something I don't appreciate or understand by keeping the focus on how important it is to the adolescent?*

If the parents are flexible, these questions might be answered in the affirmative. A willingness to explore an activity the adolescent enjoys just might lead to the discovery that the swim meet is intriguing, the lacrosse game exciting, the Impressionist exhibit fascinating.

It is far easier for parents to be flexible than it is for the adolescent. Adolescence is a time of living what the child believes to be an authentic life, and there's not much room for bending. Parents should not expect the highly competitive athlete to be more interested in how the team plays than in winning the game or the delicate ballerina to develop a fondness for strenuous hikes. Instead, if the parents are willing to step out of the box and support the adolescent's interests, their willingness to adapt and try new things can go a long way toward building a lasting connection with their adolescent.

JUST WHEN YOU THOUGHT IT COULDN'T GET ANY WORSE

Physical and Sexual Development, Sexuality, and Sexual Behavior

Puberty is a time that many parents dread. They associate it with emotional instability, heightened sexual awareness and feelings, and potential sexual behavior—all of which are valid concerns.

Puberty marks the onset of adolescence, and, as such, it is the beginning of a developmental period that may span ten or more years. In addition to being the longest phase of human development, it is also the most complex, involving physiological, cognitive, social, and emotional changes. The process integrates many components of the child's life, and it is the last leg of development prior to adulthood.

Before you decide that neither you nor your adolescent will survive this time of life, remember that your parents survived it when you crossed the threshold into puberty, and you made it safely to the other side too. To be sure, it's not an easy transition, but if you're both prepared, the journey might be somewhat less precarious than you anticipate. To help with that preparation, let's take a look at some issues you might confront when nature kicks in.

PHYSICAL AND SEXUAL DEVELOPMENT

With the onset of puberty comes a host of physiological changes. The body's timetable has reached the point at which something new and different is happening nearly all the time. For starters, the pace of growth accelerates—sometimes very quickly. If an adolescent gets very tall very fast, he may find it difficult to coordinate his new body. He might feel awkward, self-conscious, and unattractive.

In truth, most adolescents do not feel good about their bodies. While they perceive others—even their peers—as normal, they see themselves as flawed. *I'm too fat. I'm too skinny. My arms are too long. My legs are too short. My nose and my feet are way too big.* Whatever they consider important, they're convinced they don't have enough of it.

Take acne, for example. Many adolescents don't just *have* acne—they feel as if they *are* acne. Where others see a few isolated zits, they see a massive forest of screaming red bumps. And if this is what they perceive, it becomes their reality. Going to school becomes more than just going to school. It becomes, *How can I go to school and make sure no one sees my pizza face?* Real or not, that's how they view their dilemma, and for them, minor issues can become larger than life.

Adolescents are constantly faced with bad-hair days, bad-zit days, bad-clothes days, and bad-friends days. Yet we tell them that these are the best years of their lives. I often think we're doing adolescents a great disservice when we go on and on about how wonderful everything should be when they're in high school. Imagine feeling utterly miserable about your life and hearing those words. It's a wonder they don't decide that if this is as good as it gets, they might as well give up on the spot.

Prior to this stage, children do not engage in such intense self-evaluation. Their day-to-day lives are devoid of self-criticism and self-loathing, and they simply "are." Little boys run around with dirt-streaked faces and torn socks, oblivious to how they appear to others. Little girls play and chat with their friends, not caring if their pigtails are slightly askew or if their thighs are a bit chubby. They don't compare themselves to others because personal competition is simply not within their frame of reference.

But when adolescence hits, everything changes. Comparisons to one's peers are rampant, and words like *taller, thinner, prettier, cuter, cooler, smarter, funnier,* even *sexier* become part of the vocabulary. An adopted adolescent may experience a heightened sense of not fitting in, and he may extend the comparisons to his family. It's common for him to begin to wonder why he doesn't look like his parents and why people are suddenly mentioning the fact. It wasn't an issue earlier because his friends were too busy playing and being kids to notice that his mom and dad have dark eyes but his are baby blue. And even if the differences were mentioned when he was younger, the disparities take on a new meaning in adolescence.

When a growth spurt occurs, the adolescent may suddenly be a head taller than his father. This, of course, prompts questions such as, "Wow, who did you get your height from?" Although this may happen within birth families as well, the question doesn't trigger anything deeper. Even a benign question about height may cause the adopted adolescent to feel unauthentic if he doesn't answer the question with, "Oh, I was adopted."

As children begin to show signs of growing, they are also experiencing physical changes related to sexual development, and this can be a source of intense emotional discomfort. Take the case of the early bloomers, who may feel like total misfits. *Body hair in fourth grade? Breasts in fifth? This isn't happening to any of my classmates, so I must be a freak.* While they're stressing over too much too soon, the late bloomer in the high school across town is anxiously waiting for that first armpit hair.

Marvin, age fourteen, was about to be adopted and was in therapy to help him with the transition. He was very concerned that little had changed about his body other than his height. He checked his armpits more often than he brushed his teeth, and he was euphoric when he found those first few hairs. For him, they represented being a man, and he could hardly wait to tell me about this new development at his next appointment. In fact, before I was able to close the office door behind us, he attempted to show me his new growth!

Marvin had been embarrassed by his lack of armpit hair every time he played basketball, and he was sure that his teammates and everyone else within viewing distance noticed he had none. Of course, he couldn't help but focus on the fact that all the other players sported evidence that they were maturing. When his mother-to-be joined us in the session, he startled her by hiking up his shirt and proudly showing her his latest acquisition. She was completely taken by surprise, and it took her awhile to realize just how critical this discovery was to Marvin's sense of well-being.

Eleven-year-old Rebecca had been sexually abused for several years in her birth family prior to being adopted at age four. Research suggests that girls who have experienced this kind of trauma begin puberty earlier than their non-abused age-mates. Rebecca had already developed breasts and began her menstrual cycle by the time she was ten. No one else in her fourth-grade class had breasts, and she became a target for the boys' raucous teasing and the girls' quiet whispers. Because she was emotionally immature, she faced a double whammy: a maturing body and a little girl's view of the world. This disparity is seen often, and it becomes the parents' task to help bridge the gap.

Many adults forget just how stressful the physical changes in puberty can be, and there's probably not a kid on the planet who thinks he's right on course in terms of timing. For some, the mere thought of changing clothes for gym class fills them with dread. The notion becomes so traumatic that they refuse to participate, preferring to fail rather than disrobe in front of their peers.

Parents can help keep lines of communication open by periodically mentioning issues related to physical changes. In most cases, mothers talk to daughters about what happens as they mature more often than either parent talks to a son. Parents feel they must prepare a girl for her first period because it's an occurrence that can't very well be ignored. Boys, on the other hand, tend to get a bit lost since they do not experience a comparable landmark event for which they must be prepared.

As parents see changes emerging, they can address them in a neutral manner. Some adolescents are so sensitive about these changes that they attempt to hide them.

Tanya, age thirteen, started to get noticeable hair growth on her legs. She didn't like the way it looked, so she set out to shave without first talking about it with her mother. Because she didn't know the proper way to handle a razor, she cut herself several times, which drew more attention to her legs. Her brothers were relentless in their teasing, and her embarrassment was acute.

Tanya's parents tried to minimize the damage that their sons had caused, but they didn't meet with much success. What began as a private issue for Tanya ended up being far too public, and the entire incident grew significantly out of proportion. It is my guess that if Tanya had been able to talk to her mother about her concerns, her mom could have helped avoid the problem of all the nicks, cuts, and bandages.

As mentioned, boys often get little information from their families. They sometimes get even less from sex-education classes in school because they're too busy snickering at what they see and hear and then getting in trouble for laughing at something they're sternly told "is not funny." Of course, it's giggle time for fifth-grade boys when the serious teacher attempts to talk about the things they've been joking about at recess.

Bradley, a young adolescent who was in therapy, was very confused when he had his first ejaculation. It happened in the shower, and he was sure that somehow the soap had mysteriously gotten into his body and was just as mysteriously coming out. He thought he must have done something to damage his body, and he was terrified. Again, some basic information from his parents might have helped Bradley avoid the anxiety he experienced.

As adolescents grow into their new bodies, they develop more comfort with them. Each adolescent has a unique spin on how he handles the changes over which he has little control. Once the changes are relatively complete, he is better able to develop some mastery over his body and his life.

By middle adolescence, most young people have settled into their new packages. If physical changes have not occurred by this time, parents should consult with a pediatrician or endocrinologist so an evaluation can be made.

SEXUALITY

For the purpose of this book, I am defining sexuality as the psychological underpinnings of how individuals understand their feelings about sexual matters. How do they manage sexual thoughts? How do they inhibit sexual impulses? How do they see themselves from a sexual perspective? If they have been sexually abused prior to puberty, how has that impacted their answers to the first three questions?

Sexuality, an identity component of a maturing adolescent, should not be the result of sexual behavior. Instead, it should be the integration and internalization of self-attitudes, the family's value system, the individual's moral point of view, and the perspective of his faith. It is, in essence, a compilation of life experiences as they relate to matters of sex. Rather than being a separate identity system, sexuality is a component of the overall sense of who a person has been, who he has become, and who he perceives he will be.

This identity aspect helps guide the individual through the complex issues he faces, the difficult decisions he may have to make, and the challenging peer and social pressures. If an adolescent has established a clear sense of self and has a strong moral standpoint, he will have some immunity from the onslaught of sexual messages he is exposed to in almost all spheres of his life.

Premature exposure to sexual activity—such as the sexual abuse that is so prevalent among children in the child-welfare system—takes a huge toll on development. Sexual abuse impacts every area of the victim's life, forcing the child to engage in activities that are harmful in a myriad of ways. Furthermore, it places sexual behavior prior to puberty, skewing the natural sexual progression and causing the child's perspective about almost everything to be out of order. When sexuality is the result of sexual behavior, the individual faces the world primarily from a sexual perspective, which impairs development in many ways.

SEXUAL BEHAVIOR

Sexual behavior and adolescence are developmentally incompatible. Most adults believe that adolescents should not engage in sexual activity. Many adolescents themselves feel that they should not have sex before marriage and certainly not during adolescence. From a faith-based perspective, regardless of which religion, doing so is forbidden. From a practical and health perspective, it is high-risk behavior. From an interpersonal perspective, it is emotionally demanding and complicated. From a psychological perspective, it compromises the adolescent's ability to master the tasks associated with normal adolescent development. Additionally, it often leaves the adolescence with a jumble of feelings, including shame, remorse, betrayal, insecurity, and anxiety. If there was some level of coercion or even strong persuasion, a sense of being violated is added to the mix.

Sigmund Freud said that newly emerging sexual energies and impulses during adolescence are channeled by the adolescent and redirected toward accomplishing typical developmental tasks, such as academic learning, sports performance, artistic expression, identity seeking, peer-relationship development, and dating involvements. In other words, the adolescent requires a lot of focused energy just to master the responsibilities associated with being an adolescent.

If he is sexually active, the energy that would otherwise be available for him to carry out the typical developmental tasks is used up and cannot help him with industry and productivity. Instead, his focus is on sexual behavior—and perhaps not even on the person with whom he is involved. So in addition to moral and spiritual reasons for adolescents to refrain from sexual activity, there are also practical reasons.

SEXUAL ABUSE

If an adolescent has been victimized by sexual abuse—either early in life prior to adoption or since adoption—the onset of puberty might be more complicated than it would be for the typically developing child. Premature exposure to sex and sexually related issues often results in intense responses to the physical and psychological changes that occur. It is important to remember that individuals who have been sexualized have had sexual awareness for a long period of time, and surging hormones may lead to intense impulses that are difficult to manage effectively.

Children who have been sexualized often relate to adults and peers in a sexual manner. They tend to see themselves as being sexual and may actively seek sexual encounters—almost as a way to gain some mastery over what was once out of their control. Some children who have been sexualized by adults have a sense that the activity felt good to them, and it may have. This complicates the issue for two primary reasons: It leads the child to think that he caused his abuse, and it leads him to believe that he should continue engaging in such activities with others because it generates a pleasurable feeling.

Even when the actual abuse ends—usually when the child is removed from the birth family or orphanage—the reality of it does not. It is replayed over and over again in thoughts, feelings, sensory experiences, and, in some cases, with other children. When abused children reach puberty, they often experience a surge of sexual feelings. Faced with an increasing libido, the adolescent who has already had many sexual experiences is likely to seek sexual activity. He may put himself in high-risk situations in which he might be victimized again. Because he has had many sexual experiences prior to adolescence, he does not have much fear about doing what he's done before. He has defined himself as a sexual being, and his sexuality—his identity—is the result of earlier sexual behavior.

Sometimes sexual abuse drives adolescent sexual activity. Many boys who have been abused by male perpetrators feel that they may be homosexual—a belief further reinforced if the sexual activities felt good physically. The fear of being homosexual may drive them to try to conquer as many girls as possible, just to prove to themselves and others that they are not gay. They are preoccupied with sexual matters, and they may have histories of perpetrating against others throughout childhood and adolescence. This preoccupation clearly interferes with the adolescent's capacity to complete the developmental tasks required of him.

Boys who have been sexualized by older girls or women will also face complications in adolescence. They may be completely uncomfortable with females and, as a result, might find that their sexual identities are in a constant state of confusion.

Often girls who have been sexually abused by males feel disgusted about sex and anything associated with boys or men. They may identify themselves as being bisexual or exclusively attracted to females. Yet other girls who are abused by men seem almost driven to be sexually promiscuous throughout adolescence and perhaps into adulthood. Girls who have been abused by their mothers or other women are equally confused and driven to wonder about what their experiences mean in terms of their own sexuality.

Parenting an adolescent with a history of sexual abuse requires absolute vigilance of emerging sexual issues. Some studies suggest that about 30 percent of children who were sexually abused repeat perpetrating behavior. The good news, then, is that 70 percent do not continue the pattern. However, there may be an increased likelihood that the adolescent who has had sexual experiences in childhood will become sexually active.

Parents must take an active role in the adolescent's life when there are concerns that sexual activity is on the horizon. Although parents can't always prevent sexual activity, they *can* address the issue long before adolescence, just as they do other critical issues, such as the use of alcohol and drugs. Ongoing discussions about the importance of abstinence should be referenced from as many perspectives as possible. This may offer psychological immunization that will pay off when the adolescent finally hits those hormonally driven years.

A strong parental stance may allow the adolescent to feel comfortable about choosing not to engage in sexual activity. Many adolescents feel rescued from peer pressure when their parents have discussed and explored the many facets of sexual development. They can always use Mom and Dad as the reason why they can't do anything sexual, as in, "My parents would kill me if I did anything like that! I think they must have a GPS connected to me because I get caught every time I do something they don't approve of."

Adoptees may fear rejection by a boyfriend or girlfriend if they do not do what seems to be expected, so in an effort to be accepted, they may engage in sexual activities against their better judgment. To help diffuse these situations, it would be helpful for them to have a repertoire of responses to offer a persistent suitor. Parents might discuss some options with their children—again, well in advance of adolescence. The children may dismiss the parents' suggestions as "stupid," but their advice just might come in handy in the future if such a situation arises.

EXPOSURE TO SEXUAL MATERIAL

Children and adolescents are bombarded with sexual material via television, print media, music, music videos, and Internet sites. Never before in history has there been such easy access to graphic images and pornography. Anything that anyone is curious about is just a click away.

Such exposure is rampant throughout the world, and it has a serious negative impact on the developing child and adolescent. Short of pornography, adolescents are at the mercy of network television shows that feature sexualized content. Even female characters with professional jobs—from detectives to doctors—wear skin-tight clothing and show an inordinate amount of cleavage. Cable stations are worse still, with their endless parade of visual obscenities. Commercials run all hours of the day and night touting pills to enhance a man's performance, exposing the entire viewing family to a laundry list of possible bizarre side effects. It is not uncommon for parents to be asked questions about bodily functions by children far too young to make sense of such information.

Adolescents who get involved with pornography do so at great emotional expense. They are worried about some of the things they see; they compare themselves to characters in adult movies; their hormones are overstimulated; and they seem to lose their own capacity to form psychological fantasy and images. They become reliant on actual images and video to provide them with the sexual stimulation they should be able to construct without the help of concrete examples.

They begin to objectify women, men, sex, and themselves, and once this happens they begin to objectify their relationships with their peers. Objectification of anything allows for experimentation with it, and in the case of sex, it becomes easier to engage in activity without any inhibition or regard for the people involved in it. It also brings about the circumvention of moral thinking, which leads to moral relativism. When rules or morals are allowed to be relative, the individual is less likely to internalize a permanent set of values by which he judges himself and others. Objectification and moral relativism can ultimately lead to a floating, fluid conscience, and the loss of a guiding set of values is a huge price to pay.

To avoid or at least lessen these problems, parents of children and adolescents must do whatever they can to ensure that their computers are well monitored and properly protected by the latest technology. They must also communicate openly and clearly about the issues of sex. When I ask parents whether or not they have parental controls on their computers, I often hear, "Oh, no, but I don't think he'd go to those sites. I trust him." I generally reply with, "He's an adolescent, and what you *should* trust is the fact that, if given the opportunity, he will follow his sexual curiosity directly to all the wrong sites."

DATING PARENTS

Divorced parents who are dating may find that their adolescent does not approve of their new significant other. An adopted adolescent may feel especially rejected and abandoned by the absent mom or dad and may respond to this loss in a way that his parents did not consider. He may hope that they will get back together, but when divorced individuals begin to date, it usually diminishes the chances of a possible reunification.

Another complicating factor is the sexual component. If an adolescent suspects or knows for a fact that his parent is in a sexual relationship, he may feel extremely uncomfortable. And let's be honest here: No one wants to think about his parents having sex!

Given the fact that between 50 and 60 percent of marriages end in divorce, more adolescents than ever before have dating parents. It used to be that parents witnessed their kids going out on dates; now parents and their adolescents might be engaged in parallel activities. This can be unsettling for the adolescent, who is ill-prepared at this stage of life to deal with a parent's dating crisis. After all, up to this point, he's the one who's been in charge of the drama in the family.

Parents should keep their adolescent in mind when they embark on a new relationship. Their child must still be their primary interest, even if he is an adolescent who spends far less time at home than he used to. Dating parents have an opportunity to be role models, exhibiting behavior they would like their adolescent to emulate. If, however, there is a revolving door of partners, parents must realize that this will have an adverse effect on the child. In fact, I believe such conduct compromises the security that an adolescent needs in his relationship with his parent.

If the dating includes overnight stays, the adolescent might become even angrier. This kind of situation almost forces the adolescent to sexualize the parent, which is an unnecessary and unhealthy complication. I am surprised when adults forget the possible consequences their behavior has on their children.

Tara, age fifteen, was brought to therapy as the result of her anger and her tempestuous outbursts. She had been adopted by a single mother when she was twelve, and the two had developed a close, comfortable relationship. When Tara was about fourteen, her mother began dating someone — something she had not done since Tara came into her life. Tara immediately felt displaced by having to share her mother for the first time. What was once an important primary relationship with strong connections now felt secondary.

From Tara's perspective, it seemed that every time she suggested going out to dinner, her mother would reply with something along the lines of, "Oh, that sounds like fun. I'll call Rob to see if he wants to join us," which infuriated Tara. Whenever she rejected the idea and suggested that they engage in a mother-and-daughter-only activity, her mom accused her of being selfish. Eventually, Tara simply kept her mouth shut since her mom seemed bent on inviting Rob regardless of Tara's wishes.

In therapy, it became clear to me that Tara was feeling excluded, minimized, rejected, and replaced. Whenever she expressed her intense feelings, her mother was dismissive, saying, "See how selfish she is? All she thinks about is herself. Well, what about *me*? I need to have a life too. She's going to college in three years, and then what am I going to do? I'll be alone forever, that's what. No — Tara is not going to control my life!"

Tara would cry and scream and call her mother horrible names. "When Rob spends the night, it makes me sick! You're a slut, and it's embarrassing to see the two of you acting like teenagers in public. You even dress like a slut since you met him. I hate you, and all of my friends hate you too! I wish you had never adopted me!"

I could see that Tara and her mother were having parallel problems. Tara was losing her mother, so to speak, and her mother was gearing up to lose Tara when she left for college. The hurt, or anticipated hurt, they were feeling was disguised by the intense anger they shared.

Fortunately, the relationship Tara and her mom shared pre-Rob was strong, and they were able to reactivate it to help remedy the crisis. Tara's mom saw how important their relationship was. She had thought that because Tara was spending more time with her friends, she wouldn't mind if her mom added a new dimension to her life. Initially, Tara was actually fine with it. She liked Rob, and she enjoyed the time away from her mother when the two went out on a date. But those feelings soon faded, and Tara felt more and more tangential in her family. Her loss issues were triggered, and once that happened, she began acting as if she were losing everything in her life. Because her mother had become so important to her — in a very real sense, her "everything" — she was indeed losing all she cared about.

Tara's mom made some changes. She arranged to do things with Tara alone — just like they had done for two and a half years — and Rob stopped spending the night at their home. Both of these adjustments seemed to bring about a greater sense of security and comfort for Tara. She even was less antagonistic when the three of them spent time together.

SEX EDUCATION

I'm not sure when we, as a society, decided to give up things that were once the domain of the family and assign them to public education. When I hear parents talking about just how much the schools want them to be involved in homework and all things school related, I think that since we've asked the schools to raise our children — to talk to them about drugs, alcohol, physical abuse, and sexual issues — the schools are simply getting even when they say that parents should help their kids with geometry.

Because public-school teachers and administrators live in terror of addressing anything within a moral context — lest it look or sound like religion — they approach the sensitive issues from an amoral perspective, a mechanical perspective, a technical perspective. While that may be a helpful approach for many academic areas, it is not an effective approach for the moral arenas in our lives. When adults teach adolescents who are not their own children, they do it in a different way — an objective way that is not loaded with any moral message. Because they do not have any emotional investment in how the students respond to what they learn, they are free to exclude anything that comes close to being judgmental or moral.

It is my belief that sex education is best accomplished within the context of the family. The school could handle the "plumbing" parts from a technical and biological perspective, and the family could address the moral, emotional, and spiritual components.

Some sex-education classes teach the students how to have consequence-free sex, but there is no such thing. For adolescents, psychologically safe sex simply does not exist, and to call it "safe" is misleading. On some level, they get the inaccurate message, *If it's safe, why not do it?*

While I think that adolescents should have as much information as possible about all the complicating factors in life, I do not think it is helpful to have something as important as sexual issues presented in a solely objective and relativistic manner. A recent government survey suggests that adolescent sexual activity is going up, while condom use is dropping. Another study indicates that one in four teenage girls has a sexually transmitted disease. This information shows that, after years of declines in teenage pregnancy and disease, a new trend has emerged.[1] The only possible conclusion to draw is that our school-based sex education may not be as effective as some people think.

To be sure, we do not want our children and adolescents to engage in sexual activity, but after saying that, we teach them how to do it "safely." I understand why we have approached this area in the way we have, but it falls short of a complete, integrative way of addressing the issue of sexual activity.

I can't imagine a substance-abuse class taking the stance, "If you're going to do drugs, marijuana is a better choice than methamphetamines. Your teeth won't fall out, and you won't look twenty years older in a few months." Or a parental lecture advising, "We don't want you to rob a bank, but if you do, don't use a gun because you could shoot someone and you'll go to jail for a longer period of time." Surely, the former example would include specific information on the dangers of all drugs, and the latter would add some sort of moral arguments about stealing and respecting others.

The bottom line is that families must step up to the plate regarding sex education. Parents should talk with their child's teacher, review the course material, and discuss things at home, long before sexual activity is even a blip on the child's radar. It is essential to maintain open communication and to talk about *everything*, even the things that your adolescent thinks are far too dumb for his totally cool self. Ask for his opinions, his thoughts. Open-ended questions can often be productive. When adolescents say they don't want to discuss something, many times they actually mean that they don't know what to say, how to say it, whether or not they should say it, or how their parents might feel about it. It is therefore helpful to explore issues with them not as an interrogation but as you might do with a friend or another adolescent.

TRANSRACIAL AND TRANSCULTURAL ADOPTIONS

Where Does Your Child Fit In?

The words *transracial* and *transcultural* are sometimes used interchangeably, but I believe that it is important to differentiate between them because they are distinct.

> Race refers to an anthropological system of classification of humans based upon physical characteristics determined by heredity. People who share a genetic heritage and who, as a result, have very similar physical characteristics, constitute a racial group. The characteristics that determine one's race are strictly biological and can include color and texture of hair, color of skin and eyes, stature, bodily proportions and bone structure, tooth formation, and many other less visible biological traits.
>
> Culture is a system of values, beliefs, attitudes, traditions, and standards of behavior that govern the organization of both individual and group behavior. Culture is adaptive; it is created by groups of individuals and incorporated into group life to assure survival and well-being to the group's members.[1]

In addition to the cognitive systems mentioned, culture includes norms that in some way regulate each individual's behavior.

Everyone is a part of multiple cultures, and each of us must be able to navigate among the various cultures in which we live. It is doubtful that anyone has only one cultural perspective. A person lives within a family culture, a workplace culture, a faith culture, an academic culture, and a social culture. This list can likely be expanded to include even more arenas. Culture is transmitted and perpetuated through life experiences; race is perpetuated genetically.

In this chapter, *transracial adoption* refers to a situation in which the adoptee is of a different race than one or both of his parents. Because culture has to do with the individual's unique life experiences, it is not only possible but also probable that cultural differences will exist even within a same-race adoption. It is likely that any adoption that did not take place during infancy will have transcultural features.

I find it interesting that many parents use the term *transcultural* to conveniently describe their child's adoption. For example, when they use this word to reference an adoption from Vietnam, they are sidestepping the fact that they actually have a transracial adoption. If the child was adopted in infancy, he has lost the possibility of ever having any part of the culture into which he was born. He will never have the chance to *be* Vietnamese. However, people outside his circle of family and friends may assume, based on his physical appearance alone, that he knows more than he actually does about his culture of origin.

RACE MATTERS

Ours is a society in which we often find it difficult to talk about race, so instead we dance around it. When a person has grown up in a one-race environment, he knows very little about other races. His only points of reference are his parents' attitudes toward members of other races, the media, his peers, and stereotyped images.

Many parents who are involved in a transracial, intercountry adoption do not always acknowledge the transracial component. I know of one family who adopted a black child from Brazil, and they express surprise whenever he is teased about being black or is faced with other negative experiences as the result of racism. "Why do people think he's black," they asked me, "when he's from Brazil?" My answer was short and sweet: "Because he *is* black." People seldom consider the part of the world where the child was born and respond instead to how he looks.

In chapter 2, I addressed identity formation and the fact that adolescents are often mired in this potentially intense process. An adolescent in a transracial adoption will almost definitely explore racial differences in a way marked by the zeal and intensity typical of his age. If his parents have addressed race as an integral component of life throughout his childhood, his exploration may be more tempered. If, on the other hand, the family operated as if race doesn't matter, the adolescent will most assuredly make it matter, and he will probably do so as loudly as possible.

Dr. Joseph Crumbley, one of this country's leading authorities on transracial adoption, shares,

> Our role as professionals is to help adoptive and foster parents
> recognize the complexity of transracial placements. While most
> parents are familiar with the stages of child development, based
> on their own experiences with children, they are unaware of racial
> and cultural identity development. Such identity development
> does not mesh in a tidy way with the universal stages of cognitive,
> psychological, and emotional development that are clearly tied to
> the age of the child. Rather, demographic and sociological factors
> play a strong intervening role regarding perceptions of, and attitudes
> toward, identity.[2]

Race matters in most cultures and societies. Given this country's historically raced-based problems, it matters a lot. White adoptive parents must lead the way in helping their children of color build an understanding of the relevance of race, preparing them for what they may face in the world. As with other critical issues I have discussed—drugs, alcohol, and sex—race needs to be addressed at an early age, not during adolescence. Race is central in our culture, and embracing a mentality of "We're all the same" doesn't begin to do it justice.

One difficulty white parents have in dealing with race is they often don't know much about it. As members of the majority, they can usually live their lives with little or no regard to race. If they have not lived in a multi-racial community or had much contact with individuals of other races, they are poorly suited to helping their child face racism issues as he grows up. Furthermore, if the parents do not have a racially diverse set of friends, that, too, sends a negative message to the child.

Multirace families will likely have faced many questions, insults, and ignorance by the time their children have become adolescents. Most adoptive families face a host of rude and thoughtless questions from others, but mixed-race families are more likely to be approached by complete strangers who sling a barrage of questions: "They're not yours, are they?" "What happened to their real parents?" "Do you have children of your own? Do they live with you?" "Was it expensive to adopt the Chinese kid?"

There is wide variability in how families define themselves and how they are defined by others. Multiple motivations prompt people to adopt, and this is also true for families who decide to adopt transracially. The following questions should be answered honestly when considering a transracial adoption:

- How diverse are your social relationships? Is your community accustomed to people of color? Does your school district include children of color? How willing are you to make changes in your lifestyle to accommodate your adolescent's need for ongoing involvement with peers who are like him?

- How do members of your extended family feel about racial minorities? Is your faith community integrated? Can you embrace, not just accept or tolerate, your adolescent's racial and cultural heritage? Are you willing to have friends of his race spend time at your home? What are your feelings about interracial dating and/or marriage?

- Are you willing to advocate actively for your adolescent when he experiences the fallout of racism? Can you comfort him when he tries to date someone he's been friends with for years but is now seen by her family as a young black man instead of a cute little African boy? Can you do so without trying to explain or defend the other parents' feelings?

- How will you feel if your adopted son calls you white? Or black, if you are a person of color who has adopted a Caucasian child? A racist? Not really his parent? How will you manage things when you see your child socializing with adolescents who may be of a different class? What does it mean to you when your adolescent tries to be more black, white, Asian, or Latino than he used to be? If your adolescent suddenly hates everything relating to a color other than his own, including you, how will you respond?

Because adolescence is a time of identity exploration and experimentation, some adolescents will overidentify with the negative stereotypes of their respective racial groups. Their attempts to get in touch with their roots may cause them to engage in the primetime-television behavior they associate with their race. Unfortunately, this means they're more likely to emulate the cop-show street thug than the senior class president who is also of their race. They might start to associate with the kinds of kids their parents find undesirable. They might trade in their preppy duds for clothes that will help them fit in with and identify with their racial peers, who may or may not be their social peers.

Bobby, a seventeen-year-old African American, was adopted when he was about a year old. His parents were both white, as was his entire social world. There were few other black kids in his small Midwest town, and they were not among his circle of friends. They were poor, and Bobby's world did not come into contact with theirs. Bobby's parents did not have any black friends, and all the members of their church were white. Bobby's soccer teammates were white, and so were all the teachers in his school. None of this seemed problematic — until Bobby was about sixteen.

An excellent student, Bobby wanted to attend a six-week summer program at a large urban university in his state. When he arrived on campus, he noticed that he was no longer the only black kid on the block. He also realized that he was different from the other black students and that the white students, none of whom he knew, reacted to him differently than did the white kids in his hometown. The upshot was that he felt completely out of place. Some of the black kids made remarks about his acting and talking white. The white kids did not say anything mean to him, but they didn't include him in their social activities either. Bobby, trapped between two worlds, was utterly alone.

Some of the black students commented that "Bobby" was such a white name and that soccer was way too white. They tormented him about not being able to play basketball. When they asked about his life, they learned that his parents, his friends, and his whole world were white. They were somewhat incredulous, and for the first time in Bobby's life, he began to wonder what he would need to do to be more "black."

First off, his new friends called him "Robert." He began listening to rap music with them, and that seemed to be his foray into a new world. The music taught him a new language and gave him something in common with the other black students. He started to think about reflecting his race and fitting in with the other kids at the summer program.

As with most adolescents who dabble at being different than they have been throughout their childhood, Bobby immersed himself in his new identity. After about three weeks, he felt like a new person. Because he was not in a position to go shopping for clothes, he could only change how he talked and walked, and he observed a few gestures that he began to use. He no longer needed to be accepted by the white kids in the program; his new friends were exclusively black.

When Bobby's parents called him, they noticed his new language and different inflections and thought he "sounded black." They weren't particularly concerned, but they did begin to wonder what had happened to bring about this change. They were somewhat confused at his insistence that they call him "Robert," but they agreed to do so out of respect for him.

They talked with each other about how to address their son's new identity, but they had little knowledge about race, adolescence, identity, and diversity. They had no black friends with whom they could talk, and they weren't about to bring it up with their white friends. After all, they had raised Bobby as a person, not as a black adopted kid. In fact, whenever anyone asked them about Bobby's being black, they most often said, "You know, we don't even see him as black; we see him as our son."

Unfortunately, Bobby's parents had not prepared for this moment, and no one along the way had given them any idea that race was something they should be concerned about. It would be easy to judge Bobby's parents and find them guilty of color blindness to a fault, but that would not be productive. They decided that this was a temporary glitch, and they were sure that when Bobby came home, everything would be the same again. Call it hope, call it denial, but that's where they landed. And they were dead wrong.

Bobby, now Robert, was on a journey to becoming who he really was and who he wanted to be. He returned from the summer program an almost unrecognizable person. His new music offended his parents, and they didn't realize that many black parents wouldn't want their adolescents listening to hard-core rap in their homes either. They knew little about the style of the sagging, oversized clothes their son insisted on buying. They had no idea how to deal with their once-little boy who now seemed like an unknown person to them, and they felt like strangers in their own home.

Not knowing how to proceed, Robert's parents called me to set up an evaluation. After gathering a lot of information prior to meeting with the three of them, I was fairly certain Robert was in the midst of an adolescent identity search. This process is typical for any adolescent, and its content — the search for racial identity — was to be expected in a transracial adoption in which race had never been discussed.

When I met with Robert, he was angry about being in my office. He insisted that nothing was wrong with him, and he said he didn't care what his parents thought about how he was acting. "I'm black," he sneered, "and they better get used to it!"

Despite being angry, he appeared to want to talk to me. He continued, "What were they thinking? Did they think I was just going to end up being white? Didn't they know this would happen when they adopted me? I had to learn about my people all on my own, and that sucks!"

Robert thought he knew a lot about his people, but he was able to hear me when I suggested that he knew something about some blacks but that there was much more to learn. Knowing the lyrics to as many rap songs as possible might help him fit in with some of his peers, but that was just a small part of his race. More knowledge and experiences with a wider range of black people would deepen and strengthen his identity, which was somewhat superficial and new.

Although Robert didn't think he needed to see me again, he agreed to do so. His parents were relieved when he said he would follow up with more appointments.

He did not have psychological disorder, unless one looks at adolescent development as pathological, which it most definitely is not. My role with Robert and his family was to be a bridge between what appeared to be two sides of a huge chasm. Robert needed to know that someone had an understanding of what he was experiencing, and he needed an arena in which to discuss race, identity, adoption, and his relationship with his parents. The family needed a lot of belated psycho-education about transracial adoption and related issues.

After I met with Robert and his family for about a year, they developed a new level of interacting marked by less volatility, more mutual respect, and more balance.

When Robert started looking at colleges, two historically black universities were included on his list. Upon visiting the black schools, Robert felt a level of comfort that he had not known before. Conversely, his parents felt extremely out of place and conspicuous, convinced that people were staring at them — which they probably were. Never having been in a minority position, they were startled into a new degree of awareness. The visit provided them with a glimpse of what Robert had experienced throughout his life, and it opened up expansive communication between parents and son.

Robert ultimately chose to attend the larger of the two black schools, and the summer prior to his enrollment, he and his parents participated in a two-day freshman orientation program. There were joint sessions of students and parents as well as meetings just for students and others just for parents. Robert's mom and dad were immersed in yet another new situation as the only white parents in the group.

Robert was happy that his parents supported his decision about where to go to school, and his parents were pleased with their new understanding about something they wished they had addressed years before. Once Robert gained more confidence about his identity, he, like all older adolescents, began to mellow. He no longer had to "act black," because he had grown into who he was becoming. He clearly saw himself as a black man, and this new security allowed him to be a more psychologically integrated and complex person.

Traci, age eighteen, was adopted when she was three. She was biracial, and her single mother was white. Although the two lived in a primarily white community, Traci's mom had friends who were of varying races, and Traci had many friends of many colors.

Traci was an easygoing child who flowed with just about everything that crossed her path. She did well in school, was very sociable, maintained a positive attitude throughout adolescence, and made good decisions. She was planning to go to college, and she consistently indicated that she wanted to go to a school close to home so she could continue to spend time with her mom and stay in touch with her friends.

Traci and her mom had talked about adoption and race throughout their lives together, and Traci's even temperament allowed her to relate to many people in different situations. When her friends were having conflict in their relationships, Traci was the go-to person for balance and resolution.

I had no professional contact with Traci, but I had met her and her mom through an adoption organization in which they had been involved. Traci wanted to enter a profession that would allow her to work with children. She had some interest in knowing more about her birth family, yet she did not pursue a search for either information or names of relatives. Her level of contentedness was apparent.

Traci's life certainly had the ingredients that could have created chaos for her. However, her close and open relationship with her mother seemed to serve her well in all spheres of her life, providing her with a sense of internal security that allowed for complete balance.

Traditionally, transracial adoption has referred to white parents adopting children of color. In recent times, however, more black families are adopting white children and adolescents. While I have no knowledge of anything having been written about this, it seems to be an increasing phenomenon. Part of the reason for this new trend is the fact that more foster parents are adopting their foster children than ever before. Fourteen percent of white children available for adoption in the Cleveland, Ohio, area were adopted by black families, and 17 percent of adoption-available black children in the region were adopted by white families.[3] It will be interesting to see if this direction of transracial adoption will be examined as closely as transracial adoptions have been thus far. It will also be interesting to gain insight into what the special concerns of these adoptees and their families will be.

TRANSCULTURAL ADOPTIONS

As previously stated, culture is transmitted through life experiences from generation to generation. Therefore, adolescents who have been adopted in childhood or later will have had some exposure to their birth family's culture. Depending on the age at which he was adopted, a child whose early years were traumatic may internalize those emotional wounds and bring pieces of his fractured culture into his adoptive home. If he was in an orphanage for a long period of time, he will have remnants of institutionalization — the orphanage culture.

Because much of what the abused adolescent carries with him is dysfunctional, the adoptive family must be prepared to live with the old and simultaneously introduce new elements to the adoptee's cultural world. The new will come from the adoptive family's life, and over time it should be expected that these new experiences will be embraced by the adolescent. It should not be assumed that he will abandon the cultural factors that developed prior to adoption but rather that input from his adoptive family will replace the dysfunctional components of his personality. Parents and professionals should remember that the culture of trauma is tenacious and resistant to change, but that should not preclude attempting to modify it via therapy and new life experiences. In *Adopting the Hurt Child*, coauthor Regina Kupecky and I examine this issue at length in the chapter titled "The Toll of Impermanence."

Transcultural adoptions typically refer to intercountry adoptions. These days, many children and adolescents are being adopted from a variety of countries throughout the world. If a child is adopted in infancy, cultural issues will be nonexistent. However, that does not suggest that the adoptive family should ignore the need to have information about the child's country of origin. Such data could prove helpful in answering any questions the child may have as he gets older and his curiosity increases.

Some adolescents will be interested in talking about their birth countries. They may want to do a homeland tour or try to find their birth families. Today's technology simplifies the process of an international search, but the vast majority of adoptees from other countries will not have successful searches and reunions. Many of them were abandoned, and there is no information whatsoever about their birth families.

During adolescence, some adoptees will identify with an aspect of their country of origin, while others will have little interest. The adoptive family should be open about discussing the adolescent's country of birth, and they should be willing to get information about things in which the adolescent has expressed interest. However, I think it is best to follow the lead of the adolescent in terms of keeping his cultural issues alive.

Some adoptive parents want to expose their child to the language of his country. If the child wants to learn Chinese, his desire should be supported. But if the purpose of sending him to language classes is to satisfy the parents' need to do the right thing, the goal should be reexamined.

While adoption professionals continue to encourage families to promote involvement in cultural activities, sometimes it simply does not interest the child. I have seen parents get giddy with excitement over the prospect of attending a cultural event, while their adolescent's apathy about the whole scene is almost tangible. If we remember that culture is transmitted by experience, we must realize that if an adolescent has been raised in the United States, his culture is American. His heritage may be Korean, Russian, or Ethiopian, but going to a rap or heavy-metal concert may be much more appealing to him than attending a culture camp. It should be up to him to decide whether or not he wants to participate.

Jake was adopted from Korea when he was a year and a half old. By the age of thirteen, he had grown into an all-American kid with one consuming interest: his skateboard. He skated day and night, and he was rarely seen walking anywhere without his board.

Jake's parents felt strongly that they needed to keep his awareness about Korea very much alive. Each summer, they sent him to Korean culture camp, and each year, he seemed more resistant. When he was twelve, he really dug in his heels, but his parents forced the issue and he gave in. Jake was so miserable and uncooperative at the camp that he came very close to being sent home.

At thirteen, he had become more involved with his friends and planned to spend most of the summer skating with them at the local skate park. He also hoped to travel to a park in a neighboring town that was considered *the* place to skate.

When his parents broached the issue of the culture camp again, Jake exploded. "I am *not* going to that stupid camp this year! I am *not* giving up a whole week of being with my friends. I don't care about Korea, I hate Korean food, and I don't even have one Korean friend. I'm not Korean! I was born there, but I've lived here my whole life. Why would I want to go hang out with a bunch of Asian kids I don't even know? If you like Korea so much, why don't you guys go to camp?"

Jake made it clear that his interests in Korea were nonexistent. It seemed to me that his parents should have been paying closer attention to what he was saying. Korea was *his* birth country, so *his* needs, relative to his former culture, needed to be respected. Actually, I think that his parents' attempts to keep Korea alive for Jake ended up exacerbating his hatred of all things Korean.

Angela, age sixteen, was also from Korea. She had been adopted in infancy, and she always seemed interested in things related to her country of birth. She liked her Korean dolls, and she enjoyed dressing in Korean clothes. She was especially fond of reading books about Korea, and she enjoyed talking about her adoption story with her mother. She loved going to culture camp in the summer and made a point of keeping in touch with the kids from camp throughout the school year.

Angela frequently begged her mom to take her to the Korean grocery store so she could buy food that she would prepare using recipes she had gotten from camp. She dreamed of taking a homeland tour and perhaps visiting her foster mother in Korea. She also hoped that one day she could meet her birth mother and find out if she had any siblings.

Angela told me, "I really love going to camp every year, and this year, because I'm sixteen, I'm going to be a junior counselor. When I go to college, I want to be able to work at the camp every summer. It feels so good to be with other adopted kids. There are more Asian kids at camp than there are in my entire town! It's just a special place."

Jake and Angela: two adolescents, two very similar backgrounds and adoptive homes, two entirely different reactions to the cultural component. Whatever the case, each adolescent's feelings and needs must be honored and respected. Most children alter their interests throughout their lives, and it makes sense for parents to take note of these changes. I am always surprised when moms and dads don't seem to notice that their sixteen-year-old has morphed from what he was at age eight. It might have been cool for him to wear his Russian outfit to the adoption picnic when he was in third grade, but it's a ridiculous and embarrassing getup for the high school sophomore.

INDIVIDUAL UNIQUENESS

As you can see from the cases mentioned in this chapter, responses to transracial adoptions fall all along the spectrum. Every individual has his own beliefs, feelings, and reactions. It is therefore important for adoption professionals to remain open about how to work with adoptive families. If we decide there is only one right way to handle an issue, that way may not fit in with the family's own style and culture. Perhaps they do not want to do *the* right thing. If that's the case, we must work with them within the context of their wishes and situations.

We also need to be aware of adoption trends. Many behavior that is considered right today was once probably seen as the wrong way to do things. Just think about openness in adoption—at one time it wasn't even considered. There was also a time when agencies wouldn't dream of a transracial adoption. Same-race placements were not only encouraged but often demanded. White families adopting children of color were required to attend training about race and culture, and it was necessary for them to have a "cultural competency plan." Today the phrase is unheard of. In fact, some agencies are so afraid of violating the provisions of the Multiethnic Placement Act (MEPA) that they provide absolutely no training—sometimes no discussion whatsoever—about race and culture. I believe that such fear hinders having an open discussion about one of our country's most sensitive issues: race.

In closing this chapter, I've chosen to include two poems written by transracial adoptees. The first is by James Hall-Gallagher, an African American adolescent who was adopted by white parents. The second is by Sara B., age twenty-one, who wrote her poem when she was nineteen. Sara is multiracial and was adopted by white parents.

I Have Four Last Names

Complicated.
Cool.
Wonderful.
Interesting.
My first name was
Jason Terralonge Arterberry.
My second name was
James Hall-Gallagher.
These magnificent names
have two meanings
for me

and for the people I see every day
in and out of school.

My first name
is what I really am
and what is truly me
on the inside
and the out.
It is what I was born with.
What my true parents,
my first parents,
gave to me,
so I could become me.
This name is me,
a black boy
who is becoming
a man.

Terralonge is a name from Jamaica;
Arterberry is an English name.
My mom gave me Terralonge
and my dad gave me Arterberry.
These names
are more than just words
scrambled together
to make a sound.
They are
who I am
and who I will be,
for the rest of my life.
My second name
is James Hall-Gallagher
This name is my name,
but not by birth.
It is the name

my second family
gave me.
This name
is not
as important
to me
as my first.
I feel
like
this name
is what the government sees
as me
but not
what I see
as myself.
Since I am not
in the custody of
my first parents,
I can't use my
real name.

My second name
is like a mask
that is covering my true self,
that one day
I will take off.
And then
I will show people
my true name
and who I really am.
But my second name
is still important
since this name
was given by the people

who will take care of me
my whole life.

Both of these names
are beautiful,
confusing,
and real.
They will stay with me
my whole life
and
I will
never forget
that they both
define
who I am.
Both of these names
are who I am.
I am called
one more
than the other,
but
both
are very
meaningful
to me.

TRA (Transracial Adoptee): Understanding and Love

2 mothers, 2 fathers, 1 sister, 1 brother
Inside me burns a fiery hunger
A loss of never meeting
No birthday or holiday greetings
From biological family

While my friends are smiling
Sadness harbors itself in my soul

I am falling into a black and white hole
No bottom or end in sight
Nightmares end in fright

Those around me who know my name
Don't realize there is more to my life
Struggle, pain, and endless strife
Underneath a rich, white light
Covers me in a warm glow every night

My adoptive parents find it hard to understand
Race relations
Judgment and discrimination
Drive this nation
Somehow not touching the lives of my parents
But for me, in my life, it is inherent

EIGHT

TURNING EIGHTEEN

What Does It Mean?

Adolescents and their parents reference the eighteenth birthday so frequently that it merits a place in the Hall of Fame of Meaningless Statements. Adolescents use, "When I'm eighteen . . ." as an introductory phrase for every proclamation of their upcoming emancipation. Parents use it as a reminder that expresses just a hint of threat: "When you're eighteen, you can do whatever you want, but as long as you live under my roof . . ." On particularly bad days, the line usually goes something like, "When you're eighteen, you're outa here!"

The truth is, when the adolescent turns eighteen, not much changes. Most eighteen-year-olds are still in high school and coming up with answers to the commonly asked question "What are you going to do when you graduate?" Some adolescents know precisely what they'll be doing—heading off to college, attending a trade school, starting a new job, joining the military—but others seem almost paralyzed by fear. "What *am* I going to do? I need to be planning my future, but I don't even know where to start."

Adolescents who were adopted later in childhood or adolescence might be very concerned that they will have to leave the family. They might have no idea what they are going to do once they turn eighteen, and if they have had significant trauma, they might be so developmentally delayed that they are not in a position to make any kind of decision about their future.

Adoption offers an individual permanent membership in a family for a lifetime. The manner in which the parents demonstrate this permanency is of critical importance. Many adoptees have heightened sensitivity about developmental transitions. If they have experienced or created significant chaos in their families throughout their lives, they will probably wonder if turning eighteen will prompt their parents to think about asking them to leave home. If they have had a calmer life with little or few difficulties, turning eighteen may not mean much at all.

As you will see from the stories in this chapter, the milestone of turning eighteen affects adoptees and their parents in many different ways. To some, it has a dramatic impact, but to others, it's barely a blip.

L. G. MANSFIELD,[1] ON HER SON:

Of all the challenges I've faced in my lifetime, launching my grown kids into adulthood has been the toughest one. It all began when my oldest son, Ty, turned eighteen and announced with a flourish that he was now a "legal adult." He promptly dropped out of high school, quit a lucrative job as a Web designer, and assumed a self-absorbed, arrogant attitude worthy of a street thug. He was pumped. I was crushed.

I was a single parent at the time, and I had no idea how to respond to this belligerent and disrespectful stranger. My initial shock gave way to hurt, which finally exploded in outright fury.

"How could you do this to me?" I bellowed. "After all I've done for you!" Oh, I was the irate parent, all right. And I made it all about *me*.

I had lost control of both my sanity and my ability to respond appropriately to the situation. I knew I was out of my league, so I prayed for the strength to get back in harmony with my son. My prayers were answered with startling simplicity when I realized that I couldn't control the actions of Ty any more than I could control the phases of the moon or the changes of the season. So I let go.

It was clear that my son wanted to experience the world by his rules — rules that I, in my infinite parental wisdom, knew would not work. But I decided to give him the freedom to try it his way.

"It's a big world, kiddo," I said as I packed his belongings, "and now it's yours. I'm going to give you the gift of a lifetime—the chance to go out there and sample it all."

He looked a little baffled as I walked him to the front door, and for the first time in a long time, he didn't have anything to say. I tried to keep my voice steady as I continued my little speech.

"This isn't exactly what I had in mind for you," I said, "but I can't handle your lack of respect. Since you refuse to behave with any decency, I'm setting you free. Go out there and put your rules into play. I hope it works."

I kissed him on the cheek and gave him a huge hug.

"I love you," I whispered. "Be safe. And remember, the door is always open."

I watched as he walked down the front steps and loaded his things into his car. I waved as he drove away. And then I unleashed the tears.

So far, despite a minimum of grace, he's surviving his solo flight. I swear I can still hear his wings flapping in his room late at night.

BETH HALL,[2] ON HER DAUGHTER:

I feel as if my hair is flying straight away from my face and I'm grabbing the bar of the roller-coaster car so hard my hands ache. When it's time to get off the ride, I exit on legs like Jell-O. My brain keeps telling me to get up and walk away, but my limbs have trouble cooperating because the rush of the ride is still fresh in my cells. I have been parenting a child for eighteen years, and now I'm watching her leave for the first time.

There were so many moments when I meant to be the perfect parent, and they passed me by before I had time to complete them. There were so many times I meant to tell her what was right and good about her instead of focusing on the little suggestions for what she could do better. There were so many times that I meant to take care of myself so I wouldn't be a burden or hold her back from the hopes and dreams she has for herself. There are so many ways that I forgot to prepare for this moment.

Before I understand what is happening, I am sobbing, surprised by the strength of my emotion and stunned by the depth of my despair. When did I begin living through her as if I had no life of my own? How did I forget to remind myself that she is an independent being, blossoming into an adult?

She is a young woman off to begin her own journey of independence, which necessitates leaving me behind. Consumed with the task of mothering, why did I think so many silly moments would be so easily remembered or brought back to mind? Like the photo books I mean to put together each year, I find myself with only boxes of pictures thrown together haphazardly. The first time she raised her dark-haired head and discovered a world beyond her bassinet—my husband and I continue to be the only two who seem capable of understanding the magic and the hilarity of that moment.

Her first step, first day of school, first broken bone, first overnight, first boyfriend, first time behind the wheel of the car, and, of course, all the seconds, thirds, and one hundredths—these memories slide into a blur that seems to have slipped by with impossible speed. This young lifetime as a family that has now so quickly passed is like the roller-coaster ride—over before it has even begun.

Of course I know she will return—many times. Of course I know that our relationship is deep and reaches far beyond the bond of living under the same roof. Of course I know that college will involve steps back to the safety and comfort of home in between the surges outward. Of course I know, but right now I just can't seem to care.

I sit in my car while my sixteen-year-old gets his hair cut. I have no more than twenty minutes to myself. My husband and my daughter have headed south to the college of her choice, where she is enrolled in a summer institute—living in a dorm, taking her first classes. My baby is a college student. She is ready—I hope. She is excited and scared. So much of the preparation has been about her that I forgot to pay attention to the feeling of loss for myself.

I always meant to try letting go—to raise my hands high on those roller-coaster rides of yore. I always admired the willingness of others to lift their hands in the air and let the ride simply happen. It was harder for me to trust that somehow gravity and nature would hold my body on this earth rather than fling me, or the car itself, into the atmosphere. I never have been able to let go—until now.

I am amazed by how deeply and truly my confidence and trust in my daughter matter to her as she sets forth. It is clear to me now that she has always needed to be seen and validated more than she needed to be corrected or cajoled. Did I encourage enough? Does she know I believe in her?

We recently had a moment when I let her have it after a missed curfew. She defended her position with indignant logic and a splash of pleading, to which I responded, "You are so self-absorbed! It's like you don't even care how we feel." Her eyes told the story: I had cut her to the bone. Although I knew I had gone too far, I wanted to feel justified for the years of worry and the fear that never goes away. A lifetime later, after we had made up and slogged through our own versions of the truth, she hit the nail on the head when she said, "Everything I do is basically to make you proud."

I could fill all the oceans with the tears this evokes in me and how it reminds me of a truth I have known from the beginning—that children's esteem is based in large part on their parents' positive view of them. But as my buttons were pushed, I forgot to remember and stay vigilant. I pray that I have conveyed my trust enough to hold her steady.

I know she is ready to try her own version of a first step, just as she was on her first birthday when she stood up and walked from her father to me, six baby steps before she landed on her padded bottom and laughed with the pride that only a baby can embody. And as I weep and experience the devastation of losing her, I know in my heart of hearts that she needs me to let go. This time, I really will hold my arms in the air and trust the world, because this time I understand. It is these moments of trust that mean everything and bind us for life. The sharing of the real joy and the real pain. Her fears. My fears. Our joining in support of each other as a family—not to hold on for dear life but to let go because we know that our connection is meant to be. The tie that binds us is not the iron bar that clamps us into the ride but the one that is forged in love and trust.

Letting go can be done in many ways. In both of the stories, it did not mean ending a relationship; it meant mothers understanding and appreciating the journeys of their almost-grown-up adolescents. Letting go is more like standing beside someone instead of prodding from behind or leading from in front. Whatever the specifics, it is not about abandonment.

JANET ALSTON JACKSON,[3] ON HER SON:

When I think back to when my son Devon turned eighteen, two things come to mind: freedom and fear. Freedom for Devon, and fear for me.

On Devon's eighteenth birthday, he was returning home after three years of living in Devereux, a nonprofit institution for children with emotional, developmental, and educational disabilities. He was placed there because he was not only out of control but violent as well. The six-month program had turned into three years for him. The staff told my husband, Walter, and me that Devon had been the most difficult client to deal with out of all the young people in his unit who came from homes around the country.

Devon was three years old when we adopted him. Each passing year, he grew increasingly more argumentative and difficult. Our entire household—which included my oldest son, Ryan, and my adopted daughter, Jada—all felt trapped in his emotional bondage. We struggled to keep our sanity while living in Devon's cesspool of lies, deceit, thievery, and complete unrest. There was no peace in our house.

Back then I was a publicist for a major television network. I was trained to be aggressive in that job and in my previous job with a different network, which entailed getting publicity for shows and actors in lightning speed at any cost. However, even with my twenty years of experience tracking down information for the national press and the networks, I could not find help for Devon.

Fruitlessly, I dragged my son to twenty-two different therapists over the course of eleven years. I was determined to get this child "fixed." He was driving everyone crazy—our family, his teachers, his classmates—and no one could stand him. Devon seemed to relish antagonizing other children and pitting adults against one another. I was constantly in battles with his teachers over his "crazy lying"—lying with nothing at stake.

We had no clue that he was suffering from attachment disorder. When a child doesn't get his needs met during the first few years of his life, he cannot bond with his caretakers. He doesn't trust adults, and he is detached from his own feelings. Deep down, he thinks no one cares. Separation from birth parents, emotionally and physically, leads such a child to feel that he will always be abandoned. He protects himself with an emotional shield to keep everyone at a distance. In extreme cases of this self-survival disorder, a child can become antisocial and may end up leading a life of crime.

Devon was born with PCP, cocaine, and alcohol in his system, and in his first few years of life, he had been sexually and physically abused. By the age of three, he had lived in two different foster homes. In spite of his history, Walt and I fell in love with him at an adoption party. Something spiritually happened. We were galvanized to this child. We were not naive enough to think that life with Devon would be easy, but we didn't know that we wouldn't be able to find the necessary resources to help us through the tumultuous years ahead.

Like many families, Walt and I both worked, but I ended up quitting my job at the television network because Devon required constant supervision. My occupation became running to his school and heeding teachers' desperate calls to take him home because of his unruly behavior.

When Devon reached his teens, he grew violent. I could have saved myself those agonizing years sitting in mental-health waiting rooms if I knew then that effective therapy is built on trust. Devon, like other children with attachment issues, didn't trust. The therapists couldn't figure him out, even though they diagnosed him as ADHD, bipolar, and oppositional defiant. They didn't know he had attachment disorder because, like me, they didn't know what it was.

Devon manipulated his therapists as he did his teachers. He brought out the worst in them and seemed to enjoy being the ringmaster in the chaotic three-ring circus he created.

During those years, I was constantly on high alert and exhausted from dragging him to different therapists. But all of that came to a halt when he showed signs of violence with his brother and at school. It culminated with his arrest after he was caught stealing at Wal-Mart.

When Walt and I went to pick him up from the police station, we knew this was it. We had suffered through his emotional issues, but we refused to go down his path of breaking the law. We were not going to be dragged through the penal system with him. We thought about his violence and how fast he was growing up. We talked of the horror stories in the news of teens out of control, hurting and killing others. It haunted us. We then came to grips with the fact that we simply could not help him and had to find a live-in facility with mental-health experts who could.

After we walked through what seemed like fire with the system and dealt with school psychologists, social workers, and his therapist, Devon ended up being placed in Devereux. Located in Texas, it was hundreds of miles from home because there was no program in California that could handle his unique case. He hadn't committed a crime severe enough to be placed in juvenile hall, and he could not be trusted enough to live at home. (Actually Devereux was Devon's second placement. We had begged the officials at Hathaway Children and Family Services, which dealt with mental issues, to accept him into their program since he was already an outpatient. The home was just ten minutes from where we lived. They reluctantly agreed, and Devon was there about a month before they kicked him out.)

Devon's stay in Texas was supposed to be for only six months, but he ended up sitting in his room for six months, refusing to cooperate with the staff. Medication and therapy did not seem to help him, so his stay kept getting extended. In the meantime, Walt and I feared he would be kicked out of Devereux, too — boomeranging back home with open emotional wounds from incomplete therapy and anger with us for sending him away.

Our weekly family phone-therapy sessions were supplemented by exhausting red-eye flights to visit Devon every other month. In the first two years that he was at Devereux, we felt as if we were on lockdown, just like our son. He could not have the same off-campus privileges the other kids enjoyed with their parents, such as trips to the amusement park or dining at a restaurant. Because he would not cooperate with the program, he was sentenced to his small, stark green room. Even though the room was nice, it was as if we were flying to Texas to sit in a jail cell with him.

One day something magical happened with Devon. He began to turn around, and he was no longer the kid his peers hated and the staff struggled to help; he'd become a model citizen. His therapist called to say that Devon would be coming home on his eighteenth birthday. He was being released.

Devon was thrilled and excited. Freedom on his eighteenth birthday! For the rest of our family, it meant back to hell and turmoil. How could we live with him? Had he really changed as the staff said he had? Would we go back to knotted stomachs and stashed possessions? Would life revert to arguing, shouting, and not being able to truly relax in our own home?

As the time grew closer to his birthday, Devon called daily with growing excitement.

One of the things Devon lacked was fear. He had grown accustomed to losing his privileges, but he never feared that the road he was on would lead him to lifelong consequences, such as going to jail. Not only did we have these fears for him, his teachers and therapists did as well.

When Devon returned home, our entire family stood in the airport waiting like soldiers on high alert watching for a terrorist. It took about a month before we began to relax and feel that he was no longer the enemy.

Devon showed that he had learned many lessons. He had a healthy fear that if he did not follow the rules and regulations of both our home and society, he would pay a higher price than he'd paid living at Devereux. In addition, it wouldn't be like stealing from Wal-Mart, where they had dropped charges because it was his first offense.

I had to work on a lot of fears, like the backlash from Devon going off his medications. He had refused to take them the last few months at Devereux, and at one time he was on suicide watch. But the doctors reported that he had adjusted well after a few months, and, as Devon said, he did not need the pills anymore.

In time I came to realize that the fears that haunted me were the result of my living in the past. Yes, I should be concerned that he could relapse, but I couldn't allow myself to live my life in fear. It attracts even more fear, and it could attract the very thing I resisted.

So how could I let go of the fear and enjoy the newfound change in my eighteen-year-old? I learned that the best way for me to relieve the stress and fear was to live in the moment. When fear came up, it was my alarm and direction to focus on the present. I kept my mind on whatever task I was doing. I concentrated on my breathing when my mind would wander off into that dangerous territory of what-ifs. I mindfully embraced my emotions and thoughts with love instead of pushing them away.

I didn't know that Devon also had fears deep inside. One evening after his return, we were shopping together to buy him new clothes. We were laughing and kidding one another when he said, "I'm glad everything is working out." When I questioned him about his statement, he began to open up, which was another sign that he had grown and matured. Before Devereux, he had held his feelings inside and then exploded. Now he was talkative and expressing his feelings.

"I was afraid of how the family would feel about me coming back," said Devon. "I was afraid you guys wouldn't accept me. I was also afraid that I would mess up and have to leave home again."

He told me that some of the parents of his friends at Devereux didn't allow their child to return home. A few had turned their backs and didn't even take their child's calls from the facility. I knew from Devon's therapist that we were the parents who visited their child most often, even though we lived the farthest distance away.

Listening to Devon express his fears—and admitting my fears to him—was a pivotal moment in our relationship. He apologized again to me, as he had done when he first returned home. He took Walt and me aside separately and expressed how sorry he was for all the trouble he had caused us in the past. Walt told me later that when Devon apologized, it brought tears to his eyes, and it was in that moment that he forgave our son.

Despite our family's fears of Devon returning home on his eighteenth birthday, we all managed to be civil and kind to him. I guess you could say we put up a good front to keep peace in the house. Although Devon said he felt happy and relaxed to be home, it was going to take time for our other son and daughter to develop trust in him and feel comfortable. In the meantime, we were all "faking it until we could make it."

Our conversation on fears that day showed me the remorseful side of Devon. My guard tumbled down like an Alaskan glacier breaking off and sliding into the ocean. It was the day when I saw the transformation I had always hoped for. I suddenly realized that Devon had left home as a fifteen-year-old unruly child and returned a mature eighteen-year-old young man.

Today Devon is serving in the United States Marine Corps, stationed in Washington, D.C. Just a week before I sat down to write these words, he called to tell me he was getting married and wanted to be sure the family could attend the wedding. I was proud to say, "Of course we'll be there."

Hanging up the phone, I realized that his engagement was another sign that he had truly grown up and moved beyond the past. I thought how great it felt that he had transformed into a responsible, disciplined soul and how much I, too, had grown. Looking back, I know I had let go of my fears, and that gave me my freedom.

RICHARD, ON HIS SON:

I adopted Carlos when he was sixteen, so eighteen was right around the corner. He had grown up in more than thirty foster homes and had experienced several failed adoptive placements. I hadn't given much thought to how long Carlos would be part of our family. He had been expecting to be on his own for several years, as his prospects for adoption seemed to fade each time he moved to a new place. The agency that had custody of him had enrolled him in an independent-living program because they, too, believed he was unadoptable.

Carlos had moved so many times that he assumed I would be kicking him out sometime soon after he arrived. This assumption seemed to provide him with immunity from being hurt, but it also interfered with his ability to develop strong connections to the rest of the family or to anyone else. As time went on, though, our relationship grew closer and Carlos settled in. He frequently asked if he would have to leave when he graduated from high school, and I always assured him that he could stay at home as long as necessary. I knew he was unprepared for the world, as are most kids his age.

Carlos planned to attend college, but he was having a hard time deciding where to go. He wanted to live on campus somewhere, yet he was afraid of leaving home. One day he said, "I know this is stupid and would never happen, but I sometimes think that if I go away to school, you might sell the house and move without telling me where I can find you."

I was stunned. I knew that he lived life with a sense that everything — including family — was temporary. I felt his pain and wondered if I had somehow sent him a message that our family, too, was temporary. How horrible it must be to live in a constant state of wondering where you will be next and if you'll be able to take care of yourself.

I was profoundly sad that Carlos had been so injured and broken by his crazy journey through foster care. I had a new level of understanding of the depth of his pain and why he approached so many basic things as if they were complex and difficult. Seemingly minor slights represented a huge threat to him, and I suddenly understood why he reacted with such emotional vigor to a simple corrective comment. Carlos was in a constant state of being prepared to get the boot. Anticipating rejection at any and every moment, it's no wonder he always seemed loaded for bear!

Carlos decided to attend a local community college, which was probably driven by his need to stay at home, and I was happy with his decision. We now had the opportunity to spend two more years together, which is exactly what he needed. After all, he had been in the family only since he was sixteen, and there's no way he'd be ready to launch after just two years.

After earning his associate's degree, Carlos was accepted to an out-of-state college on a full athletic scholarship. As I watched him drive away, I was overcome with sadness. Here he was, leaving, as he had left so many homes before. But this time, he would be returning for Thanksgiving. It was a moment I will never forget.

CARLOS, AGE TWENTY-TWO:

I had a horrible history. I was in lots of foster homes and had about four placements that were supposed to be adoptive homes, but they all fell through. I never knew why the families got rid of me. A social worker would just show up at school or "my" house to say I was moving again. I always wondered why, what was wrong with me, why didn't they want me, why was this happening to me.

Question after question ran through my mind: *I can't be that bad—can I? Why don't they like me? I do everything they ask me to do; I clean my room, I take out the trash, I help with the dishes after dinner, yet I'm gone.* Family after family, no one wanted me. I was a useless person with no future. What a mess I must have been.

When I got to my final adoptive home, I didn't believe I would stay there. It was a great place, but I kept thinking that they would get rid of me as soon as they could. That had been the story of my life: Go somewhere, and then they get rid of you. *You are not normal. Something is very wrong with you, and you will never have a family. You must not deserve a family.*

However, my dad, a single parent, was able to meet my needs. He was so accepting, and even though we had many conflicts and struggles, everything worked out well. I finally understood how to fit into a family. The best thing in the world for me is that I was finally adopted. When I have normal life struggles, I always call my dad and tell him that no matter whatever conflict or problem I have, at least I have a family.

AMANDA, AGE TWENTY:

Turning eighteen meant becoming an adult and being on my own — my own car, my own house, my own rules. It meant being in total control. It also meant being alone.

I was so torn about becoming an adult because it meant I controlled my life, and as a child, I had never been in control. I wasn't the one deciding which guy my birth mom was going to bring home that night. I couldn't choose whether or not the man she did bring home was going to sexually assault my sister and me. I didn't know whether my family would eat that day or where we'd sleep that night. I never knew what would happen next. So being an adult and making all my own choices, being in full control, seemed so safe.

When you grow up in the system, eighteen is the magic number. Social workers are always talking about it. When I was eleven and working on my second foster home, a social worker told me, "You're young. You've got quite a bit before you turn eighteen. You need to make the best of it. You need to behave." I heard that and thought, *Eighteen and I can go home. I can be with my birth mom. We can be a family again, and I'll be older, so I can help her.* Back then that's what I wanted most: to be with my birth mother.

The older I got, the more the meaning of eighteen changed. I grew to believe that eighteen meant that no one would be there to take care of me. Throughout my life, that "someone" wasn't consistent — it was always a different foster parent — but at least I hadn't been alone. I had someone. I had a John Doe to make me feel a little better.

At sixteen, I was adopted, giving eighteen a whole new definition once again. I had a family, but it was only until I turned eighteen. I believed that as soon as I turned eighteen, I was out. So I got out before they could kick me out. In my mind, it seemed like the least painful path. It wasn't. I became my birth mother. At sixteen, I was shacked up with my high school dropout boyfriend at his mom's house. Totally classy, right? I partied all the time and skipped school. There was only one thing different: I'd been through enough counseling to know better. I knew that this path wasn't the right one and that I had chosen it. So one day, out of the blue, I woke up and wanted to change. I needed something more. I called my adoptive mother, and we fought for two days. Finally she agreed to let me move back in. I was shocked, stunned, and in complete awe. I had been thrown out of many homes for far less.

A day later, I moved home and I changed. It took me long enough, but I did it. My thoughts on eighteen, changed as well. I guess a little part of me believed that when I turned eighteen, I would become my birth mother. But maybe if I behaved long enough, my family wouldn't leave when I did turn eighteen. So I tried. I tried in school, at home, and even in counseling. My mom and I still fought, and when I turned eighteen, I moved out. So now eighteen meant bills, responsibility, and a job. It was hard. Surprisingly, my family didn't leave. They actually supported me every step of the way.

I'm twenty now, and looking back, eighteen is no different from any other age. Yes, you have the option of moving out and starting the beginning of the rest of your life. It's great, though, because you still have your family. I still call my mother almost every day. It's tough, scary, and a little lonely at times, but it's also fun, new, and adventurous. Don't get me wrong: Sometimes I wish I could move home until I'm thirty-five. But I love being on my own. So I guess eighteen is what you make of it. It's different for everyone, but not that different. I mean, the sky doesn't fall, you don't magically turn into someone else, and the whole world doesn't turn its back on you. For me it meant being on my own, making good decisions, and still having a loving family to go home to.

As you can see, there are variations of what turning eighteen means. Each family and each adolescent can be expected to have some sort of response to reaching the so-called age of majority.

NINE

THE CLINICIAN'S ROLE

Helping to Correct the Disequilibrium

When families with adopted children are in therapy, parents often get the feeling that they are not being understood. While it is important that therapists who work with children and adolescents make it a priority to develop connections with their primary clients, it is equally critical that all mental-health professionals who deal with adoptive families maintain an all-inclusive perspective.

Parents frequently lament that they find it difficult to locate professionals who are sensitive to adoption issues. Some therapists dismiss or minimize adoption, convinced it is not a contributing factor to the presenting problem. Others blame all of the child's difficulties on the fact that he was adopted. As with most things, the truth of the matter lies somewhere between these two polarities.

The adoption-sensitive therapist should be well aware of both adolescent developmental processes and adoption-related concerns. In framing issues related to adoption, the therapist can think about the seven core issues discussed in chapter 3 and combine them with the developmental issues presented in chapter 1.

Brett, age fourteen, was adopted at the beginning of the summer before his freshman year in high school. He participated in summer football workouts and began making friends. He was terrified that someone would find out that he was in the process of being adopted, so he invented a believable history to share with his inquiring friends.

He told them that he had recently moved from a nearby community after his parents' divorce. He said he currently lived with his dad, which is why he transferred to a new school. Brett was worried that if people knew he was adopted, they would wonder why his "real" family didn't want him. He understood that to be adopted at age fourteen must mean that something had gone horribly wrong in his life. He was aware that his birth parents were undesirable people with criminal histories. His guilt and shame were strong, and he felt tarnished by his background.

Brett's adoptive family lived in an upscale community, and his friends were among the most popular athletes in the school. Just the thought that they might find out where he really came from was paralyzing. His fear was intense, and as it grew, so did his sense of shame. The result was guilt about his past and about the string of lies he was planting among his new friends. Of course, each lie led to a new one, so Brett had to be constantly vigilant about keeping track of all the untruths.

His older brother, Jack, who had been adopted by a different family, was well known in the community for having started a successful computer business at the young age of eighteen. Local business owners frequently sought him out for his expertise, expanding his popularity. When an article appeared in the community newspaper about his business, it included a reference to the fact that he'd been adopted when he was fifteen. When Brett read the article, he felt alternately sick and terrified. He assumed that if his friends who knew of Jack read the paper (realistically, how many adolescents do?), they would know that he, too, was adopted. His lies would be exposed, and a flood of questions would ensue. They would know that his family had gotten rid of him or that he had been taken away from them or that he was unwanted. They would know that he wasn't really who he pretended to be. So while Brett was trying to establish a new identity and connect to his new family, his social world was collapsing around him.

Brett knew he would be seeing his therapist the day after the article appeared, but at that moment, he was in a state of flight. After his parents went to bed, he sneaked out of the house and simply sat in the woods — alone, sad, fearful, ashamed, and guilty. He was trying to be a new person, but now he feared that his cover had been blown. What was he going to do?

Brett's therapist was able to help him look at the many components of his panic. Together they examined his feelings and actions as they related to the core issues of adoption and to the kinds of things adolescents are addressing developmentally, such as identity formation and separation and individuation. Brett also had to contend with his position in a new family and his attempt to establish a meaningful attachment to them. When you think about all the things Brett was trying to balance and coordinate socially and psychologically, it is somewhat amazing he could function at all.

Different individuals move through the phases of adolescence with different styles. Some progress with grace and few ripples, while others create waves that wash over the family like a tsunami. The therapist must find a way to be a stabilizer — to have a steadying presence that enables parents to develop a sense of hope and allows the adolescent to feel better understood and appreciated. If the therapist models a balanced approach to understanding what's going on, all members of the family may find that they have a shared vision of the future.

STRIKING THE PERFECT BALANCE

Parents want their adolescent to be an autonomous, successful, thinking, productive, and energetic contributor to society. Sometimes they don't realize that their adolescent may actually want the same thing. Because young people at this stage often do not express their feelings clearly and openly, their parents have no idea what kind of goals their children have set for themselves.

Most adolescents hope their lives will be as good as their parents would like them to be. I don't recall any young client ever saying that he wanted to be a dependent, underachieving, nonproductive, glued-to-the-couch loser.

The key in therapy is to help both the adolescent and his parents more accurately view each other's perspective. The clinician can help the parents understand why the adolescent wants what he wants, does what he does, and thinks like he thinks. The professional role is to help close the gap that may appear huge at first glance. But upon further inspection and interpretation, the gap may prove to be smaller than either the parent or the adolescent realizes.

If the therapist develops an exclusive relationship with the adolescent, he may lose his credibility with the parents. Conversely, if the adolescent thinks the therapist is too closely aligned with the parents, he may feel as if the adults are ganging up on him. Imagine a married couple in therapy with a counselor who always sides with the wife. There's no way on earth the husband is going to consider that a beneficial, productive experience!

When helping a family establish some sort of balance, a good clinician assumes multiple roles and perspectives within the therapeutic relationship. At times he may be a rudder, carefully guiding the parents and the adolescent toward each other. At other times he may be more like an engine, driving the process toward a mutual comfort zone. At still other times he may be a magnet, drawing broken relationships back together.

The adoption-sensitive therapist must maintain a constant awareness that he often serves as a bridge between parties in a somewhat strained relationship. His primary focus must be on restoring the equilibrium that once existed. He must remind parents that the chaos will end, balance will be restored, and the family relationships will be okay, even though it may be some time before resolution occurs. This dynamic is typical of many parent-adolescent relationships, whether or not the child is adopted.

Certain situations require a therapist to make firm decisions, such as hospitalizing an adolescent who talks of suicide. Under such circumstances, the adolescent may or may not be in agreement with the therapist. Even the parents might feel there is no need for such extreme measures because they assume their child is being overdramatic. Ultimately, the parents are the ones who make the final decision as to whether or not they will head to the emergency room for an evaluation. However, if the therapist is very concerned about the danger of a particular situation, he should use whatever authority he has to ensure that the adolescent will be safe.

TO SHARE OR NOT TO SHARE

Some therapists follow very strict guidelines about the privacy of therapy. And sometimes I scratch my head in disbelief.

A mother recently called to ask about my practice's confidentiality policy regarding children. She had been in touch with a psychoanalytically oriented therapist who announced at the first visit that everything discussed in session was completely private. As a result, she would not share anything that the woman's daughter, who was *three years of age*, talked about—unless it involved abuse, which the therapist would have to report. This seems beyond ridiculous to me, not to mention extremely irresponsible. What could a three-year-old possibly talk about in session that would better serve her by keeping it a secret from her parents?

When parents bring an adolescent to therapy, I discuss the kinds of things that will not be confidential, such as physical abuse, sexual abuse, dangerous drug or alcohol use, and issues related to safety. Typically, there is an understanding that family matters will be shared with the individuals who are involved in the treatment process. In many cases, before revealing something to me, an adolescent will ask if I'm going to tell his parents. My usual reply is, "It depends on what you tell me." I then proceed to go over the kinds of things that I would either need or want to share.

Adolescents who ask to attend therapy do so for a variety of reasons, including anxiety, relationship problems, and depression. If the individual's issues are not related to the family in any way, I might agree to see the adolescent only and to have limited contact with his parents. Some families prefer this arrangement, and, in such cases, the adolescent often schedules his own appointments and attends sessions on his own. I keep the parents in the loop via phone calls or by having them attend sessions with their adolescent occasionally, and I always let the adolescent know when these contacts will be made.

If problems related to attachment, adoption, and family relationships are present, therapy is structured to involve participation by parents and the adolescent. For therapy to be effective, everyone involved in the troubling dynamic must take part.

Ted, age seventeen, came to therapy at his request. His mother had no idea what he wanted to discuss, nor did she think she should be involved. In addition, Ted had told her that he wanted to keep the content of his sessions private.

She did not mention adoption when she called to set up his initial appointment, so I assumed that Ted was a birth child. However, when they arrived at my office, I saw that Ted was Asian and his mother was Caucasian. I thought there might be a chance the child's father was Asian, but my first guess was that Ted was adopted.

When I questioned the mom to confirm my belief, she expressed surprise. "Well, yes," she replied, "we did adopt him, but what does that have to do with anything?"

Her comment suggested that there had probably been little discussion in the home of anything adoption related, anything racial, anything regarding identity. When Ted's mother left the room, I brought up the adoption issue again. I asked him if being adopted had anything to do with why he requested therapy. His eyes filled with tears, and he answered, "That's not why I wanted to come here, but I think about it all the time — just about every day. Something always comes up that reminds me that I was adopted. I just wonder how they could do that to me."

I asked him if he meant his birth family, and he started crying harder. It turns out that Ted had been abandoned at a train station in Vietnam shortly after his birth, and the missionaries who found him took him to an orphanage. He was adopted when he was a year old.

Ted's parents had adopted other children as well, and as we continued to talk, it was clear that the family never talked about adoption. As a result, Ted thought he shouldn't talk about it either. In fact, he felt guilty for having such frequent thoughts about being adopted, convinced that something was very wrong with him for doing so.

I was able to help Ted approach his parents with some of the questions he had. In this case, his parents simply didn't think they should "make a big deal" about adoption. They felt it would make their kids too sensitive and self-conscious about not being in their birth families, and they didn't want to cause any unnecessary pain. Obviously, their adoption agency did not prepare them for what their kids would be addressing as they got older. Once the parents were aware of adoption-related issues, they became more comfortable talking about their kids' adoption stories and sharing the information that they had about their children's lives in their respective countries of origin. Even though they did not have much information about Ted, he seemed thrilled with each morsel he received.

In spite of Ted's initial request for privacy in therapy, he ultimately decided to share our discussions with his parents. He felt more comfortable asking them questions, he no longer feared that they would be mad at him for wondering about his birth family, and he felt as if he were opening doors for his siblings to talk about adoption freely. By expressing his thoughts and wishes, Ted helped his parents realize they could discuss adoption with their children without risking hurt feelings.

Even though Ted's parents became involved in his therapy regarding adoption, the other matters he wanted to discuss with me were never revealed to them. In fact, they were so minor — involving advice on how to handle arguments among friends and other social situations — that his parents did not even need to be remotely concerned about them.

When considering whether or not to divulge, the therapist must balance professional ethics, local laws, and the parents' rights to know about their minor adolescent's treatment with the adolescent's need for privacy. When a therapist considers and respects all family members, situations are generally resolved to everyone's satisfaction.

THE EVOLVING IMPACT OF ADOPTION

The clinician must never lose sight of the fact that adoption is a permanent factor for adoptees, but it should not be assumed that it is the source of every problem. Instead, it should be explored as a possibility — nothing more. If an adolescent says that adoption is not related to his current concerns, his claim should be accepted as the truth. If it turns out to be exerting more influence than the adolescent originally thought, that fact will surface over time. While adoption does not necessarily have an overriding presence in the adolescent's life, it does have relevance in therapy and should be examined on an individual basis. The therapist's agenda in treatment must be directly related to the identified problem areas.

People born into a family have a complete accounting of their histories and have no need to wonder about basic things such as, *Who do I look like? Who do I act like? Whose talents did I inherit? Am I Italian or Irish? Does anyone in my birth family have a serious disease?* The unknown is powerful, so the more information a person has about his life, the better equipped he is to pull all the pieces together, draw some accurate conclusions, and gain an element of comfort from having a more comprehensive idea of who he is and where he came from. Even bits of information that may seem insignificant to non-adopted people can be very important to the adoptee.

Jeff, age thirteen, was adopted at birth. His life was uncomplicated and typical in almost all ways. He began to experience some minor anxiety in early adolescence, so his pediatrician referred him for an evaluation. Jeff's parents had not discussed adoption very often. They said that Jeff always knew he was adopted and never asked any questions about his birth family or the situation that led to his being placed for adoption. He told them he never thought about it.

When I first brought up adoption in therapy, Jeff dismissed it as being completely insignificant. He went on to add, "Besides, I can't find out anything about my birth family until I turn eighteen, and that means I have to wait five more years." That comment led me to think that he must have some interest in his background or, at the very least, some questions. I explained that if his parents wanted to get information from the adoption agency that had placed him, they could request it. There were no guarantees due to a host of complex reasons, but they could certainly try.

Jeff and I sat down with his parents to discuss the ramifications of getting information from the agency. Such searches have an element of risk because the details could range from fascinating to horrendous and fall anywhere in between. It would be one thing for Jeff to learn that his birth mother was a dancer and his father was a director — that they felt they couldn't raise a baby because they were on the road so much. But it would be very much another thing if Jeff's birth mom was a heroin addict, if he was one of multiple siblings who were scattered to adoptive and foster homes throughout several states, or if his birth dad was serving time in prison for armed robbery. The negative possibilities could go on forever, and Jeff and his parents needed to understand that.

In spite of the risks, the three of them decided to go forward. Jeff's dad wrote a letter to the placing agency requesting information, and the agency replied with a two-page document that offered scant details. As I read it, disappointment set in. There was little more than a physical description of Jeff's birth mother and some basic information that included her age, height, and weight. When I gave it to Jeff to review, he read it slowly as if savoring each word. Suddenly, a huge smile radiated across his face. When I asked him why, he replied, "It says here that she has a dimple in her chin! It must be just like the one I have." He was so happy to know they had a trait in common, and I was reminded that something small is better than nothing at all. Never underestimate what a seemingly minute piece of information might mean to someone who is trying to put together the puzzle of his life.

Dennis, adopted at seventeen, had a lifebook that included several photos of his birth family. They were not particularly revealing, but there was one photo that was very special to him. In it he was being held by his birth mother. Dennis was the focal point of the shot, and the only part of his mom that was visible was her elbow. In spite of this, the photo held great importance for him. He looked at it repeatedly, remarking to his adoptive family, "This is my birth mom's elbow." It was all he had to remind him of her, and, sadly, his new family didn't quite get just how important this photograph was to him.

Adoption issues arise at different points in the adoptee's life span. What may not be important in childhood may be relevant in adolescence, and what is irrelevant in adolescence may surface in adulthood. Although somewhat stereotypical, many practitioners report that adolescent girls are more often interested in adoption-related issues than are their male counterparts because females usually have greater concern about relational connections. Male adoptees may develop a more focused interest in their own adoption at the point when they become fathers. There is no specific timetable for when individuals want to address adoption-related matters. Some adolescents are extremely focused on issues surrounding their adoption, while others have not framed their identity around being adopted.

Nick, age seventeen, seemed almost obsessed with wanting to meet his birth mother. He had been adopted as an infant, and his parents had very little information about his birth mother and no information whatsoever about his birth father.

After several months of therapy, it became clear that Nick's preoccupation with undertaking a search was interfering with his overall functioning. I spoke with his parents about it, and they were surprised about their son's desire. He had never mentioned anything about adoption to them, so they assumed the details of his birth family were of no interest to him. Once they became aware of his wishes, they were very supportive of his quest.

I managed to connect them with a search group who helped them locate Nick's maternal birth relatives within days. They met first with his grandparents, and soon thereafter they had a visit with his birth mom. The meetings went well, and answers were provided to many of Nick's questions, including a few about his birth father.

Once these connections were made, Nick's birth mother wanted to stay in touch with him via phone and e-mail. Nick, on the other hand, had no interest in maintaining contact. When his parents questioned him about it, he indicated that he had satisfied his curiosity by meeting her and did not want an ongoing relationship with her. He was comfortable with his life and had no desire to shake things up any further.

His parents felt he was being rude by not responding to his birth mother's attempts at communication, but Nick's feelings had to be validated and respected just as they were when he requested the search. When I suggested that he and his family determine a way to tell his birth mother about his feelings, Nick decided to send her an e-mail explaining his decision. He said he hoped she would not be offended, but he did not want continued contact. He left the door open by adding that he might choose to get in touch with her again at a later point in his life, and he thanked her for agreeing to see him when he'd requested it.

Nick's parents were a bit offended and disappointed, as they had done a lot to help him with his search. They had driven out of state so he could visit his birth relatives, and they truly liked his birth mother and would have preferred to foster a friendship. I reminded them that the decision belonged solely to Nick and that it would not be fair for them to try to influence him in any way.

IT'S *HIS* LIFE — LET HIM KNOW ABOUT IT

Everything that parents and social workers know about an adolescent's pre-adoptive life should be shared with him. Secrets have no place in adoption, and withholding information is never helpful. It serves no purpose to conceal any detail that might help an adolescent form a more complete and accurate picture of his earlier years.

Any client, including the adopted adolescent, brings a multitude of dimensions into therapy. The adoptee does not have the benefit of complete awareness of his medical and emotional history. He may have no information whatsoever about his birth family's fragile mental health or problems with substance abuse. This is particularly true for adolescents who were adopted from orphanages in other countries. Adolescents who were in foster care prior to adoption may have more information that might prove helpful to the therapist who is attempting to fine-tune a diagnosis.

Certain biogenic disorders — such as schizophrenia, bipolar disorder, and depression — are more likely to occur if there is a family history of them. Although such knowledge won't prevent a condition from developing, it may lead to a better understanding of what the adolescent is experiencing.

Some families wonder how old a child should be before being told something truly disturbing about his background. I have found that the best time for parents to tell is when they find out. Chances are, the adolescent may already know what his parents are worried about sharing. And even if he doesn't, it might not seem as powerful or dreadful to him as it does to the grown-ups in his life. Keep in mind that a neglected or abused child often builds up a great level of resiliency over the years, and his ability to accept negative information may be surprisingly strong.

So many well-meaning parents attempt to protect their adopted child by keeping information about his life from him. While their motivation may have merit, the failure to provide details about another's life does not. When parents keep a child in the dark, they border dangerously close to compromising his ability to trust that they will always be honest and open with him.

Sometimes parents' own anxieties and discomfort interfere with their capacity to share emotionally charged information. Subject matter such as sexual abuse, an incarcerated parent, or a history of parental drug addiction can cause them to feel awkward and uncertain about how their adolescent will respond. If they cannot handle such discussions on their own, the clinician can provide assistance within the context of the therapeutic environment.

It is always more helpful to read material from the actual case record than it is to tell the story from memory. When parents share information without documentation, the adolescent may think they are just making up stories in an attempt to disrespect the birth family or to make themselves look better by comparison. When the information is in writing, it is less likely the adoptee will distrust it.

Some professionals and parents think that if the adolescent is told that his birth parents had serious difficulties, he may feel as if he is doomed to follow in their footsteps—that he will develop a poor self-image. I do not believe this is true. In the first place, if the adolescent was older when he was removed from his birth family or adopted from an orphanage, he probably knows more about his history than even the professionals involved. In this case, it is ludicrous to think that he doesn't have details to discuss. When parents are able to validate the adolescent's memories with facts, they are better able to deal with whatever trauma he experienced. Instead of feeling that he will grow up to mimic his birth parents' failures, he can find encouragement in the support and understanding of his adoptive parents.

Full disclosure from the placing agency empowers parents to help their adolescent deal with his past. When they make it apparent to him that they are open to talking about the serious issues, he can feel more comfortable about facing them as well. And once he realizes that his parents know the good, the bad, and the ugly aspects of his life and still accept him as he is, he doesn't need to keep any secrets from them. A secret-free family works together more smoothly, and openness during adolescence will ultimately have big payoffs.

INCLUDING SIBLINGS IN THERAPY

Some of the most ignored people in the adoptive family are the siblings who are developing normally and do not have any serious problems or issues. It is not unusual for parents with an adequately functioning family system to suddenly decide to add another child or adolescent to the mix. Let's say they adopt an adolescent who has been in the foster-care system for years. It is extremely likely that this new kid will bring more than his physical baggage with him. He is bound to have psychological baggage resulting from early trauma in his birth home as well as from multiple placements.

Most parents know very little about the difficulties they may face when they adopt a child or adolescent, and the children in the family know even less. They assume that the new addition will move in and be just like they are. In all probability, that assumption is false.

The adoption-preparation process oftentimes does not include the children, and their parents exacerbate the problem by not revealing the reality of what it might be like to share their home with a new sibling whose life experiences may complicate day-to-day living for everyone. Instead, the parents focus on being helpful to someone who needs a home, and they may not realize what their other kids will lose as a result of what the new adoptee will gain: a family.

Arleta James has developed a curriculum, "Supporting Brothers and Sisters," to help professionals prepare entire families for the addition of a new member. In her new book, James enumerates the losses that children already in the family, either by birth or adoption, may experience when a child with difficulties joins them: parental time and attention, privacy, family resources, a peaceful family, a safe environment, happy parents and a comfortable emotional climate, the family they had grown to know, the brother or sister that they had expected, and possibly birth order.[1]

I have seen many children whose lives have been turned upside down by the introduction of a troubled sibling into the family. Before his arrival, they didn't have to keep all of their belongings securely hidden away or the bedroom door locked at night to ensure their safety. The losses they experience may lead to a wide variety of feelings, including anger, resentment, frustration, embarrassment, guilt, sadness, isolation, loneliness, confusion, jealousy, and anxiety.[2]

As a result, the siblings may need to be included in whatever therapy is going on. They may prefer to have their own therapy that is not associated with the sibling who has been identified as the problem in the family. If that is the case, their wishes must be respected and understood. After all, they had nothing to do with the situation that has now created havoc for them.

I cannot stress enough that the family therapist must be able to support different perspectives at different points in time. The clinician's agenda must match the family's agenda if he is to succeed in uniting them. To achieve the greatest degree of effectiveness, he must be flexible in both approach and focus.

TEN

DEVELOPING EMPATHY

How Animals Can Help

"Empathy is to see with the eyes of another, to hear with the ears of another, and to feel with the heart of another." — Alfred Adler

The following was written by Katherine A. Petefish, MS, LPC, a child and family therapist and certified pet dog trainer (CPDT). It is reproduced here with her kind permission.

Empathy is arguably the single most important component in healthy relationships and attachments. Sadly, children who have undergone trauma, abuse, or neglect often lack this critical ability. When this emotional void exists in its most extreme form, it is a predicator for bullying, aggression, and violence to both people and animals. Lack of empathy allows people to exploit others without remorse because a relational barrier prevents the perpetrator from identifying his victim as someone with feelings, hopes, and dreams similar to his own.

So what exactly is empathy? Although commonly mistaken as synonymous with sympathy — the capacity to feel pity or compassion without necessarily relating to another's plight — there is a significant difference. Empathy is the ability to identify with, and understand, the feelings and motives of another. Being empathetic means that you feel the person's pain and honor his connection with you as a living, breathing, and feeling being. Empathy is a learned behavior, and it is something that is generally taught in the course of normal development.

For example, if two young children are playing in the sandbox and one child hits the other a little too hard with a plastic shovel, what will happen? The hit child will cry, and the parent of the hitter will ask her child, "How would you feel if someone were to hit *you* like that?" If all goes well, the hitting child will apologize and be forgiven, and a drop will be added to the empathy bucket.

Notice that there are two elements of empathy in this example. First is the act of being *aware* ("I would not like to be hit that way") and second is that a *follow-up behavior* occurs after this awareness (an apology). Teaching empathy provides children with the perception that others have feelings like their own and that their actions have an impact on both their lives and the lives of others.

But what happens when a child is a victim of abuse or neglect or there is a lack of focus on empathy development in childhood? Because empathy is a learned behavior, it can be taught at any stage of life, although it is arguably more difficult to teach when the child in question is an angry and confused teenager. At this stage, the adolescent has learned that relationships with people are complex, confusing, and full of mixed signals that are difficult, if not impossible, to understand.

This is where the power of animals comes into play. Animals are not as socially complex as humans, tending instead to live in the moment. Dogs, in particular, are forgiving and loving creatures that do not play the same mind games and dance the same confusing social dance as humans are so wont to do. Because of their purity and simplicity, it is frequently easier to teach basic empathic skills to older children and adolescents by beginning the work with man's best friend. Then, after the child has learned to build relationships with an animal, his new skills can be transferred to building relationships with people, which ultimately translates to greater emotional and behavioral well-being.

When working with adolescent clients who have a lack of empathy, the help of animals can be put into play in a variety of ways. In severe cases, the process of developing empathy begins without direct animal interactions. Methods might include storytelling, visitations to animal shelters, and other activities in which the child is taught and encouraged to understand the world from the animal's point of view. In less pronounced cases, simply being around animals and participating in structured activities — such as grooming, caretaking, and obedience training — allow empathy-teaching moments between the therapist and the client to occur naturally.

The following case studies are examples of how working with animals has resulted in an increased capacity for, and demonstration of, empathy.

DEVELOPING EMPATHY AWARENESS

David was an angry and lonely fourteen-year-old who had endured severe abuse and neglect throughout his lifetime. His history had resulted in an internal sense of fear that manifested itself outwardly in angry and bullying behavior. He was enrolled in an animal-assisted interventions therapy group that focused on empathy development through positive motivational dog training.

One day, David entered the gymnasium with a scowl on his face, cursing under his breath and glaring at Blake, a two-year-old rescued mixed-breed sheltie who was sitting with the boys and girls in the group. "Why do I have to do this?" David asked. "That dog gets enough attention from everyone else. I'm not his keeper."

Despite his frustration, David reluctantly agreed to participate in the afternoon's activities. The group was given the task of competing in an obedience exercise with Blake as their teammate. Each student had the opportunity to give the dog a series of obedience commands, such as "heel," "down," "sit," and "come." They were judged on the use of praise for Blake, their ability to follow directions, and their demonstration of good sportsmanship with each other and with the dog. The competitors were told they would be judged solely on their own performance and not on whether Blake actually obeyed the commands.

As each student took a turn, it became apparent that Blake was having a difficult time with some of the commands. Before long, the frustration that both he and the students were experiencing was becoming obvious. When

David's turn came, all eyes were on him as the group anticipated his usual glowering expression, brusque commands, and lots of criticism for the poor dog. What happened instead brought tears to the eyes of more than one person in the room that day.

Instead of using harsh words or an angry tone, David knelt on the ground next to Blake and said softly, "You're a good dog, Blake. I can see you're trying, and I know it can be tough when you try so hard and you can't seem to get it right. But I'll be here to help you through it." The pair went on to give a flawless performance with joy and precision, winning the competition hands down.

At the end of the routine, I asked David how he had known what to say to Blake. He gave Blake a big hug, handed the leash to me, and said, "I knew exactly how Blake must have been feeling."

The use of positive motivational dog training is perhaps one of the most powerful tools for the development of empathy in teenagers. Dog training is inherently interesting to most teens, although they soon learn that it is far more challenging than they had anticipated. It requires an acute understanding of animal behavior that lends itself naturally to the development of empathy.

When a dog fails to sit when he is told, it is a beautiful teaching moment for the children. *How is the dog feeling: confused, stubborn, overwhelmed? Is he refusing to sit because he wants to make you mad? How would you like to be treated if you were the dog in the same situation?* Adolescents quickly learn that when they interact with the dog in a more positive way, they are more likely to get the desired response. More important, they are able to develop awareness that other living creatures share the same emotions and feelings that they do.

DEVELOPING EMPATHIC BEHAVIOR

When people think of animal-assisted therapy or pet-assisted therapy, they generally envision a nicely trained dog that visits a nursing home or a children's hospital to provide emotional support to the patients. Perhaps they might even recall programs in which children or adults in correction centers learn how to train service dogs. But some of the most therapeutic moments in my career have occurred when working with a very different and very heartbreaking type of dog.

These animals are the victims of severe trauma, abuse, and neglect that caused them to have an intense—and very understandable—mistrust of humans. They might be nervous, hypervigilant, anxious, fearful, and possibly aggressive. Need I state the obvious parallels between the dogs' behavior and that of abused or traumatized children? When a traumatized child who has a lack of empathy is confronted with working with a traumatized dog that is terrified and anxious, powerful opportunities for empathy development abound.

In most cases, rehabilitating these dogs is very difficult. Because safety issues are involved for the children, I rarely allow them to work with dogs that have an extreme history of abuse and trauma. However, I once met a dog who changed my life and the lives of many of my clients.

Sebastian was a year-old, mixed-breed hound dog who had been rescued from an abusive home by the folks at a veterinary hospital. I received a call from these kind people asking if I could do anything for this needy creature. When I went to meet Sebastian, I was very skeptical. I tried to engage with him, but he was far too afraid. Yet no matter how hard I might have challenged his fears, he never became aggressive in any way. Something made me take the chance to decide to work with him with the adolescent clients enrolled in my animal-assisted empathy-building therapy group.

Before I introduced Sebastian to the group of children with whom he would be working, I told them about his fear and the need for us to move very slowly in the process of rehabilitation. Within a moment of meeting the dog, who was cringing back in the safety of his kennel, one of the children said these words, which I will never forget: "He has been hurt. Like us. It's in his eyes. We have to help him." And all the children nodded.

If I had any prior hesitation about trying to help this dog, it disappeared in that moment. As I looked at the children, I began to cry. As the children looked at the dog, they, too, began to cry. And we became a group with a single, zealous purpose: to help Sebastian.

Because of his great need, the usual two-hours-a-week group schedule went right out the window. For the next several weeks, the children spent many extra hours at the kennel, talking to Sebastian in gentle, low voices and encouraging him to take treats from their hands. They worked together and took turns to make sure that someone was there for several hours every day.

Eventually, after many months, Sebastian was able to come out of his kennel on his own and accept being petted with a wagging tail. With the help of the children, this sweet-hearted dog was ultimately ready for adoption by a kind and loving family.

What occurred with Sebastian is a wonderful example of empathy in action. It is one thing to be aware of the feelings of others, and it is another thing to act on the awareness of these feelings. The adolescents in this group were not only able to empathize with Sebastian, they were able to learn how to act appropriately on this empathic awareness.

THE HUMAN-ANIMAL-VIOLENCE LINK

Thus far, empathy development has been discussed within the context of animals helping children who *like* animals. But what about the child who has a history of animal cruelty? There are those who would say that children who abuse animals should not be allowed around animals due to safety concerns for the pets. This is a very valid concern, and the welfare of all animals should be of paramount importance. Certainly, all interactions between pets and these children must absolutely be supervised. But let's look at the situation from another perspective.

If a child has been aggressive toward people, should he be strictly forbidden to associate with others? Not only is that unrealistic, it is not a solution at all. The child who has been aggressive toward people should receive treatment and learn to relate to others with respect and compassion. Otherwise, it is likely that he will continue to be combative and will, in many cases, escalate his behavior.

The same principle holds true for aggression toward animals. If specific treatment interventions are not put in place to resolve this problem, the child will probably continue his hostility and might, in fact, transfer it toward people. It is therefore vital that an intervention occur at the first sign of any animal abuse.

Before interventions are discussed, however, let's take a look at why people are cruel to animals. Animal cruelty, like any other form of violence, is often committed by a person who feels powerless, unnoticed, and under the control of others. The motive may be to shock, threaten, intimidate, or offend others or to demonstrate rejection of the rules of society. Some people who are cruel to animals copy behavior they have seen or that has been imposed on them. Others see harming an animal as a safe way to get revenge on someone who cares about that animal.

Animals are victims of abuse for many of the same reasons that children are victims of abuse: They hold little power in a world governed by powerful adults. Both children and animals do not have a voice to condemn those who wound them. And, unfortunately, the perpetrators of animal cruelty are frequently the very children who share the same fate of abuse. Driven by emotional turmoil and pain, they will often act out this pain on those victims who, like themselves, cannot speak out or provide an adequate defense. If they're clever enough to manufacture plausible explanations or excuses for the animal's injury or death, they can get away with abominable acts with little or no repercussions.

Cruelty to animals is symptomatic of underlying rage with the world and the people in it—a rage that often finds its roots in attachment and trauma issues that resulted from the neglect or mistreatment by primary caregivers. Often the abuse to animals can be traced to the child's earliest, most dysfunctional relationships in which he has been the victim of similar behavior or has witnessed it imposed on other children, one or more of his caregivers, or animals. Cruelty to animals is typically a form of displacement of this anger. The confused and rage-filled child may find targeting animals to be a safe outlet for the anger he is loathe to express toward people who may retaliate.

Intentional cruelty to animals is a significant concern because it is a sign of psychological distress and often indicates that an individual has already experienced violence and may be predisposed to committing acts of violence to humans. Most criminals who have been violent toward people share a common history of cruelty toward animals. Aggression among adult criminals may be strongly correlated with a history of family abuse and childhood cruelty to animals. The FBI has recognized the connection since the 1970s, when its analysis of the lives of serial killers suggested that most had killed or tortured animals as children.

STOPPING THE VIOLENCE WITH EMPATHY

In recent years, an assessment for both adult and juvenile animal abusers has been created to help identify them. Created in 1999 by the Psychologists for the Ethical Treatment of Animals (PSYETA) — now called the Society and Animals Forum — in a unique partnership with the Doris Day Animal Foundation, the AniCare Model of Treatment for Animal Abuse is the first professionally developed psychological intervention program for animal abusers over the age of seventeen. The Society and Animals Forum has also created AniCare Child, an assessment and treatment approach for childhood animal abusers. The key to helping children who have abused animals is to help them develop empathy.

Several years ago, I was working with Karen, a thirteen-year-old girl who had an extensive history of cruelty to animals. As is so often the situation in these cases, her cruelty was symptomatic of the terrific amount of emotional pain she was experiencing due to the early abuse and neglect of her primary caregivers. Karen had a strong lack of empathy and an inability to perceive that animals experienced emotional states similar to her own. It was this relational barrier that justified her cruel actions. If she saw animals as objects without feelings, then her actions could not hurt them and she would not have to experience any feelings of guilt or shame.

As I typically do in animal-assisted therapy sessions, I began by working with Karen to write stories from the perspectives of animals. We did role-playing, and I would be the voice of the animal. We performed animal puppet shows. We visited animal shelters, where I showed Karen how to be attuned to the body language of animals through their tails, ears, eyes, and body posture. All of this was to no avail. Karen remained convinced that animals were not capable of emotions.

I was ultimately forced to be more creative in my endeavors and decided to help Karen teach Chance, my therapy dog, how to express emotions on cue. For hours, she and I discussed what Chance might do *if* he were capable of emotions. We decided that for "mad," he might growl. For "sad," he might lie down and put his chin on the floor. For "glad," he might spin around or roll over. And for "scared," he might crawl backward and whine. I then taught Karen how to teach Chance to express these emotions of mad, sad, glad, and scared on cue. In addition, I worked with her to teach Chance to "use his words" where he barked on cue to "talk" to us.

Throughout the process of working with Karen to train Chance, I helped her connect the importance of her own tone of voice and body language. When she asked Chance to be sad, she would give the command in a sad tone and manner. When she asked Chance to be scared, she simulated a fearful tone of voice.

We taught Chance the commands through positive motivation training techniques. Karen would frequently become frustrated during the sessions, but I noticed that she was becoming more responsive to Chance's emotions and needs as they went through the training together.

The breakthrough came when we began to teach Chance to be "afraid" on cue. As we struggled with teaching him how to take a step backward by using a food lure, Karen asked, "Why don't we just move toward him like we're going to hit him? That would be faster." While the suggestion was certainly not a positive motivational suggestion, it implied something very important for Karen's treatment.

"But that would mean that Chance would have to have *real* feelings, wouldn't it?" I asked. "Because it seems as if you're saying that the way in which we behave toward him *could make him afraid*."

And that was the moment that Karen got it. She began to cry real tears as she suddenly realized what she had done to other dogs just like Chance. And so her healing began—most likely saving the lives of many other dogs, and possibly humans, in the process.

If a child demonstrates a severe lack of empathy, such as in Karen's case, it is recommended that therapeutic services be obtained and animal-assisted interventions considered for treatment. The abuse of animals, much like sexual abuse, should be treated as a primary issue. It should not be assumed that general treatment for emotional disturbances will be effective to generate empathy for animals or people.

In mild instances where empathy is lacking, parents can help their children work with animals to learn empathy in the home environment by engaging in some of the following activities:

- Fund-raising together for animal-welfare agencies
- Participating in animal awareness and safety classes to help the child know how to respectfully interact with pets in the community

- Visiting the zoo and writing a story or play from the perspective of the animals there
- Reading stories about animals and encouraging the child to discuss the feelings, emotions, and thoughts of the animals in the story
- Encouraging the child to research and present information on pets and pet care
- Helping the child to volunteer at animal shelters and animal-rescue groups

Although dogs were the animal helpers primarily discussed in this chapter, there are many ways in which empathy can be developed with the help of animals. Different programs utilize the talents of horses, cats, llamas, rabbits, and farm animals. Green Chimneys Children's Services in Brewster, New York, is a residential treatment center in a farm environment that focuses primarily on the healing power of human/animal interactions utilizing farm animals. Recovery Ranch in Tennessee and Hooves for the Heart in Colorado are excellent examples of using horses in equine-assisted therapy. For additional information about animal-assisted interventions and the development of empathy, please contact The Latham Foundation or the Society and Animals Forum, both of which are listed in the Related Resources section near the end of this book.

ELEVEN

STORIES OF HOPE

Parents and Adolescents Share Their Stories

This chapter is composed of stories from parents and children who have shared their journeys.

HEIDI, MOTHER OF DANIEL:

Parenting Daniel has been the most painful, challenging, and rewarding aspect of my life. He gives me great anguish and great joy. Even on days when he acts absolutely maddening, I am so glad he is part of our family.

I think the teen years are particularly difficult for Daniel. He is still trying to catch up from the severe deprivation and neglect he had suffered during his seven and a half years in a Romanian orphanage. It seems that Daniel's biological clock and his developmental clock are operating in two different time zones. He has the body of a typical teen, but developmentally and emotionally he is not at the same place.

Daniel has certainly put us through a lot, but we have put him through a lot too. All those times when he acted like a wild animal, I tried to remind myself that for the first years of his life, he was treated like a wild animal. I am sure our world of rules, structure, and family values made no sense to him. While many kids have eighteen years in the comfort of a family before having to accept adult responsibilities, Daniel had less than eleven years to learn what he would need to know. He has hiked a challenging (uphill) road. He has reached high school graduation, so he must be hiking in the right direction.

DANIEL, AGE NINETEEN, ADOPTED AT SEVEN:

The path of my life has been very bumpy. By age ten, I was filled with rage. I expressed myself through aggression. One time I was removed from school by Mobile Crisis because I wanted to harm the principal and a social worker. Later I wanted to kill my mother and myself. I was hospitalized at mental-health institutions multiple times. My family was falling apart, and I was close to being sent to juvenile detention.

Over the years, my parents took me to many therapists and doctors. They tried every intervention possible. Eventually, they found doctors who could help me. Slowly, I started to change. First, I gave up my aggression. Several years later, I gave up stealing. Last, I gave up trying to destroy my family. By giving these things up, I gained a lot. I gained a chance to become a person who can succeed in life.

For most people, loving their parents is natural, but for me, it was a foreign concept. However, during high school, I let go of my anger. I started to see my parents as people. I started to allow my parents to help me, and this has made a big difference in my life.

Following are portions of the speech Daniel gave at his confirmation, where he was the recipient of the esteemed Brickner Award:

I spent the first half of my childhood in an orphanage in Romania. So for those years, I had no family, no love, no fun, no music, no toys, no nutrition, and no Judaism. At the age of seven and a half, my life changed: I was adopted. This is really when my world began. Now, you might think that everything would suddenly become beautiful and easy, but life was pretty challenging. Here is just one example.

I had no education—no books, no pencils, no alphabet—and one week after arriving in America, I was plopped into a first-grade classroom. The teacher said, "Today is Monday, October 21, 1996." I didn't know that there were days of the week, months of the year, numbers, or dates—not to mention I didn't know English, and I barely knew Romanian. After two seconds, I was totally confused. This was only a taste of the hurdles I would have to jump through every day.

My participation at the temple has not always been smooth. My dad felt I should call this speech "From Banned to Brickner." My behavior was so out of control that at one point I felt banned from the temple. I had been removed from Sunday school for disruptive behavior, and, in fact, my family was told that we needed to call ahead and get permission to attend services if I would be there. Several times I was so out of control that I had to leave in a police car.

So how did I get from that point to this point? I guess this is the amazing part. There are many factors involved—doctors, therapists, and so on—and Fairmount Temple has been a *big* factor. It is a place where I can be myself. I don't have to fit into a mold like I do at school. From playing guitar at High Holy Day services to riding a bus bound for a D.C. rally, Fairmount Temple offers me opportunities to do things I would not be able to do anywhere else.

As the recipient of the Brickner Award, I am charged with the mission of representing the confirmation class. I hope that I can stand here with my classmates and be a positive symbol. We are getting confirmed together. We have reached this landmark occasion in many different ways, and my path has veered off course at times. But what is important in life is reaching the finish line feeling proud, despite the trips, falls, and hurdles. We all have trips, falls, and hurdles, but let's focus on our powerful strides, our strengths, our talents. That is what helps us reach our goals.

Before I finish, I would like to thank two people: my mom and dad. If I could use one word to tell someone what I think of you, I would say *amazing*. The reason that I am even here today and the kind of person I am is because of you. Even when we had our hard times, you never gave up on me, and that is what's amazing. You have instilled in me your beliefs on how my helping others ultimately helps me. I don't know how I could have reached my goals and become the person I am today if I didn't have you. I love you very much.

ELLE, MOTHER OF MARCO:

Until my son turned twelve, he was an easy child. He seemed genuinely relieved to have been removed from the chaos of his birth home, and being loving and agreeable came naturally to him. But with the onset of adolescence, everything changed.

To say that his progress came to a screeching halt is an understatement. In truth, all of his forward momentum ceased. He refused to do any schoolwork. He lied constantly—about big things, little things, and completely insignificant and irrelevant things. Compliance flew right out the window, and he defied me at every turn. By the time he was sixteen, drugs were a big part of the equation, and it became painfully clear that some sort of major intervention was required.

Marco entered a residential treatment facility to give him the structure and support he needed to get back on track. I'll never forget the first time I visited him there—how he begged me, with tears streaming down his face, to take him home. As much as I wanted to gather him in my arms and whisk him away, I knew that wasn't the solution.

Over time, Marco came to realize that he had to work at getting his life in order. He adapted to the strict rules of the school and became a positive role model for the newer residents. Sure, there were moments of defiance—like the time he snuck out a window in the wee hours of the morning, landed hard and broke a water pipe when he hit the ground, and cut off the water supply to the entire school for two days. But he was making progress—the staff saw it, I saw it, and he felt it.

Marco earned his high school diploma a year ahead of schedule and transitioned into the school's independent-living program, where he chose to stay for nearly another year. At that point, the security felt confining to him, and he felt a strong need to see if he could make it on his own without a live-in support system. Shortly after his nineteenth birthday, with mixed feelings and sad good-byes, he left the program and reentered the "real world."

Today Marco has a lucrative job in sales—a position that suits his outgoing personality. He works hard, has many friends, and remains drug free. He and I are closer than ever before, and when I look at this six-foot-two young man, I once again see the sweet, happy toddler who first became part of our family.

MARCO, AGE NINETEEN, ADOPTED AT THREE:

Being adopted is the best thing that happened to me; I can't imagine what kind of person I would have become otherwise. Just the thought of that life makes me sick because I had a small taste of it when I started the addiction that my biological mother had.

I got into trouble with the law and the court system, and my life went downhill. I could not stop the drugs. I just needed more — no matter what, I needed it. I would steal from my dad and was terrible to my mom. I was just a different person.

I was sent to a treatment center on July 3, 2004 — I'll never forget that date. I hated my life, and I hated my parents. The day my mom came to see me, I was so confident she was going to get me out of that place. When she said no, I told myself that I was never going to talk to her or my dad again.

With a little bit of time and some wise words from the staff and counselors, I realized that what my parents did was give me a second chance at life; if they did not send me to that school, I know I would have been in jail or dead. While I was there, I became closer with my mother and father than I'd ever been before, and I did something that made my parents proud: I graduated high school a year early. Since I have been out of the center, I have played on a college football team, I have supported myself, and I have a successful job. I could not have done any of it without the help of two special people, my parents. I love you guys, and I owe everything I have and have become to you.

LARANDA, AN ADULT WHO GREW UP IN THE FOSTER SYSTEM:

When I really take the time to look back, I can see that my life has unfolded in ways that are truly remarkable. As I began to write my story, I found that I was amazed at the turns and bends along the way and how resilient a child can be. Mostly I am in awe of how a little girl at the age of three (where my memories begin) with many adversities to overcome can grow into a woman who finds herself living a life that brings her happiness and contentment.

My second foster family, with whom I lived most of my young life, gave me an existence — a foundation — I never would have known if my birth mother had been allowed to care for me. I know now that because of my foster mother's unconditional love, I am a success story in the world of foster care. Although I was never adopted (my choice), my foster mother and father are, to this day, my parents and my children's grandparents and my grandson's great-grandparents. And life comes full circle.

DEBBIE AND KEN, PARENTS OF BRANDON:

Brandon was almost ten when we adopted him. We'd read the books and taken the classes, but nothing could have prepared us for the kind of defiance, opposition, and stubbornness he brought to our home.

He refused to comply with the mildest request—wouldn't go to bed at night, get up in the morning, brush his teeth, take a shower. Everything had to be *his* way, which was how he felt he maintained control of his life.

For a long time, it seemed hopeless. He was ruining our lives, and we were afraid we were ruining his. We were supposed to be turning him around, making him feel safe and loved, but we spent most of our time punishing him.

Gradually there were small improvements. Holding therapy helped him trust us enough to relinquish a little control. We learned to stop arguing and to let a lot of unimportant things go. We didn't nag him to brush his teeth, even if he went days without doing it. We stopped expecting him to do chores. We simply made fewer rules. We discovered some strategies that worked. He might miss the school bus but then would have to hand over five dollars for Dad's "taxi" to school, even though he hated it. We had "lying days," where we said the opposite of what we meant when his untruthfulness got bad. And we started to show him the most love when he seemed to deserve it least, because that's when he needed it most.

Now, at sixteen, Brandon is much more responsible and cooperative. He still won't do many chores and intentionally leaves his plate on the dinner table every night, as ways to show he's still in control. But he also does his homework without a fight and gets good grades at the private school he attends. Oh, and he goes to bed on time, as long as Mom comes up shortly to do a puzzle with him.

Being with us has opened so many doors for Brandon. At ten, he was so socially backward, he'd stand in the driveway wearing a plastic Halloween mask so he could watch other kids without them seeing him; today he has a few friends. At ten, he'd never put on a baseball glove; today he's a pitcher on his high school; team. He's on his way to being an Eagle Scout; he made the honor roll at school, and he volunteers with disabled kids.

We both feel we were meant to adopt Brandon—that everything in our lives led us to the point when we would find him and become a family. We're sure we would have done a lot of interesting and fun things in our life together had we not adopted Brandon, but none of it could have been as meaningful, important, or rewarding as our life with him. Birth parents say a child changes everything. Adoptive parents—particularly those who adopt older children—don't have the energy to contemplate such things. They're too busy looking at a world turned upside down.

If not for a family therapist who "got" Brandon and us, we'd still be frustrated, angry, and making a lot of rules. He helped us turn things around. Now there is still frustration, but there is still plenty of love and joy—and hope.

BRANDON, AGE SIXTEEN, ADOPTED AT NINE:

Since I was adopted, I've been able to do a lot of things I never imagined I would do. I am now a really good pitcher for my school, and I can run and play other sports. Ever since I was adopted, I have someone to finally trust in my life. If I wasn't adopted, I probably wouldn't know what baseball is, and I could never trust anybody.

LYNNE AND JIM, PARENTS OF ETHAN:

Adolescents who are adopted not only have to make sense of who they are, they have to figure out who they were before they joined their family and integrate that person into the mix. I know that Ethan, our second son, struggles to sort out who he would have been in Honduras with who he is in this country. In Honduras, he most likely would not have attended school, he would have fished most of his life, and he would have been very poor. Here he lives in a nice neighborhood, has a GPA of 3.5, runs cross-country, works a part-time job, and takes fun family vacations.

Sometimes I feel he struggles with survivor's guilt. We have visited his birth family in Honduras several times, and one of his brothers has pleaded with us to give him money so he can hire a jackal to smuggle him into the United States Of course, we refused. Although his family is doing better financially, they are still abjectly poor by American standards.

While we have had a few bumps in the road, all four of our adopted children are doing well as adolescents. They are generally enjoyable, and we have fun as a family. It has been challenging at times as parents, but with support from counselors, friends, and family, we are making the adjustments we need to make to help our children be successful. We are finding that it is less about what we do and more about who we have become as parents.

ETHAN, AGE SIXTEEN, ADOPTED AT NINE MONTHS:

I was born in Honduras. My birth family was going through a rough time, and I probably would not have survived if I had stayed with them. My family was large and hardworking, but no matter how hard they worked, there was just not enough food and money to take care of everyone. I had two older siblings who died from disease.

I was given to a foster family until all the paperwork could be completed for my adoption. When I was nine months old, my adoptive parents brought me home. I was raised in a Christian home, and I am very grateful for the family God chose for me.

My life would definitely be very different if my birth family had kept me. They live in wood houses with concrete floors, and they sleep in hammocks. They fish and don't make a lot of money. None of my brothers or sisters graduated from high school. I have visited my birth family on two occasions, and I am happy to know them. During my last visit, I learned a lot about them. Most of it was good, but some of it was not. Things are better now for my birth family than they were when I was born. For instance, they now have electricity in one of the houses, and they also have television. I don't have any doubt that the family I'm with now is who I should be with.

SOFIA, AGE EIGHTEEN, ADOPTED AT BIRTH:

My heart always skips a beat when I see a sign for San Bernardino, California. Everything that I may have been thinking about—the weather, what exit I need to take, L.A. traffic—somehow runs out of my mind, and I am left with thoughts about her: Ana Arroyo, my birth mother.

I was born at the San Bernardino County Hospital. When I was only a day old, eleven hours old to be exact, I was adopted by my white parents and left my first mother behind. I am eighteen years old now and have visited my birth mother only twice. I have pictures of me—only a few weeks old, in an outfit especially picked out by her, and one of the two of us during my visit when I was not even two. Every time I show that picture to my friends, they all comment on how much I look like her. Now that I am officially an adult, I am questioning my identity in a new way: *Who am I? What does it mean to be me?*

Living in Los Angeles at Occidental College, so close to the place of my birth, has opened up new questions: *Is she out there? Where? Does she miss me? Or even think of me?* At night I look across the hills scattered with lights and wonder. Although she is so close, I feel as if there is an invisible wall preventing me from getting to her. I know so little about her. She may not want to see me. I do not even know her address. Without answers to my questions about who she is, it is as if I am stuck in a bottomless pit, unable to fill in the missing pieces of myself.

The barrier of distance and knowledge between my first mother and myself is a boundary that keeps me from feeling as if I can truly know who I am. Living here, so near to her, means I am at the brink of a connection that defines me. It is exciting and terrifying at the same time. Once I am able to cross over this border between things that I have known my whole life and the vast unknown that resides within the history and body of Ana, I will have a much better knowledge of who I am and my own cultural identity.

Ever since I was a little girl, I have always felt as though people who were not adopted knew more about themselves than I did. I envied the questions they were able to ask their parents and get easy answers to. The first time I filled out medical forms on my own, I sat in the doctor's office going down the list of facts, realizing I had no idea whether or not high blood pressure ran in my family. It was déjà vu all over again filling out my school's medical history forms, but this time was different.

As I sat in my dorm room, avoiding my homework, I started thinking about her. I was in Los Angeles, and if I wanted to I could try to find her. Maybe I could finally *know* my medical history instead of always guessing. She was here, eighteen years ago, so close to where I am now, and maybe she still is.

It's not like my questions are the most important questions in the world, but I can't help feeling they would help me enter a new frontier of knowing myself. I sit on my bed imagining the stories—stories that would go along with the answers to my questions. Stories of a great-uncle pushing through and living an extra three years even though doctors told him he had only six months before the cancer spread throughout his body. Stories of my dad, coming to Los Angeles from Guatemala, getting sick from too much fast food. Stories of special secret family concoctions guaranteed to get rid of an ear infection. Those family stories that most people my age ignore, but the fact remains that they shape who we are. In her body, small and compact like mine, does Ana even realize that she holds so many of the pieces to the puzzle called me that I have been missing? Does she even know that she holds the key to creating a whole new identity—a whole new me?

People tell me that college is the time when you find yourself. It is a time when adolescents take their first steps into life on their own. But for me, as an adopted Latina first-generation college student, my questions seem to stretch out to forever—or at least across the freeway to the place of my birth. I know that sometime soon I will have to take a risky step into the contact zone—into the place where I need to let go of my fear of rejection in order to open the door to the possibility of a reunion. Although I did not realize it, I have been constantly negotiating with my identity. I know that I have another mother who cares about me more than anything, but do I actually belong to her? To anyone? To myself?

There is a border called belonging. At this border is a space—a place where negotiations happen and decisions are made. For me, defining my belonging to my birth mother feels like a border between two worlds. It is a border because it is where conflict within myself about who I am occurs. It is where negotiations of my first family history and past and that of my adoptive family all take place. Will I be able to call myself Ana Arroyo's daughter and feel that I actually belong? Do I risk my other family membership if I explore this relationship with Ana? Can I negotiate with not only each of them but also myself to find a way to be whole, without barriers between these two mothers, two families, both of whom have, up until now, been on opposite sides of my true self, splitting me in half in a way that makes me feel less than strong. I need to ask all my questions. I need to get my answers. I need to finally belong in both worlds. I need to belong to both families. I need to know and love both my mothers because then I can become my own self, create my own personal and cultural identity. A place to be me—really, truly me. A place without borders.

MARA, AGE SEVENTEEN, ADOPTED AT FOUR MONTHS:

I believe that living in society today as a young adoptee can be pretty challenging, especially because everyone is so judgmental.

Many adoptees I know tend to think they're not like everyone else (usually in a negative manner) and that they don't fit in just because they weren't raised by their birth family. My adoption experiences haven't been so much embarrassing as they have been fragile, because it feels as though once you let people know you're adopted, they want to treat you differently in some way.

I've never been in contact with my birth family, but I do wish to search for them when I'm older. I just don't feel I'm ready at the moment to meet them, but I'm hoping to one day. I was adopted when I was four months old. I was taken care of in a foster home before I came to the United States from Korea.

I know that many adopted kids, teens, and adults have asked themselves at least once in their life the infamous question "Why did my birth parents put me up for adoption?" Some of my friends believe that their birth families put them up for adoption because they didn't want them. At times, adoption is difficult because some people who are adopted don't understand the true reason why they were put up for adoption and they think they weren't loved by their birth family and weren't wanted. This could lead to problems in the future for not only the adoptee but also the people involved (the birth family, the family that adopted, and so on). On the other hand, adoption can be a good thing because it helps you look at life a little differently. It helps you understand the different lives people live and why they make the choices they do. It can really help you grow if you allow it to.

As a Korean adoptee, I believe that being adopted is a big eye-opener. It has made me mentally tough when I've had to deal with stereotypes about being Asian and adopted, and, in turn, I've grown from my experiences. Not only have I learned more about my Korean heritage than most Korean teens living here in the United States have, but it has given me a chance to really find out who I am and who I'm going to be in the future.

I've been fortunate to learn a lot about my Korean heritage through the Olympic sport of Tae Kwon Do. I began taking classes when I was five years old, and I've been doing it ever since. My grandmaster and coach are both Korean (father and son), and many of my teammates are Korean as well. So through my daily interactions with my teammates and friends, I've learned a fair amount about my Korean heritage.

What is also important is that my mother is extremely involved in the Korean adoption network and has created the nonprofit organization Korean Focus. She is always asking me if I want to volunteer at or attend different events and activities that her organization is involved in. These events always give me a deeper insight into my Korean heritage. My parents have been as supportive as they can be with everything in my life—not just adoption and helping me be connected to the Korean community but in everything I do.

I also attend Teen Weekends with Adoption Service Information Agency (ASIA), and we discuss different topics and watch different films on adoption. I have several adopted friends, and I feel as though I make new ones every year because of the different events and activities I attend with my parents and on my own.

My friends' experiences are similar to mine and I think probably to every adoptee's. Because my adopted friends are mostly Korean American, we relate to one another—not just on the level of adoption but also on the fact that we're all Asian. Some experiences we've had include people reacting in a weird manner when we mention we're adopted or people stereotyping us because we're Asian. For example, they think all Asian people look alike or that all of us are Chinese.

Since I don't feel ready to pursue anything bigger through adoption, my parents have just been supporting me, and when I'm ready, they'll be there for me.

Above everything, adoption has shaped me into the person I am today, and I'm very grateful for that. There's no need for the pressures of society to tell you what's good and bad; it's your choice and your life to live.

SHERRY, MOTHER OF AMANDA:

I adopted Amanda when she was sixteen. I was a single mother at the time and was looking for some meaning in my life.

Amanda never really "moved in," preferring instead to watch and participate from a distance. Throughout her adolescence, I continued to give her rules, taught her ways of self-respect, and took her to therapy to help her figure out her life. I remained consistent and let her know she was a worthy person.

I certainly would not have experienced as much stress if I had not adopted her. I had hoped to travel, but that was not to be, given my responsibilities at home. When I look at the young adult Amanda has become, it is clear that the sacrifices were well worth the cost. She values what I taught her, and she knows that she always has a family to come home to, and I think that's very meaningful to both of us.

Adopting Amanda caused my life to take a big turn in more ways than one, as I met my really fantastic-wonderful-stupendous husband through an adoption support group.

JAN FISHLER,[1] AN ADULT ADOPTEE WHO WAS GIVEN TEMPORARY CUSTODY OF AN ADOPTED ADOLESCENT:

This story takes place in 1984. I was in my early thirties and had just left the corporate world to start my freelance writing career. I was living alone in a one-bedroom flat in Oakland, California, when my cousin called to talk about her thirteen-year-old adopted niece, Sara. During our conversation, I learned that Sara—who was living in Ohio with her mother and two younger brothers (one adopted, one biological) — had become increasingly disrespectful to her mom, was engaged in risky sexual behavior, and had run away more than once. Foul language, hitting, screaming, and destruction of property were commonplace, and Sara's mother — after being struck more than once — was afraid of her daughter and concerned about her influence on the boys.

Therapy, including a stay in a psychiatric ward, had done nothing to improve the situation. My cousin, a psychotherapist, believed that Sara's anger was, in part, due to her parents' recent divorce, and she offered to have her niece come to California for a visit of indeterminate length. Two weeks had gone by, and the visit wasn't going well.

Because I, too, was adopted, my cousin suggested that Sara stay with me. "She needs one-on-one attention and someone who can relate to her," she began. "With my practice and the children, I don't have enough time to spend with her exclusively."

It had been several years since I had seen Sara, so I suggested we meet and see how we might feel with one another. I must admit it was difficult for me to believe that the adorable five-foot, blue-eyed blonde could wreak so much havoc on a household. In the end, I jumped in with an open heart and a willingness to do whatever was required.

I gave Sara my bedroom and moved into the space I used for my office. For the first two weeks, I put my business on hold and spent all my time getting to know her; we shopped, decorated, listened to music, danced, and talked. During this time, I never witnessed the anger I had heard so much about. What I saw was a bright, fun-loving child who needed room to express herself. When Sara's mother heard that living with me was going so well, she suggested that Sara stay and start the school year in Oakland. I had concerns about this but was willing to give it a try.

The school district where I lived was predominantly black. How would this light-eyed cherub fit in? The first few days went well but deteriorated quickly when Sara fell back on her old behavior patterns. It was one thing to be a tough kid in an upper-middle-class neighborhood in Ohio and quite another to aim for the same status in the inner city.

When Sara realized that she had backed herself into a corner — that she was in what could only be viewed as a no-win situation — she changed.

Suddenly, she wanted to go back home. Her mother was no longer the "bad guy" and was, instead, her savior. Her brothers were no longer annoying, irresponsible brats — they were her family. Promising to "be good," Sara begged me to convince her mother to let her return home.

I arranged an appointment with a therapist, her mother flew out to California, behavioral terms were discussed, agreements were made, and Sara went back to Ohio. Today she is married and the mother of a five-year-old boy who was adopted as a two-year-old from Ukraine. She and her husband are currently trying to adopt another child from the same town.

Sara's turnaround was truly the result of being "scared straight." As a student in Oakland, she came face-to-face with the reality that no matter how well she acted the part of the little toughie, she'd always be up against someone tougher, meaner, more dangerous. The harsh wake-up call of the inner city made her tranquil Ohio lifestyle and the gentleness of her family look more appealing. It was a hard life lesson, to be sure, but it allowed Sara to grow into a happy and contented young woman who embraces family and responsibility with fervent enthusiasm.

ZACH, AGE SEVENTEEN, CURRENTLY IN FOSTER CARE:

It is important for families to adopt teenagers because it gives kids a chance at life and a chance with a family. To me, the closest thing to a family was my grandma, and she passed away a year ago. It has made my life a lot more difficult since she passed away, so I would really like another chance for a family. There are a lot of kids out there who would like to have a family, and I am one of them. I think that kids need another chance at a family. I would really like another shot at a family — and soon.

BROUNAN, AGE SIXTEEN, RECENTLY PLACED IN AN ADOPTIVE HOME:

When I was sixteen and back in foster care after one adoption had fallen through, I thought I could never be adopted. But when a matching family was found, I was shocked. The first thought that came into my head was,

You've got to be kidding me. But they weren't! Now here I am living with a family that loves me. But not all kids have that.

Most kids in foster care pray to either be put back with their families or be out of foster care as fast as they can. Teenagers on the adoption listings have less chance of being adopted. This is because most recruited families want younger children so they can spend more time with them. When I met my new family, I asked many questions, one of them being, "What will happen when I turn eighteen?" Their answer was that I'm welcome to stay. It feels good to have a real family, even after I graduate.

LIZ, AGE SEVENTEEN, ADOPTED AT SEVENTEEN:

My name is Elizabeth. I am seventeen years old. I was brought into the custody of children services when I was twelve. I was there for six months and then went home for three months to see if anything had changed for the better, but it hadn't. I went back into custody for a little over five years.

During that time, I lost my real mother, whom I was very close to. She had been very sick. I have a sister who is twenty years old. I have her on my side no matter what I do, and I love her so dearly. No, she was never adopted. She has had some hard times, but she's now on her feet, and I'm so happy for that. I know that some foster kids don't have that family connection or anything. Luckily, that's not the case for me. I hope that someday all kids will find, like I have, the best family for them that will love and care for them.

One day, two or three summers ago, my caseworker asked me about adoption. The first thought that came to my mind was that this could be a good thing or a bad thing for me. Either I could stay in foster care and go on my own, not knowing what to do, or I could be with a family that could teach me things about life. The thing is, when you think you want something good and it gets to the point where there's no turning back, you begin to feel scared.

I had also been staying with a family that was so amazing, and I started to want to live with them. Then my caseworker told me about another family. I liked them, too, but I didn't want to leave behind all my friends and the people I considered family to move in with them. It was all very confusing and I couldn't make the decision myself, so they made the decision for me. At the time, I didn't like the choice they made, but I wouldn't have liked either choice, as I didn't want to be adopted; I wanted to be living with my real mom. But that wasn't possible.

My feelings about getting adopted are so many because the friends and family I had developed before just went bye-bye. I have to remind myself that if they're that good to me, they won't forget me. Always hold on and don't let go! I've just had to be strong and start over — that's all I can do. Now I am finally legally adopted. Since I have been with my new family, I have discovered new areas, people, family, and friends. I can have my driver's license and my cell phone and spend the night with friends like typical teenagers do. I have a job at a Wendy's that my adoptive family owns. I am happy. I so hope that all foster kids will find that special family — like I have.

STEVE, FATHER OF SIX ADOPTED CHILDREN:

I have always been a strong believer in adoption, and I recently had the opportunity to join the board of directors of an adoption agency. But even before joining the board, while doing parent presentations on adoption, I would always look at the books of kids waiting for permanent homes. Even though all the children tugged at my heartstrings, seeing the older, harder-to-place children made me ask myself some difficult questions: *What was going to happen to these kids when they age out of the system at eighteen and the state no longer has a legal responsibility for them? Where will they go? Who will they turn to for guidance and support? Where will they live? Will they just be put out on the street with nowhere to go? How will they find a job or go on to college if they so desire? Without someone to provide guidance and a place to call home, will their destination be the streets or jail or even a violent death?*

Those thoughts haunted me as I kept going back to the picture of one boy, almost seventeen years old, who had lived in nine different foster homes and two residential treatment facilities during his nearly ten years in the system.

Adoption was not new to me since I had adopted five children, two girls and three boys, over the last forty years. The two still living at home, now eighteen and sixteen, had been with me since they were three years old and fourteen months old. *How would this young man fit into the family? How would he get along with my son, who is his same age? Would I be able to handle — and could the family adjust to — the multiple issues of ADD, ADHD, and ODD?*

Would I have support from the adoption agency if I needed help? What would it do to him if it just didn't work and he was rejected once again?

These were among the many concerns and fears that I had to face as an adoptive parent. Of my kids still living at home, my son was against the idea of adopting this sixth child, although my daughter was more open-minded. With all this in mind, I agreed to have a foster child placed with me for adoption.

During the past two years, as a family, we have worked through some difficult and challenging times, but they were also coupled with rewarding and heart-filled experiences. If you are considering adopting an older child, you need to be prepared for disruptions to your normal household, and you must have patience, trust, and the belief that through love, understanding, firmness, fairness, and sometimes just plain old tough love, adoption of an older child can be both successful and rewarding. Through all the pain, heartache, and accomplishments, there is nothing more powerful than the words "I love you, Dad." It is then that you know you have made it. After all, love makes a family.

EDD, FATHER OF AN ADOPTED ADOLESCENT:

I recently completed the process of adopting a sixteen-year-old boy who had been living in foster care most of his life. Many people asked me why I would want to adopt a teenager, and, to me, the answer was easy: He was a child in need of a family and all that comes with it.

We often hear people say that they "take care of their own." There are thousands of kids in Ohio who are in the same situation my son was in. I feel that these kids are "our own," and we are responsible for giving them at least the basics: a home, a family, security, and hope for the future. I specifically looked to adopt an older teenager to avoid having him age out at eighteen and be out in the world with no resources and no family to support him.

Although I knew that adopting was something I wanted to do, it was not a decision I made overnight. I had many doubts and fears about what the future might hold for both the child and me. My main concern was whether or not I could accept this person as my own son and whether he would accept me, as well. I also wondered how my friends and family would react to my decision and to the son I wanted to adopt. What if we didn't get along or have things in common? Although I worried about such issues, my determination was stronger than my fears.

Here was a child who had been through an unimaginable experience. For whatever reason, he was separated from his birth parents and moved from place to place for more than half of his young life. He had no stability, no control, no lasting friendships. I thought about how fortunate I had been as a child, growing up with my family in a structured and loving environment. Then I thought about the children growing up with none of these things, knowing that at any time they might be moved to yet another unfamiliar situation.

Many of the concerns I have for my son are the same concerns that birth parents have for their children. Like all families, there are good days and bad, bumpy roads and smooth ones. You do your best and hope for the best. Whether I am appreciated or not isn't important. Few teenagers tell their parents how much they appreciate them. My reward is knowing how much I am giving this child. I feel more fortunate than a birth parent because although I did not create this child, I am able to give him the things in life that are truly important and necessary and that he has never had before, and this is something that every child deserves.

MARY, MOTHER OF GEORGE:

Following is an interview with a woman who is the mother of several adopted adolescents.

Question: How has adoption impacted your adopted adolescents?

Answer: They finally get to settle in one home. They don't have to worry about waking up and wondering where they're going next.

Question: How do you think your life would have been different had you not adopted your children?

Answer: Had I not adopted my children, my life would be empty and lifeless.

GEORGE, AGE FIFTEEN, ADOPTED AT TWELVE:

> *Question:* How do you think your life as an adolescent is different because you were adopted?
>
> *Answer:* I think my life is different because I didn't get to live a normal life as normal kids do. I was always traveling from house to house and meeting new people, but I will say it made me a stronger person.
>
> *Question:* How do you think your life would have been different if you had remained with your birth parents?
>
> *Answer:* I believe that I wouldn't be the well-mannered young man I am today. I believe that I would be just another stereotype of a black man.

BRIAN KECK, AGE THIRTY-SIX, ADOPTED AT SIXTEEN:

I was sixteen years old when I came to the realization that I was going to live my life without a family. I had been in and out of twenty-seven different adoptive and foster homes over a period of twelve years. Not only did I give up hope, but so did the social services people in charge of finding me a placement. When I turned sixteen, they decided to move me to Cleveland, Ohio, to a group home far from where I was living in Columbus. I felt as though I did not belong in the home because I was living with a bunch of juvenile delinquents. My life had hit rock bottom.

After living in the group home for about two months, I met Regina Kupecky, who was working for Northeast Ohio Adoption Services. The day we met, she promised me that I would be adopted before I graduated high school. Of course, I laughed at her and did not believe a word she said. At this point in my life, I did not trust anyone. Why would I?

Three months after I met Regina, I found myself at a hayride where I would meet Gregory Keck. Little did I know but this was a planned meeting arranged by Regina to introduce Greg and me. From what I knew, he was just another guy at the hayride. I really liked him because he was just a cool guy who had a cool car. I was able to spend a lot of time with him that day, and I remember telling Regina a couple days later that he was the type of guy I would love to be adopted by.

A few months after that, I was informed that Greg was interested in adopting me. I couldn't have been happier. I thought that maybe I'd get lucky and actually be adopted before I graduated high school. I started going on weekend visits with him, and things were great. Before I knew it, I was living with Greg permanently.

Things were great at first. Then, just like at every other home I lived in, things started to go bad, so I expected that I would be leaving this home just like I left the twenty-seven homes before.

The thing was, my new father was *nothing* like any parent I'd had before. No matter what happened, he did not throw me out. He was so stubborn. I remember testing him to see if he would kick me out just as everyone else had before. He never did.

It took me awhile, but I started to trust that my new father was in it for the long haul. After we started to trust each other, our relationship began to grow. Everything in my life started to improve. I became my high school's first-ever state champion in wrestling. I was able to graduate from a very respected private high school in Cleveland. I went to college on a full wrestling scholarship, and I graduated with a degree in social welfare.

Being adopted has meant everything to me. I will always have a family to go home to. I remember someone having asked my dad why he would adopt such an older child, and I remember his response. He said that a child needs a family not just for his adolescence but for his whole life. A parent does not stop being a parent when his child leaves and goes to college. I will always have a dad. I will always have a dad to call when things are not going well in my life. I will always have a dad to call and tell of the good news that has happened in my life. I will always have a family to go to during the holidays. I feel that my dad will always be there for me no matter what happens to me in my personal life.

I had a very bad childhood; a lot of bad things happened to me when I was young. If I had to do it all over again to end up with my father, I would do it in a heartbeat. I feel like the luckiest person in the world to end up with a father who did not give up on me. I could not even imagine where I would have ended up if I had not met him twenty years ago at the infamous hayride. Thank God I did.

JAMES KECK, AGE TWENTY-FOUR, ADOPTED AT THIRTEEN:

Being adopted was one of the hardest things I've had to go through in my life. I was thirteen years old at the time my father told me that he wanted me to be his son. Never having a father, I was scared for what life might bring me. I had no clue what path my life was going to take after being adopted.

The only person who knew that everything was going to be okay was my father. He didn't know how things were going to turn out, and chances are he was probably more scared than I was. But no matter what I did at the start of my adoption, he wouldn't give up. My father showed me the love I deserved on the first day I was living with him. He showed me the way to be a part of a real family. I graduated high school and am currently in college. I played football in Australia right out of high school for the Pennsylvania/Ohio all-star team. All of these things most likely would not have happened if it weren't for him.

My dad has made all of my dreams come true just by staying here by my side. Life takes many twists and turns, but never giving up is something my dad has taught me. He is the reason I can go on; he filled a hole in my heart that I thought would always be empty.

LAUREN, MOTHER OF AN ADOPTED ADOLESCENT:

We're a united front, we parents of adopted children. We've all survived a lot of the same episodes, endured the same miseries, celebrated the same small victories. We've leaned on one another, supported one another, encouraged one another. When we accepted the responsibility of bringing these children into our lives, we bought an unlimited ticket for the roller-coaster ride: "Just sign right here and go up and down as many times as you like."

We've all had our share of the down times. For some of us, it has been an all-consuming experience. I, for one, have often found it difficult to focus on anything else when my adolescent son declares, "I was born to a useless woman; I'm doomed to be useless," and proceeds to flush his 130+ IQ down the toilet. When he's in this frame of mind, he feeds on bad decisions, finds some sort of bizarre sustenance in them. At these times, he is a child sentenced to a purgatory of his own creation.

And I watch. And I ache. And I try to understand. Mostly I feel utterly helpless because only he can stop the downward spiral. Sometimes he has to hit rock bottom before he looks up and discovers he doesn't really want to be there. I'm not sure what the fall feels like to him. To me, it all happens in slow motion—an agonizing descent that seems to go on forever.

But you probably know this saga. And I'm guessing you don't appreciate the fact that I've just reminded you how awful it can be. But let me try to save myself with a story—one that's guaranteed to make you smile, I promise.

Meet my son Beck, that adolescent I told you about. He's profoundly analytical, distractingly attractive, and too intelligent for his own good. He's the only kid in his school who gets Ds and Fs on his report card yet participates in the gifted and talented program. He's the sort of kid who doesn't do his homework, doesn't cooperate in the classroom, and rolls his eyes when I spout things like, "Gee, you're lucky, Beck, 'cause ninth grade will be there for you again next year." Like he really cares.

Two weeks ago, Beck was invaded by the body snatchers. They took away my I-don't-care-about-anything son and left in his place a model of responsibility. He came home from school with a note from his teacher stating that he had done all his homework during free period, had completed several past-due assignments, and was exhibiting a new, positive attitude. That evening, he decided to write a two-hundred-word, extra-credit essay about Isaac Newton. His rationale was that he could bring up both his language arts and science grades with this project. The next day, I received a note from the teacher saying that she had given Beck an extra A and B for the report and that, by the way, he'd had another great day.

This behavior has continued without interruption, with one positive note after another. It carries through at home. He volunteered his landscaping services to a neighbor whose lawn and garden had gotten out of hand. "I don't need money," he said to her. "It just makes me feel good to get things cleaned up." (She paid him twenty dollars anyway.)

One afternoon, he impulsively threw his arms around me and squealed, "I'm so happy!" Although his actions caught me completely by surprise, I knew that he meant it. And I knew it had surprised him, too. I grinned at him and saw that his cheeks were a little pinker, his eyes were a little brighter, and his smile went on forever.

Now, I've been on this roller coaster far too long to think that all the scary twists and turns are behind me, but the ride is slowly changing as the years slide by. The distressing parts are getting shorter, further apart. The fun parts crop up more frequently. They last longer, and they feel more real. For all of this, I am grateful.

The lesson to be learned is that there are good times in store. Not just times when my son makes it through an entire week of school without getting even one citation, but times when he actually looks his life in the eye and says, "Yes, this is good. And I deserve every ounce of joy and satisfaction you can dish out. So let's get moving—I have a lot of catching up to do."

And me? I'm going to be right there catching up with him.

BRUCE AND ANITA, PARENTS OF ALEXIS AND EMILY:

We have five children, three of whom came to us through adoption. All of our kids—both birth and adopted—had issues in adolescence, but we think adoption compounds the problems the kids have. Part of being a teen is figuring out who you are and where you fit. Being adopted, particularly in a racially mixed family, makes that more difficult.

Most teens rebel to some extent. Sometimes teens who have been adopted are afraid of any kind of confrontation with parents because they fear being removed from the family. One of our kids, Emily, had major issues with any kind of change. Whenever she ended a school year, ended a camp session, changed schools, or changed friends, it was an emotional event. Adolescence was particularly challenging for her because things like dating and making career choices made change a definite, and she was overwhelmed by it all.

Sometimes kids are not afraid of confrontation and, in fact, spend a great deal of their time trying to "persuade" you to reject them. That was the case with our son. We adopted him when he was thirteen, and he had come to us a year earlier. His adolescence was like one volcano after another erupting in our home, and there were many reasons for this. He had lived in foster care most of his life, and the damage done to him was very deep. It led to substance-abuse issues that were also very destructive. He eventually became quite violent, and he is currently incarcerated. He prefers that we not visit him; we respect that, but we do write letters and speak on the phone.

We have been, and will remain, committed to him. But this is his journey, and our role is to walk with him—letting him know we are still there but not telling him which way to go. He has had too many people in his life trying to map it all out for him, and he is incredibly confused. Our belief in the formula of three years to heal for every year in foster care (or an abusive situation) means our son could have a long way to go before he begins to figure out what he wants. And when he does, we will be there, just as we are there now.

Kids who are adopted when they are teens desperately need that unconditional support because so many times they've been told they're not worth anything. But they are. Our son is a wonderful person with a great heart who has made lousy choices based on experiences he had in the first twelve years of his life. We are allowing him to take responsibility for those choices, and we are loving him at the same time. This is a new paradigm for him—one that we believe is well worth exploring.

Our goal when we adopted our kids was twofold: First, we love parenting and thought we were pretty good at it, so we wanted to have more kids; second, as we learned more and more about the children waiting for homes, we wanted to offer a child (or two or three) a chance to know that the world can be different from what they had experienced. We wanted them to see they had choices and were not doomed to repeat what had happened to them.

Watching our kids grow and change has been such an incredible journey—sometimes joyful, sometimes heartbreaking, but never boring! Our children are members of our family, but they also belong to at least one other family. Particularly during adolescence, that was a struggle, for them and for us. However, what we came to see was that our children belong to themselves and to God, and it is an awesome responsibility to love them, guide them, and allow them to grow, in their time and in their way.

It is very hard not to take it personally at times, but it is about them, not us. We would adopt each one of ours again in a heartbeat. They are our kids, and we are grateful to have had the chance to be a part of their lives.

ALEXIS, AGE THIRTY, ADOPTED AT ONE MONTH:

Part of what was most difficult for me was wondering if my birth mother would be willing to see me and if that would be devastating to my adoptive parents. During my life, I had thought a lot about adoption and asked a great number of questions. I was always wondering who I resembled (even though I look a great deal like my adoptive mom) and what my birth family was like.

I was born blind (and am now legally blind), and I think my visual impairment was a major issue for me most of my life. When I was a sophomore in high school, I was confirmed in my church and decided to use that time to make a spiritual journey to understand who I was. My parents were very helpful.

I came to many realizations, but the most important one was that I am who I am: I am adopted, I am visually impaired, I am capable, I am determined, and I am lots of other things. I realized there were things I could change and things I could not. Being adopted was not going to change, so I decided to accept that and begin determining how I wanted that fact to figure into my life. I knew I wanted to search for my birth family, but it took me a long time to get to the point where I could actually do so. I'm glad I did, and my experiences with my birth mother and her family have been good.

I also think it was easier for me as a teenager than for my brother and sister because they are racially different from the rest of our family. Because I'm not, people did not immediately assume I was adopted. There are pros and cons to that. People often said things to me about adoption that were very hurtful since they had no clue that I was adopted. For my brother and sister, it is just out there! Our family was pretty well known in our town and most people knew that we were an adoptive family, but sometimes I slid under the radar.

EMILY, AGE TWENTY-NINE, ADOPTED AT THREE:

For me, the most difficult part of being a teenager was all the changes. I had a hard time with change, and I ran into a lot of it in high school. Because I am from India, I don't look like my adoptive family, so people knew just by looking at us that I was adopted. My brother is African American, so people knew he was adopted too.

I have very dark skin, so when I began dating, I dated more African

American boys than Indian or Caucasian boys. Once I had a problem with the father of a boy I was dating because he realized I had been adopted by a Caucasian family. He was very nasty in his opinion about it. I think being a teenager is hard enough without all the additional stuff that being adopted adds to it.

I also think that people are so intent on being happy that they don't understand the questions we, as adoptees, might have or the feelings we experience. So many people think we should just be happy to have a family. I love my family and I'm happy, but there's more to it than that.

We traveled to India together three years ago, and I was able to really get a sense of my culture, of where I came from. Now things seem to fit better for me.

LLOYD, AGE TWENTY-FOUR, ADOPTED AT EIGHT:

The following poem was written by Lloyd, a young man currently serving as a combat medic in Iraq.

The Nine of Happiness

1.

eating ice cream out of the package.

hugging all that is okay.

more milk, more cookies, more love.

an oven is often necessary to show appreciation.

a blind man can smile.

radiance is brilliance of a smile plus a giggle.

all it takes is one laugh.

2.

deny none your joy, abandon humility, and start as if done.

looking in one direction is a sure cause of eye strain.

more people will know if the sun is out.

all dance, all groove, but not all get jiggy with it.

a single candle means that more candles are to come.

ravens are never invited to a fete.

3.

good is the temporary absence of sanity.
fun is to be had by all.
no one can smile upside down.
laughter can be heard a mile away.
smile is the greatest tattletale known.
one cannot keep joy hidden.

4.

feeling like a cookie requires milk.
a good egg and a bad egg are never laid in the same nest.
perfection is not key to good.
babies know more than they tell, talk to them.
youth requires constant attention, but don't be smothering.
sunshine will dry up the rain.

5.

think of clouds, shade is good on a hot day.
more smiles means success.
objection, that was me.
a thornless rose.
yellow.

6.

fools cry when milk is spilt.
it takes a smile to make a smile.
feeling is key.
no one can fake a laugh.
it is like this: extraordinary.

7.

cannot one person see a sparkle with a smile?
the end is a prelude.
at the bottom the only way to go is up.
tears don't taste good.
joy is emotional currency, you can't have enough.
others will come to you.

8.

stars feel less alone when the moon is out.

friends always have this way of gaiety.

humor is designed to be spread.

how hard is it to dance?

joy is older than you, so age does not matter.

why do you think the fork ran away with the spoon?

9.

the Teletubbies have mastered all that is good, but speech impediments hurt
their cause.

see it, live it, and love it.

faking love is impossible, ask Romeo and Juliet.

no two friends are alike.

a tickle here and there signifies a ninja of happiness in the area, seek them
out.

family + friends + pets = you.

= winner.

NIC, AGE FIFTEEN, ADOPTED AT THREE FROM ROMANIA:

How is my life different because I was adopted? I am able to go to school, and
I live in a nice home. I am able to have a family who can take care of me at all
times. I am able to have medical care when I need it. I am able to go on trips
with my family all over the world. I feel safe living in Canada.

How would my life have been different had I remained with my birth
parents? I would not have been able to get a good education. My family might
not have been able to afford medical care. (I was born with crossed eyes and
was in an orphanage for three years with crossed eyes. My adoptive parents
immediately had my eyes fixed when I came to Canada.) My birth parents
might not have had a lot of money for food, and I would not have been able
to even leave the town.

My family and I visited Romania in August of 2008. When we flew out
of Toronto, I was fine in the airport, but once I got on the plane, I started to
get nervous—so nervous that I couldn't even eat. I was thinking about what

Romania would be like.

I was imagining and guessing what we would see. I was scared to go to the orphanage. I have no memories of that time, but I was worried I might see something and remember. I had seen videos of kids in orphanages and photos of street kids.

I kept a diary while we were on the trip, and these are some of my thoughts and observations.

■ ■ ■

I am happy to be going to Romania but scared to see where I lived for three years. I am worried about flying over the water. I already lost my dad when he died last year. Dad never saw Romania, and he is missing his chance this time. My sister and I thought we saw parts of Dad in the airline steward, with his glasses and beard. I am mad that Dad is not here on this trip. Tomorrow is the one-year anniversary of Dad dying. Mom picked now to travel so we would have a diversion tomorrow.

■ ■ ■

We have arrived in Romania and I find it scary. I have not been here in twelve years. Driving around is scary. Wild dogs roam around. People speak a different language, and we have found no one who speaks English. We were warned by the car-rental people that we could be targets for theft. I am worried about our personal safety as foreigners.

We were told to expect that the car might be stolen or broken into. People were coming up to the car and begging. The first hotel we stayed in was nice, but I found it scary, too, because it was on a crummy-looking street. People were sitting on the curb in front of the hotel. I felt safe inside our room, but I checked the car often through the night from our window.

■ ■ ■

I am happy to leave that hotel. The street people were gone in the morning. We got a GPS before leaving Bucharest to drive to Arad. At least someone can speak English and tell us directions. It helped us get out of there faster. We drove through the mountains on the way to Arad. I was scared about getting out of the car. Our car made us appear to be rich people driving in a poor town.

We stopped at a campsite/pizza place to use the bathroom. It was a dark, dingy room with a hole in the floor and feet marks on the floor indicating where to stand. Gross. It was scary walking through the campsite. We were the only English-speaking visitors. I didn't want to sit and wait for the pizza at the outdoor café even though it was a clean place.

We saw poor homes while driving. Begging families were disturbing. Boys, girls, moms and dads, even old ladies, were begging along the road. I am happy I am not one of them. I realize I could be living that life. I appreciate the life I have now. We saw deformed people on the road begging. I think I would have been one of them had I stayed with my crossed eyes.

On the main road driving with us were big transport trucks, horse and carts, wild dogs and cats, beggars. This single-lane highway is the main road, and in many towns it is the only paved road. There is no sidewalk, no shoulder, so everyone is on it. It is nothing like the roads in Canada.

Tomorrow we will be in Arad. I am scared to see where I lived and came from, but I am glad to see where I was born. I don't want to see my birth mother. My adoptive mom doesn't know where she is. I don't wonder about her, don't wonder about sisters or brothers. I am not interested in knowing what she is doing now. She had no money to take care of me at birth. She likely has no money now. I am nervous about going to the orphanage. The staff probably wouldn't recognize me.

■　■　■

Today we went to the orphanage. I was nervous and happy to see where I lived for three years. I didn't eat much at breakfast and I was quiet. When we got there, we expected to see kids sitting around outside, maybe some of them deformed. The orphanage is not an orphanage anymore but a passport office. We walked around all three floors, but I didn't remember anything. The hospital I was born in is now an apartment building.

I am happy I don't live here. I enjoyed seeing those two buildings, but I was nervous walking through them.

I hope these stories will lead you to understanding and appreciating the journeys of the kids we are interested in. They all have had bumps in their roads and parents can help smooth their paths.

TWELVE

RANDOM REFLECTIONS

Musings About Adolescents

Writing a book requires thought, organization, and production. As I was wrapping up the final chapter of this book, I discovered that I still had many thoughts to share that did not necessarily fit into the established organization of the book. I hope these random thoughts and musings will help you gain a better understanding of your adopted adolescent and how to parent him in a way that will generate harmony for all members of your family.

This is the most informal chapter in the book because I want to leave you with the sense that we've just had a casual conversation about how to strengthen — and survive — your relationship with your adopted adolescent. I also want to lighten things up a bit, because if you're too steeped in the difficulties you might be facing, your effectiveness as a parent — as well as your spirit as a person — will be compromised. So take a deep breath, relax, and read on.

EDUCATION

Based on my experience, one of the most frustrating issues facing families is how to deal with their adolescent's education. If I had a single, guaranteed-to-solve-everything answer for this issue, there would be another book in the making.

One of the most difficult problems with our educational system is that it affords little diversity. Most public schools share a similar structure and format for education. It's a good thing our hospitals are not modeled after our schools because if that were the case, everyone would be subjected to the same battery of tests, regardless of the symptoms they presented.

I find it hard to believe that we have an approach, almost a singular approach, to educating children and adolescents with little regard for their individual learning styles and preferences. I would guess that you could go into any classroom in this country and find that what is going on does not vary from school to school.

We assume that boys and girls share learning styles, and that is patently untrue. Their respective learning styles and needs are so disparate that it's no wonder boys are falling behind. Our schools are meeting the learning needs of girls more efficiently than those of boys.

I think that anyone who has ever spent time with children knows that girls mature earlier than boys. In most instances, girls are ready to sit down quietly and behave appropriately when they are about five or six. Boys, on the other hand, need more time to gain the maturity required to sit still in a classroom—or anywhere else, for that matter. In fact, classes with more active learning and movement would probably suit their needs best of all.

Author and family therapist Michael Gurian has written extensively about gender differences as they relate to many areas of life. Leonard Sax, MD, PhD, author of *Boys Adrift*, has also examined this issue. I highly recommend their work to parents who want to better understand what is occurring with their sons. (For details, see the Related Resources section, which follows this chapter.)

Traditionally, boys and adult males are overrepresented in the following arenas:

- Behavioral-handicapped classes
- Most mental-heath diagnostic categories
- Juvenile and adult justice systems
- Detentions and suspensions from schools
- The homeless population
- Mental-health settings

- Substance-abuse treatment settings
- Special-education programs

Furthermore, they are more likely than girls to be on stimulant medication for attention deficit/hyperactivity disorder (ADHD).

If you want to do an experiment, take a look at a school bus stop. Don't lurk around too long, though, because these days everyone is suspected of something! What you will see is this: The girls will be chatting with each other in small groups while they wait for the bus; the boys will not be conversing with their friends but might instead be climbing the tree next to the bus stop. They may be kicking stones or even throwing them at each other—or worse yet, at the girls.

Try out part two of the experiment by going back to the bus stop at the end of the school day. You'll see the girls stepping off the bus one by one and talking with each other as they proceed down the street. The boys, on the other hand, will fly out of the bus as if they were shot out of a cannon! I am not making this up. In fact, I recently drove by an unloading school bus and watched in awe as one boy careened off the bus steps, caught a considerable amount of air in the process, and actually landed nearly halfway up his driveway.

Several years ago, some people would have said that these boy/girl stereotypes are the result of socializing boys and girls differently. I don't think that socialization has much to do with it. Do you know of any parents who have socialized their son to skip rocks the minute he gets next to a body of water? To climb the nearest fence or tree? To pop wheelies on his bike?

So we send a typically rambunctious five-year-old boy to kindergarten with his female peers and wonder why he seems to need meds as of day one. About 50 percent of the boys and adolescents I see for an ADHD evaluation have a clear diagnosis: boy. I certainly believe that medication is invaluable when a diagnosis is accurate, but meds will not be helpful if they're being prescribed simply because a male child is doing what his gender drives him to do.

More and more school districts are taking a look at single-gender schools. Gurian and others have written about this solution, and they suggest that both girls and boys learn better in single-gender environments. We need to be more creative educationally because it does not seem that we have much to lose by trying a few viable alternatives.

When it comes to homework, it clearly takes a toll on families from September through June. It begins in kindergarten and never seems to end. In *The End of Homework*, authors Etta Kralovec and John Buell repeatedly relate that there is no evidence that homework improves learning or is even helpful at any level, particularly in elementary school. There are high school students who successfully demonstrate their mastery of a subject via an A on an exam, yet they fail the class because they did not turn in their homework on time or at all.

Does this make any sense? Does it seem right that if something is late, it is unacceptable and therefore devoid of any credit? How many adults complete their work assignments late? Do they lose their jobs? No. The real world accommodates real situations, yet we are driven to hold children and adolescents completely accountable in an unrealistic manner. If they don't want to go to school one day, they are considered truant if their parent does not call them in sick. What happens when the teacher doesn't want to go to school? He calls in sick—with pay. There seems to be little rhyme or reason when we take a close look at what we are doing in our educational system.

Schools routinely suspend students for cutting classes. How brilliant that the way we punish a child who doesn't want to be in school is by forbidding him to attend! I recall once working with an adolescent girl who had cut classes for twenty days. When she returned to school at her parents' and my urging, she was suspended for an additional ten days. When I called the school administration, they insisted that she needed a consequence. I indicated that I agreed but suggested that the consequence for missing twenty days of school might be for her to attend twenty additional days of Saturday school instead of getting rewarded by ten more days at home, precisely where she wanted to be.

I must say I understand the frustration of parents as I experience the same feeling of not being heard. Because our adolescents spend much of their lives in school, we need to help advocate for them in that arena.

KEEPING THEM WITH YOU

Too many adults buy into the adolescent's statement that he doesn't want to do family things. This may be true on some level, particularly for adolescents who have been in their families since birth or early childhood. But if the adoption took place during adolescence, the goal is for him to connect with the family, and that means spending time together — lots of time. If the adoption took place at an earlier age, the goal is to maintain the connection that has already been established, and this, too, requires time.

It doesn't even have to be the quality time that is so much the trend these days but rather quantity time. After all, the more time you spend as a family, the greater the odds that much of it will be quality time.

As children get older, they may naturally want to spend less time with their parents. However, you must make sure that you are available for your adolescents. Keep family time intact, have family meals, take family vacations. Work on the assumption that the family will continue to function as a unit, no matter how old your child gets.

Many reports in the media indicate that, when asked by researchers, adolescents report that the one thing they want is to spend *more* time with their parents. So do it, even if there are some protests. Keep in mind that an adolescent may need to protest just so he can tell his friends that he *has* to go on spring break with the family even though he would so much rather go to Cancun with his classmates.

I am always shocked when parents tell me they're going on a cruise over spring break while their kids are either staying home or going away with friends. Why would any reasonable adult choose to take a vacation and leave his adolescent at home *alone* or — even more bizarre — send him off to Mexico with a group of other adolescents? When left to their own devices, even the most well-adjusted adolescents will make decisions that are not in their best interest. Do parents think their kids will be engaged in algebra study groups while Mom and Dad are on a cruise? It's time for a wake-up call. Adolescents need parental involvement in their lives; they want parental involvement, even when they say they don't.

KNOWING THEIR FRIENDS

One of the best ways to further the relationship with your adolescent is by getting to know his friends. Inviting them into your home and making them feel welcome goes a long way toward keeping abreast of what's going on in your adolescent's life. Too many parents forbid their kids to associate with certain people, but it is nearly impossible to exercise any control over such mandates. Connections will be made in school, at basketball and football games, at the mall, and at the local hangout. Rules such as "You will *not* see that person ever again!" cannot be enforced when an adolescent is out of your sight, so unless you plan to follow him around 24/7, it makes far more sense to develop a different tack. By keeping your adolescent and his friends close, you are better able to regulate what goes on.

It is important to think outside the box, to explore opportunities for new ways to stay in touch and remain connected to your adolescent, to be experimental and have fun. If your kid's friends are that bad, they probably won't want to hang out with "old folks" like you anyway. So when they decline an invitation to visit, your adolescent gets the message that his friend has ruined the arrangement — not you — so you're off the hook.

THE SERENITY PRAYER

This is a prayer used in numerous situations, but I think it is most often associated with twelve-step groups of all kinds. It is believed to have been written by Reinhold Niebuhr in the 1930s. Since then, it has been slightly modified by Alcoholics Anonymous and could probably be of help to the parents of an adolescent, as well.

> *God, grant me the serenity*
> *to accept the things I cannot change,*
> *the courage to change the things I can,*
> *and the wisdom to know the difference.*[1]

Let's dissect it a bit and apply it to adopted adolescents.

God, Grant Me the Serenity to Accept the Things I Cannot Change

As a parent, you cannot change how your adopted child was hurt. His genetic inheritance. What he believes or thinks he believes. His behavioral choices. What he likes to eat. His refusal to do his homework. His disbelief in God. His sexual abuse. His losses, including birth parents, siblings, and other relatives. His sadness over why someone didn't want him or why someone hurt him so much. His guilt and shame. His not having friends and relationships. His identity. His loneliness and longing for a connection to someone he feels is just like him. His getting fired from a job.

His grief. His friends. His need for control. His inability to understand and make sense of his adoption. His performance in school, on the playing field, on the dance floor, in the art studio, on the mat. His choice of friends. His sense of humor. The way he dresses. The way he walks. The way he talks. How he loves you. How he hates you. His immaturity. His maturity. The way his body grows—or doesn't. The risks he takes on his skateboard, on the soccer field, behind the wheel. The adult he will become.

The Courage to Change the Things I Can

You *can* change how you interact with your adolescent. How you model what you believe. Support him in his journeys. Make yourself available to him. Show steady responses to his unsteady behavior. Show him the way. Guide and lead him when he's lost. Stand beside him in times of trouble. Hear what he has to say—whatever it may be or however disturbing you may find it—because you may be the only person with whom he can share his pain. Show an interest in the adoption-related things he talks about or thinks about, such as his birth parents and his "lost" brothers and sisters. Soothe his hurts as much as you can. Share and acknowledge his pain. Stop talking so much. Stop the lectures. Stop repeating yourself. Stop going to the worst possible outcome—it's unlikely that he'll be a failure in life just because he failed tenth-grade French.

Stop talking about money. Stop telling him he'll get pneumonia if he doesn't zip up his jacket. Show concern for his safety. Show interest in his world. Support his interests, even if they don't interest you. If he's not horrendously embarrassed to be seen with you in public, go to a concert with him instead of saying, "That's not even music!" If yours is a transracial adoption, be sure to have friends who are the same race as your child. Explore his interest in his country of origin. Would he like to take a homeland tour? If so, help him plan it. Bring up important issues in a casual manner. Talk to his friends. Talk to him like you talk to his friends. Put parental blocks on the computers in your home, keeping him safe, once again. Take family trips—to the aquarium, the amusement park, the beach, the mountains. They don't have to be exotic places.

Spend as much time as you can with your adolescent. Teach him to drive without screaming or panicking, because that only causes him to drive more erratically. Odds are he's not really going to hit that truck that seems just inches away from the hood of your car. Teach him to cook. If he's new to your family, don't assume that he knows what you think he *should* know. Observe him and then help with whatever might be posing a challenge. Play with him, cuddle with him—no matter what your adolescent's age, he's not too old for affection. Demonstrate your commitment to being there for him for life.

The Wisdom to Know the Difference

Two elements give you the wisdom to know the difference between what you can change and what you can't. The first is your ability to understand your adolescent in relationship to the world. The second is his willingness to be open to change. My guess is that most of you already have this wisdom; you may just need to rely on it and use it more.

ZERO TOLERANCE

I have to admit that I am about ready to have zero tolerance for zero tolerance! The entire concept has been so distorted that I have come to believe that our world has developed zero tolerance for children and adolescents. Adolescents today are given little or no room for typical adolescent judgments.

A growing movement among parents and even some educators is attempting to end the entire zero-tolerance movement. Frustrated and appalled by the recent criminalization of behavior that was previously considered to be pranks—and not even serious pranks, at that—they are taking a stand to get things back in proper perspective.

An adolescent was referred to me for evaluation by juvenile court because he and some friends toilet-papered a friend's house and trees. He was charged with trespassing, malicious destruction of property, and criminal mischief (which seems like an oxymoron to me because it's either criminal or mischievous behavior—it can't be both). The evaluation seemed unnecessary. The boy's school performance was exemplary, his relationship with his parents was good, and his life was perfectly fine.

He was adjudicated of the aforementioned offenses and ordered to perform community service, which consisted of washing police cars. It seems to me that cleaning up the mess he made would have sufficed because it would have spared police time, a judge's time, parents' time, and the adolescent's time. He had no diagnosis other than being a fun-loving adolescent.

Let me make it clear that I don't think what he did was right, but I find it hard to believe that we are at a point in our society where this behavior has reached the level of being considered "criminal."

Other ridiculous zero-tolerance incidents include:

A Boy Scout knife falling out of a boy's coat pocket at school. His parents confirmed for the school that their son had been at a scout campout over the weekend. He had forgotten about the knife, which he never opened. He simply picked it up and put it back in his pocket. A short while later, he was taken to the principal's office and suspended for ten days for violating the school's zero tolerance for possession of weapons.

A boy threatening to hit another boy at recess. An eight-year-old wanted to play with some kids who didn't want him on their team. He yelled that if they didn't let him play, he was going to beat up one of them. He was escorted from the playground to the principal's office. His mother was called, and he was suspended until he was psychologically evaluated. I was supposed to determine whether or not he posed a danger to others. That was laughable! He was so tiny, I wondered just whom he could harm, even if he intended to do so.

A boy kissing a girl at recess. A six-year-old was well on his way to being listed on a sex-offender registry if you read the referral from the school. He and a little girl were playing together at recess, and he kissed her very quickly. He was suspended until he was evaluated to determine if he was a sexual perpetrator. He didn't even know what sex was, and he and his parents were very anxious about their appointment with me. They were unnecessarily embarrassed, and I think they felt relieved when I said I would call the school the next day to give their son clearance to return to his first-grade classroom.

Older adolescents (ages seventeen and eighteen) driving to school with cigarettes in their cars. If caught, they are suspended immediately for violating the school's drug, alcohol, and tobacco policy. Some school systems automatically remove them from all extra-curricular activities — sports teams, band, computer club — for this kind of infraction. Cigarettes, now on par with marijuana and alcohol? What about confiscating the cigarettes and throwing them away? It seems to me that adults should encourage involvement in as many extra-curricular activities as possible. After a ten-day suspension and permanent removal from all activities until the next academic year, I guess the kids will have plenty of time to sit around and smoke even more!

Obviously, our schools have to be well regulated, and everyone's safety must be considered. However, when the consequences don't fit the crime, the adolescent starts to have disregard for all rules, including those that are relevant. If safety is the issue that zero tolerance is intended to guarantee, let's have some standards of reasonableness. If the adolescent has had a checkered past and has been fighting, cutting classes, failing almost everything, *and* threatening others, it makes sense to take some sort of action. But if all adolescent misbehavior falls under the domain of zero tolerance, we are not helping adolescents learn anything about actual accountability. Instead, we are causing them to reject authority *carte blanche* and minimize the seriousness of things that are actually important.

If you are interested in learning more about the state of zero tolerance in the country, take a look at the following website: www.ZeroIntelligence.net.

CLOTHES

Many of you have probably forgotten (or blocked) how mortified you were at different times during your adolescence. One of the greatest fears young people have is that others — most specifically, their peers — won't like them. To be considered popular as the result of athletic ability, a superior intellect, or a positively awesome nature is a blessing; to be deemed weird for any reason is a curse. A kid will do just about anything to hover under the geekdar so he can remain anonymous and unembarrassed by his absolute lack of cool (or whatever word captures the same meaning in the lexicon of his particular school these days).

One of the better parts about being an adult is that you probably got over this sort of fear a long time ago. So even though you may be dealing with wrinkles or a receding hairline, it's unlikely that you're walking around worried that everyone is looking at you, judging you, and trying to decide whether or not you're a pathetic loser.

I remember once going on a roller coaster with the adolescent son of a friend of mine. As the ride ended and the car approached the exit platform, he turned to me as he frantically tried to smooth down his windblown curls and said, "Hurry up, fix your hair so we look cool!" So adolescent, so funny, yet so important for him to look cool to a line full of complete strangers.

Although adults don't usually fret over their clothes with the intensity of an adolescent, most of us are conscious of what people are wearing, and many of us choose to dress in a way that reflects the current styles. If wide ties are in, the majority of fashion-conscious men will avoid the skinny versions popular in the fifties. If ballerina flats are all the rage, you can be sure to spot them on women who keep pace with trends.

Think about it for a minute. When was the last time you saw a woman wearing a poodle skirt and saddle shoes? Embroidered bell-bottoms and love beads? A jacket with huge padded shoulders and big hair to match? When was the last time you saw a man in a leisure suit? Really short athletic shorts with tall white socks pulled all the way up? A crew cut or a mullet? You get the point. Times change, and we change with them.

Adolescents are no different from us in this respect; it's just that they're a lot more verbal about it, and their sense of who they are is more directly tied in to how they look. They don't want to appear dorky. They don't want to look like yesterday. And many of them wouldn't be caught dead in anything that remotely resembles a hand-me-down. So what's a parent to do?

Unless the clothing your adolescent wants to wear is forbidden by his school's dress code or your religion's dictates (unless it's shockingly risqué), I'd suggest going for it and letting him make his fashion statement. This doesn't mean that you have to rush out and buy the most expensive designer duds on the market. Many retailers carry a good selection of clothes that have been designed to mimic the real thing. Discount stores and thrift shops are great sources for name-brand apparel at very good prices. Decide what you're willing to spend, let your adolescent know that you've agreed to let him pick out what he wants, and head off on your shopping spree. As he tries things on, do your best to avoid saying, "Why would any human being in his right mind want to wear *that*?"

CARS

So your adolescent is painfully embarrassed to be seen behind the wheel of the family minivan, but he *really, really, really* wants to go to the go-kart track on the other side of town. If that's the only vehicle you have, the solution is simple: He can drive it, he can talk a buddy into driving, or he can walk. If he balks and insists, "If you really loved me, you'd buy something decent," you can diffuse the situation by agreeing with him.

"Yeah, I didn't like having to drive my dad's station wagon either, but right now that's all we have. If you save some of your money, maybe we can get something cooler next summer." In this way, you're validating his fear of embarrassment instead of negating it with a comment such as, "Why do you care what other people think of you?" Or perhaps the worst of all, "When I was your age . . ."

HAIR

I often wonder how many family battles have been waged about hair: hair length and hair color, no hair and multi-length hair, gelled hair and spiked hair, dreadlocks and Mohawks, plain ol' dirty hair. You would be amazed at how often parents bring up hair issues regarding their adolescents when we're in session. I'm often tempted to say, "See that degree on the wall? It says PhD, not cosmetologist!"

Sometimes, in the adolescent's presence, parents will ask me what I think of his hair. I usually say that it's fine because it's *his* hair. If I can't see his eyes, I might ask him to move it out of the way since I like to see the person I'm talking with, but other than that, I don't take a stand.

My most frequent message to parents about hair is, "There's one thing that's guaranteed about hair: It will always revert to the way it was originally. If it's purple now, it will eventually be brown once again." Sometimes I'll ask parents if they ever had hair their parents hated. Most of them will admit that they did, and they'll continue on with a story about how stupid they once looked. I then remind them that their adolescent will one day be able to look back and laugh at how absurd his greasy green locks looked. But for now, it's a benign statement that serves him in some way. My point is not to encourage permissiveness but rather to bring balance to a relationship that is in crisis over something that is clearly not a tragedy and will not go on forever.

ELECTRONIC ENTERTAINMENT

Beep! Buzz! Ding! Does this sound like life in your household? Does a computer mouse or other type of controller seem to have permanently affixed itself to the end of your adolescent's arm? If so, welcome to the twenty-first century.

I sometimes look at the Amish families in our practice and think just how lucky they are that they won't be arguing over how much computer time their adolescent has. In such cases, not having electricity seems to be a gift.

Video game systems and computers have become the best friends of many adolescents. Don't get me wrong: I don't think there's anything intrinsically wrong with electronic entertainment. The problem is that too many adolescents and younger children miss out on developing interpersonal skills when their only interactions with people are via a game, a keyboard, or text-messaging. How will they learn to relate to others face-to-face?

I don't think we know what the long-term impact of electronic entertainment will be, but it seems to me that parents need to handle this issue like they handle any other. If your adolescent is spending an inordinate amount of time doing anything at the expense of other things he should be doing, it's time to exercise your parental role. If his room becomes his summertime haven and his waking hours are spent playing video games, cruising on the computer, or even reading (an admirable habit, but not if that's all he does), you should encourage him to do something with real-live people. Have him invite his friends over or take them to the park, the hiking trails, the skate park, even the mall. Get him out of the house and moving!

The proper adult behavior in this case, as with most other adolescent issues, is to be reasonable and keep balance in mind.

HOMESCHOOLING

Many families make the decision to homeschool their children and adolescents. Some people, particularly those who work in education, are critical of the entire homeschooling movement. Some social-service and mental-health professionals are suspicious of families who choose to educate their children at home. *What are they hiding? What are they teaching? What about the social lives of their children?*

Increasing data suggests that many homeschooled adolescents are able to compete on par with their classroom-educated peers, which would indicate that the decision to teach at home is clearly a family's choice. From an attachment perspective, I think it can be helpful.

The most critical ingredient of homeschooling is the parent who is doing the teaching. If the adolescent is demanding and difficult to be around, you must be willing and able to spend all that extra time with him. Many parents whose kids pose a heightened challenge find great relief when the long yellow cruiser pulls up in the morning, and they dread hearing it approach in the afternoon. If this is you, you probably are not a good candidate for homeschooling your adolescent.

If, on the other hand, you relish the time you spend with your adolescent, the vacations you take, holiday breaks during the academic year, and snow days, you may enjoy the experience. Enjoyment is the key. I can't imagine attempting to homeschool any child if it doesn't mesh with your personality.

Many adolescents are homeschooled in small-group settings facilitated by individuals other than their parents. These situations offer the same advantages, but they don't demand constant parental involvement.

If homeschooling works for your family, then go for it. If not, there are many educational alternatives available to you: public schools, charter schools, Catholic schools, Christian schools, boarding schools, and military schools. You have the right to choose the format of education you feel will best meet the educational needs of your child.

FAITH-BASED ISSUES

As discussed many times in this book, an adolescent is seeking some sort of identity that is distinct from that of his family. The faith he chooses to embrace is not immune from being used as a tool through which he feels he can truly prove that he is different. Of course, not all adolescents choose to distance themselves from the family's religious orientation, but many of them do. They might choose to break away by exploring other religions and perspectives. Or they might become extremely critical, making proclamations such as, "All of this church stuff is stupid. I doubt there's a heaven, and there probably isn't a God, either."

As a parent, such comments may seem sacrilegious to you, particularly if you are strongly connected to your belief system. It may be even more difficult to hear if your decision to adopt was partly the result of your belief that doing so is God's work. Many of our Christian clients cite scripture that led them to adopt, such as, "Religion that God our Father accepts as pure and faultless is this: to look after orphans and widows in their distress and to keep oneself from being polluted by the world."[2] One missionary in a workshop I was giving suggested that adoptive parents should pay as much attention to the final part of the scripture as they do to the first part. In other words, she believes that the mandate to "keep oneself from being polluted by the world" refers to the fact that parents should expect some challenges in adoption and be prepared to meet them.

Although it is difficult for parents to cope with an adolescent who strays from his beliefs, it is important to keep in mind that chances are good he will return to where he once was.

If you are parenting a child or adolescent who was sexually or physically abused or subjected to other kinds of maltreatment, you might find he has difficulty understanding how this wonderful God you worship allowed him to be so hurt. If you mention that God has a plan for everyone and everything, he probably wonders, *What kind of God would have a plan for what happened to me?*

It is essential to be prepared to address your child's questions and concerns within the context of your particular faith's perspective. You need to understand this dilemma and expect that the adolescent might not appreciate or understand what you mean when you talk about God's plan. It is important to validate his feelings and not expect him to "get it" very quickly.

Miranda and her family had no involvement whatsoever in any religious activity. They never had attended church, they had no particular beliefs, and they thought Christians were far too fanatic. When Miranda reached adolescence, she chose to immerse herself in a large nondenominational, youth-oriented church. She attended services twice on Sunday and once on Wednesday and went to youth group meetings on Friday. Her parents were displeased with how much time she was spending with her new friends, and they even suggested that the church she was attending was akin to a cult.

When they came to me for therapy to deal with this situation, I found it strange that Miranda's parents were so upset. After all, she wasn't abandoning the family's church but was embracing a new experience. I helped them understand her need to explore something, which was perfectly normal and healthy. I also suggested that they might be happy about her new friends if they thought about the fact that so many other kids were experimenting with drugs, alcohol, and sex! What possible damage could church do?

We have seen many adolescents who have disowned, at least for the moment, their family's religious perspectives. Rather than being frowned upon or disputed, this behavior should be seen for what it is: a temporary step away from what they perceive to be the old and a step toward what they see as the new.

Aaron's parents brought him to therapy for a variety of behavioral difficulties. One of their concerns related to his antagonistic attitudes toward Judaism. As Orthodox Jews, they were observant of all the laws—including dietary ones—associated with their religion. Aaron made every attempt to offend his parents and the members of their temple and break every rule at his private Jewish school. On the Sabbath, he would turn on as many electrical devices as he could, violating the law about not doing any work from sundown on Friday until sundown on Saturday. It almost seemed as if his parents' act of lighting the Sabbath candles was his signal to start doing all the things they found unacceptable. They were infuriated by their son's infractions, and they began to believe that he hated everything about being Jewish. Aaron seemed almost happy that he was successfully making such a dramatic point to them.

As we were discussing this problem in my office, Aaron took the opportunity to drive his parents to new levels of anger when he said to me, "Dr. Keck, it's not like I run around the house eating a pork chop!" As he laughed, they were not amused. I must admit that I found his attempt at humor a bit funny since it caught me off guard. I usually hear, "It's not like I killed someone!"

My efforts to placate the situation were not very successful. Aaron was on a mission, and at that point in time, he was not willing to moderate his attack on everything Jewish. My guess is, however, that when he approaches young adulthood, he will return to a place that will be comfortable for his parents. Who knows—Judaism-hating Aaron might even grow up to be a rabbi.

Both Franklin and Ned Graham, Billy and Ruth Graham's sons, have been described as having strayed from what their parents desired for them. After his mother's funeral, Ned was quoted as saying that she stayed up every night waiting for him to come home from his adolescent alcohol and marijuana partying, and he was never successful at slipping by her. She would be sitting there in her pajamas with the Bible or another book on her lap. Each time this occurred, Ned reported that she'd give him a hug, say "Thank God you're all right," smile, and go to her room.[3] I guess Mrs. Graham knew very well what she could control and what she wasn't in charge of, and she seemed content to do what she could.

In spite of the cited cases, many adolescents remain involved with their churches, temples, and other places of worship. Several of my clients go on missions trips, volunteer at food banks, sing in choirs, participate in religiously focused youth activities, play guitars and drums at church services, and worship comfortably with their families.

As with all adolescent detours, parents whose kids give up on religion should not give up the ship. There's an excellent chance they'll be back on board before too long.

FINAL THOUGHTS

And on that encouraging note, dear reader, I end my musings. I hope these random reflections have helped round out the messages and advice from the pages of this book. The single most important thought I can leave you with is this: Adolescence is a trying time. When adoption is added to the equation, the challenges for parents may be greater still. My advice is to maintain perspective, keep your wits about you, find comfort in humor, hold on to your faith, and never underestimate the power of love.

NOTES

CHAPTER 1: ADOLESCENCE

1. Arleta James, *Brothers and Sisters in Adoption: Helping Children Navigate Relationships When New Kids Join the Family* (Indianapolis: Perspectives Press, 2009).
2. James.
3. One Look Dictionary Search, onelook.com.

CHAPTER 3: LOSS OF THE BIRTH FAMILY

1. Deborah Silverstein is an adoptive parent of four special-needs youngsters and a program manager for the Kinship Center®, a private California special-needs adoption agency and mental health specialty program. Deborah is also a private-practice therapist specializing in adoption issues. Sharon Kaplan Roszia is a parent by birth, foster care, and adoption; a program manager for the Kinship Center; and an author and a lecturer. Their article previously appeared in the March/April 1999 issue of *Adoptive Families* magazine.
2. S. Wilkinson and George Hough, "Lie As Narrative Truth in Abused Adopted Adolescents," *Psychoanalytic Study of the Child,* 51 (1996): 580–596. Peter Blos, "The Second Individuation Process of Adolescence," *Psychoanalytic Study of the Child* 22 (1967): 162–186.

CHAPTER 4: FACING FRUSTRATION

1. Foster W. Cline, MD, and Jim Fay, *Parenting with Love and Logic* (Colorado Springs, CO: NavPress, 2006).
2. Jenifer Lippincott and Robin M. Deutsch, PhD, *7 Things Your Teenager Won't Tell You: And How to Talk About Them Anyway* (New York: Ballantine Books, 2005).
3. Cline and Fay.

CHAPTER 5: ADOPTING AN ADOLESCENT

1. AFCARS Report, U.S. Department of Health and Human Services, Administration for Children and Families, Administration on Children, Youth, and Families, Children's Bureau, January 2008, www.acf.hhs .gov/programs/cb.

CHAPTER 6: JUST WHEN YOU THOUGHT IT COULDN'T GET ANY WORSE

1. *The Times-Union*, Jacksonville, Florida, June 5, 2008.

CHAPTER 7: TRANSRACIAL AND TRANSCULTURAL ADOPTIONS

1. "Successful Transcultural Parenting: Dealing with the Dynamics of Difference," The Institute for Human Services, June 1, 2001, 6–7.
2. Joseph Crumbley, *Transracial Adoption and Foster Care: Practice Issues for Professionals,* Child Welfare League of America, Washington, D.C., 1999.
3. Grant Segall, "More Blacks Appear to Be Adopting White Children," *The Cleveland Plain Dealer*, December 11, 2007.

CHAPTER 8: TURNING EIGHTEEN

1. L. G. Mansfield is an author, a collaborator, a ghostwriter, and my favorite developmental editor. She has written several nonfiction books covering a variety of subjects, including adoption, lifestyle, self-help, and health care. She is the adoptive mother of Ty, now twenty-five, and Marco, nineteen.
2. Beth Hall is cofounder and director of Pact, An Adoption Alliance—a multicultural adoption organization dedicated to addressing essential

issues affecting adopted children of color. Her book *Inside Transracial Adoption*, coauthored with Gail Steinberg, reinforces the message that transracially built families can develop strong and binding ties. Beth is the white adoptive mom of two teenage children: Sofia (Latina) and James (African American).

3. Janet Alston Jackson, CSL, is a personal and spiritual-growth consultant (www.SportingtheRightAttitude.com). She often teams with her husband, Walter Jackson, MscD, to facilitate effective communications trainings for better relationships. Their audiences include corporate executives, parents, teachers, women in recovery, prison personnel, health-care workers, and entertainment-industry executives. She is the author of *A Cry for Light: A Journey into Love*, winner of the USA Book News Award for Christian Inspiration.

CHAPTER 9: THE CLINICIAN'S ROLE

1. Arleta James, *Brothers and Sisters in Adoption: Helping Children Navigate Relationships When New Kids Join the Family* (Indianapolis: Perspectives Press, 2008).
2. James.

CHAPTER 11: STORIES OF HOPE

1. Jan Fishler was adopted as an infant in Ohio. After launching a search when she was in her early forties, she discovered that she was one of eight siblings, three of whom were given up for adoption. She is currently chronicling her story in a memoir titled *Lost and Found*.

CHAPTER 12: RANDOM REFLECTIONS

1. *Grapevine*, The International Journal of Alcoholics Anonymous, 1950, 6–7.
2. James 1:27.
3. blog.christianitytoday.com/ctliveblog/archives/2007/06ruths_children.html.

RELATED RESOURCES

BOOKS

Alperson, Myra. *Dim Sum, Bagels, and Grits: A Sourcebook for Multicultural Families*. New York: Farrar, Strauss & Giroux, 2001.

Borba, Michele, EdD. *Building Moral Intelligence: The Seven Essential Virtues That Teach Kids to Do the Right Thing*. Hoboken, NJ: Jossey-Bass, 2002.

Bradley, Michael J., EdD. *Yes, Your Teen Is Crazy!: Loving Your Kid Without Losing Your Mind*. Gig Harbor, WA: Harbor Press, 2002.

Brodzinsky, David M., and Marshall D. Schechter, eds. *The Psychology of Adoption*. New York: Oxford University Press, 1990.

Cline, Foster W., MD, and Jim Fay. *Parenting with Love and Logic*. Colorado Springs, CO: NavPress, 2006.

Cline, Foster W., MD, and Jim Fay. *Parenting Teens with Love and Logic*. Colorado Springs, CO: NavPress, 2006.

Cogen, Patty. *Parenting Your Internationally Adopted Child: From Your First Hours Together Through the Teen Years*. Boston: Harvard Common Press, 2008.

Coughlin, Amy, and Caryn Abramowitz. *Cross-Cultural Adoption: How to Answer Questions from Family, Friends, and Community*. Washington, D.C.: LifeLine Press, 2004.

Cox, Susan Soon Keum, ed. *Voices from Another Place: A Collection of Works from a Generation Born in Korea and Adopted to Other Countries*. St. Paul, MN: Yeong & Yeong, 1999.

Crumbley, Joseph. *Transracial Adoption and Foster Care: Practice Issues for Professionals*. Washington, D.C.: Child Welfare League of America, 1999.

Di Prisco, Joseph, and Michael Riera. *Field Guide to the American Teenager*. Cambridge, MA: Perseus Publishing, 2000.

Dorow, Sara. *When You Were Born in China: A Memory Book for Children Adopted from China*. St. Paul, MN: Yeong & Yeong, 1997.

Eldridge, Sherrie. *Forever Fingerprints: An Amazing Discovery for Adopted Children*. Warren, NJ: EMK Press, 2007.

Eldridge, Sherrie. *Questions Adoptees Are Asking*. Rev. ed. Colorado Springs, CO: NavPress, 2009.

Eldridge, Sherrie. *Twenty Things Adopted Kids Wish Their Adoptive Parents Knew*. New York: Dell, 1999.

Elkind, David. *All Grown Up and No Place to Go: Teenagers in Crisis*. Reading, MA: Addison-Wesley, 1998.

Elkind, David. *The Hurried Child: Growing Up Too Fast Too Soon*. Reading, MA: Addison-Wesley, 1981.

Fahlberg, Vera I., MD. *A Child's Journey Through Placement*. Indianapolis: Perspectives Press, 1994.

Fay, Jim. *Helicopters, Drill Sergeants, and Consultants*. Golden, CO: Cline/Fay Institute, 1988.

Fay, Jim. *Tickets to Success*. Golden, CO: Cline/Fay Institute, 1988.

Fay, Jim, and Foster W. Cline, MD. *Grandparenting with Love and Logic: Practical Solutions to Today's Grandparenting Challenges*. Golden, CO: Love & Logic Press, 1995.

Fisher, Antwone Quenton. *Finding Fish*. New York: William Morrow, 2001.

Foli, Karen J., PhD, and John R. Thompson, MD. *The Post-Adoption Blues: Overcoming the Unforeseen Challenges of Adoption*. Emmaus, PA: Rodale Books, 2004.

Geidman, J., and L. Brown. *Birthbond: Reunions Between Birthparents and Adoptees—What Happens After*. Far Hills, NJ: New Horizon Press, 1995.

Gentile, Douglas, Paul Lynch, Jennifer Ruh Linder, and David Walsh. "The Effects of Violent Video Games on Adolescent Hostility, Aggressive Behaviors, and School Performance," *Journal of Adolescence* 27 (2004): 5–22.

Gerrold, David. *The Martian Child*. New York: Tom Doherty Associates, 2002. (This book has been made into a movie that is appropriate for families.)

Gorbett, Danea. *Adopted Teens Only: A Survival Guide to Adolescence*. Bloomington, IN: iUniverse Star, 2007.

Grandin, Temple. *Journal of Child and Adolescent Psychopharmacology*, Vol. 2, Mary Ann Liebert, Inc. Publishers, November 1, 1992.

Grandin, Temple. *Thinking in Pictures and Other Reports from My Life with Autism*. Larchmont, NY: Vintage Books, 1995.

Grandin, Temple, and Margaret M. Scariano. *Emergence: Labeled Autistic*. Novato, CA: Arena Press, 1986.

Gray, Deborah. *Attaching in Adoption: Practical Tools for Today's Parents*. Indianapolis: Perspectives Press, 2002.

Gray, Deborah. *Nurturing Adoptions: Creating Resilience After Neglect and Trauma*. Indianapolis: Perspective Press, 2007.

Hughes, Daniel A. *Attachment-Focused Family Therapy*. New York: W. W. Norton, 2007.

Hughes, Daniel A. *Building the Bonds of Attachment*. Northvale, NJ: Jason Aronson, 2006.

Hughes, Daniel A. *Facilitating Developmental Attachment*. Northvale, NJ: Jason Aronson, 1997.

Jackson, Janet Alston. *A Cry for Light: A Journey into Love.* Los Angeles: Self-Awareness Trainings, 2005.

James, Arleta. *Brothers and Sisters in Adoption: Helping Children Navigate Relationships When New Kids Join the Family.* Indianapolis: Perspectives Press, 2009.

Jernberg, Ann M., and Phyllis B. Booth. *Theraplay: Helping Parents and Children Build Better Relationships Through Attachment-Based Play.* San Francisco: Jossey-Bass, 1999.

John, Jaiya. *Black Baby, White Hands: A View from the Crib.* Silver Spring, MD: Soul Water Rising, 2005.

Johnston, Patricia Irwin. *Adopting After Infertility.* Indianapolis: Perspectives Press, 1994.

Johnston, Patricia Irwin. *Adopting: Sound Choices, Strong Families.* Indianapolis: Perspectives Press, 2008.

Johnston, Patricia Irwin. *Adoption Is a Family Affair! What Relatives and Friends Must Know.* Indianapolis: Perspectives Press, 2001.

Johnston, Patricia Irwin. *Perspectives on a Grafted Tree: Thoughts for Those Touched by Adoption.* Indianapolis: Perspectives Press, 1983.

Keck, Gregory C., PhD, and Regina M. Kupecky, LSW. *Adopting the Hurt Child: Hope for Families with Special-Needs Kids.* Rev. ed. Colorado Springs, CO: NavPress, 2009.

Keck, Gregory C., PhD, and Regina M. Kupecky, LSW. *Parenting the Hurt Child: Helping Adoptive Families Heal and Grow.* Rev. ed. Colorado Springs, CO: NavPress, 2009.

Keefer, Betsy, and Jayne E. Schooler. *Telling the Truth to Your Adopted or Foster Child: Making Sense of the Past.* Westport, CT: Bergin & Garvey, 2000.

Klaus, Marshall H., MD, and John H. Kennell, MD. *Bonding: The Beginnings of Parent-Infant Attachment.* St. Louis: Mosby, 1983.

Klaus, Marshall H., MD, and John H. Kennell, MD. *Maternal-Infant Bonding: The Impact of Early Separation or Loss on Family Development*. St. Louis: Mosby, 1976.

Klaus, Marshall H., MD, and John H. Kennell, MD. *Parent-Infant Bonding*. 2nd ed. St. Louis: Mosby, 1982.

Kleinfeld, Judith. *Fantastic Antone Grows Up: Adolescents and Adults with Fetal Alcohol Syndrome*. Fairbanks, AK: University of Alaska Press, 2000.

Kralovec, Etta, and John Buell. *The End of Homework*. Boston: Beacon Press, 2000.

Kranowitz, Carol Stock. *The Out-of-Sync Child: Recognizing and Coping with Sensory Integration Dysfunction*. New York: Perigree Books, 1998.

Kupecky, Regina M., LSW. *Siblings Are Family, Too*. Pittsburgh: Three Rivers Adoption Council, 1993.

Lanchon, Anne. *All About Adoption: How to Deal with the Questions of Your Past*. Bloomington, IN: iUniverse Star, 2007.

Lippincott, Jenifer, and Robin M. Deutsch, PhD. *7 Things Your Teenager Won't Tell You: And How to Talk About Them Anyway*. New York: Ballantine Books, 2005.

Marindin, Hope, ed. *Handbook for Single Adoptive Parents*. Chevy Chase, MD: Committee of Single Adoptive Parents, 1992.

Maskew, Trish. *Our Own: Adopting and Parenting the Older Child*. Morton Grove, IL: Snowcap Press, 1999.

Mason, Mary Martin. *Designing Rituals of Adoption: For the Religious and Secular Community*. Minneapolis: Resources for Adoptive Parents, 1995.

Mathias, Barbara, and Mary Ann French. *40 Ways to Raise a Nonracist Child*. New York: Harper Perennial, 1996.

McCreight, Brenda, PhD. *Parenting Your Adopted Older Child*. Oakland, CA: New Harbinger, 2002.

McRoy, Ruth G., Harold D. Grotevant, and Louis A. Zurcher Jr. *Emotional Disturbance in Adopted Adolescents: Origins and Development*. New York: Praeger, 1988.

Nakazawa, Donna Jackson. *Does Anybody Else Look Like Me? A Parent's Guide to Raising Multiracial Children*. Cambridge, MA: Perseus, 2003.

Papolos, Demitri, and Janice Papolos. *The Bipolar Child: The Definitive and Reassuring Guide to Childhood's Most Misunderstood Disorder*. New York: Broadway Books, 2002.

Perry, Bruce, MD, PhD, and Maia Szalavitz. *The Boy Who Was Raised as a Dog and Other Stories from a Child Psychiatrist's Notebook: What Traumatized Children Can Teach Us About Loss, Love, and Healing*. New York: Basic Books, 2006.

Pertman, Adam. *Adoption Nation: How the Adoption Revolution Is Transforming America*. New York: Basic Books, 2000.

Portner, Jessica. *One in Thirteen: The Silent Epidemic of Teen Suicide*. Beltsville, MD: Robins Lane Press, 2001.

Register, Cheri. *Are Those Kids Yours? American Families with Children Adopted from Other Countries*. New York: Free Press, 1990.

Register, Cheri. *Beyond Good Intentions: A Mother Reflects on Raising Internationally Adopted Children*. St. Paul, MN: Yeong & Yeong, 2005.

Reiff, Michael, I., MD, with Sherill Tippins, eds. *ADHD: A Complete and Authoritative Guide*. Elk Grove, IL: American Academy of Pediatrics, 2004.

Riley, Debbie, MS, with John Meeks, MD. *Beneath the Mask: Understanding Adopted Teens*. Silver Spring, MD: CASE Publications, 2005.

Rosemond, John. *Teen-Proofing: A Revolutionary Approach to Fostering Responsible Decision Making in Your Teenager*. Kansas City, MO: Andrews McMeel, 1998.

Sax, Leonard, MD, PhD. *Boys Adrift: The Five Factors Driving the Growing Epidemic of Unmotivated Boys and Underachieving Young Men.* New York: Basic Books, 2007.

Schneider, Helen, PhD, and Daniel Eisenberg, PhD. "Who Receives a Diagnosis of Attention-Deficit/Hyperactivity Disorder in the United States Elementary School Population?" *Pediatrics* 117 (2006): 601–609.

Schooler, Jayne E. *Searching for a Past.* Colorado Springs, CO: Piñon Press, 1995.

Schooler, Jayne E., and Thomas C. Atwood. *The Whole Life Adoption Book: Realistic Advice for Building a Healthy Adoptive Family.* Rev. ed. Colorado Springs, CO: NavPress, 2008.

Schore, Allan N. *Affect Regulation and the Origin of the Self: The Neurobiology of Emotional Development.* Philadelphia: Lawrence Erlbaum, 1999.

Siegel, Daniel J. *The Developing Mind: How Relationships and the Brain Interact to Shape Who We Are.* New York: Guilford Press, 2001.

Siegel Daniel J., MD, and Mary Hartzell, MEd. *Parenting from the Inside Out.* New York: Jeremy Tarcher, 2004.

Simon, Rita J., and Rhonda M. Roorda. *In Their Own Voices: Transracial Adoptees Tell Their Stories.* New York: Columbia University Press, 2000.

Steinberg, Gail, and Beth Hall. *Inside Transracial Adoption.* Indianapolis: Perspectives Press, 2000.

Streissguth, Ann. *Fetal Alcohol Syndrome: A Guide for Families and Communities.* Baltimore: Brookes Publishing Co., 1997.

Taffel, Ron. *The Second Family.* New York: St. Martin's Press, 2001.

Tatum, Beverly Daniel, PhD. *Why Are All the Black Kids Sitting Together in the Cafeteria?* New York: Basic Books, 1997.

Tranka, Jane Jeong, Julia Chinyere Oparah, and Sun Yung Shin, eds. *Outsiders Within: Writing on Transracial Adoption.* Cambridge, MA: South End Press, 2006.

Trout, Michael, and Lori Thomas. *The Jonathon Letters: One Family's Use of Support as They Took in, and Fell in Love with, a Troubled Child.* Champaign, IL: Infant-Parent Institute, 2005.

van der Kolk, Bessel A., Alexander C. McFarlane, and Lars Weisaeth, eds. *Traumatic Stress: The Effects of Overwhelming Experience on Mind, Body, and Society.* New York: Guilford Press, 1996.

Verrier, Nancy Newton. *Coming Home to Self: The Adopted Child Grows Up.* Baltimore: Gateway Press, 2003.

Verrier, Nancy Newton. *The Primal Wound: Understanding the Adopted Child.* Baltimore: Gateway Press, 1993.

Whitten, Kathleen, PhD. *Labor of the Heart: A Parent's Guide to the Decisions and Emotions in Adoption.* New York: M. Evans & Company, 2008.

Wilens, Timothy E., MD. *Straight Talk About Psychiatric Medications for Kids.* 3rd ed. New York: Guilford Press, 2008.

Wu, Frank H. *Yellow: Race in America Beyond Black and White.* New York: Basic Books, 2003.

VIDEOS

I Wonder: Teenagers Talk About Adoption

A diverse group of adolescent adoptees share their thoughts on various aspects of adoption.

Families Adopting In Response (FAIR) — www.fairfamilies.org

First Person Plural

In 1966, Deann Borshay Liem was adopted by an American family and was sent from Korea to her new home. As she grew up in California, the memory of her birth family was nearly obliterated until recurring dreams led her to discover the truth: Her Korean mother was very much alive. Bravely uniting her biological and adoptive families, Borshay Liem makes "First Person Plural" a

poignant essay on family, loss, and the reconciling of two identities.
PBS — www.pbs.org

Struggle for Identity: Issues in Transracial Adoption
Transracial adoptees and their families discuss the difficult issues of racism, identity, and sense of place.
New York State Citizen's Coalition for Children — www.nysccc.org

CURRICULUM

Jordan, Barbara. *Living with the Sexually Abused Child: A Curriculum for the Foster Parents' Own Children*. King George, VA: American Foster Care Resources, 1997.

Kupecky, Regina M. "My Brother, My Sister: Sibling Relations in Adoption and Foster Care," 2006. (For information on this curriculum, contact the Attachment and Bonding Center of Ohio, listed in Internet Resources.)

INTERNET RESOURCES

The amount of information available on the Internet is staggering. From websites to chat rooms, data on every type and every aspect of adoption can be accessed. If you do not have a computer, your local library can help.

Listed here are support groups and organizations that offer information on adoption and attachment. The websites and organizations change constantly, so if these are outdated, please try referrals from other resources.

I have not investigated all of these organizations, so inclusion on this list does not reflect my recommendation. Lack of inclusion merely indicates a lack of awareness. I offer the information to you as you start your own exploration. Begin with the following resources, and it is likely you will discover many more.

AdoptUsKids

www.adoptuskids.org

AdoptUsKids provides a national photo listing service of available children throughout the United States. The site offers an overview of "getting started" with the adoption of children from the foster care system. Parents can request to be contacted regarding questions about foster care or the adoption process. The site also hosts a prospective-parents' blog. AdoptUsKids is a valuable resource for professionals, as well.

adoption.com

www.adoption.com

This site discusses adoption from all vantage points and includes adoption stories and CDs.

Adoption Learning Partners

www.adoptionlearningpartners.org

Adoption Learning Partners provides an innovative and educational resource for adoptive parents, adopted individuals, birth parents, and the families who love them.

Adoption Today Magazine

www.adoptinfo.net

Adoption Today is the only magazine dedicated to international and transracial adoption.

Adoptive Families Magazine

www.adoptivefam.org

This national, award-winning adoption magazine offers information for families before, during, and after adoption. The site also offers a wealth of adoption-related articles and books.

American Academy of Child & Adolescent Psychiatry (AACAP)

www.aacap.org

This site provides descriptions of mental-health disorders and their treatment. It is a useful resource for parents whose adolescents have been diagnosed with mental-health problems.

American Academy of Pediatrics (AAP)

www.aap.org

The AAP is dedicated to providing information relative to medical and mental-health problems. A list of International Adoption Clinics is included.

The Annie E. Casey Foundation

www.aecf.org

This foundation fosters public policies, reforms, and support for vulnerable families and children.

Association for Treatment and Training in the Attachment of Children (ATTACh)

www.attach.org

ATTACh is an international coalition of professionals and families dedicated to helping those with attachment difficulties by sharing their knowledge, talents, and resources. The organization provides a quarterly newsletter, an annual conference, a membership directory, and other benefits to members and the public. CDs of workshops from the ATTACh annual conferences are available. The topics cover all aspects of the attachment between child and parent as well as various aspects of adoptive family life.

Attachment and Bonding Center of Ohio (ABC)

www.abcofohio.net

This organization is focused on pre- and post-adoption counseling and intensive attachment therapy. The author can be contacted at this location.

ChildTrauma Academy (CTA)

www.childtrauma.org

CTA recognizes the crucial importance of childhood experiences in shaping the health of the individual and, ultimately, society. A major activity of the CTA is to translate emerging findings about the human brain and child development into practical implications for the ways we nurture, protect, enrich, educate, and heal children.

Child Welfare League of America (CWLA)

www.cwla.org

The CWLA program spans adoption, adolescent pregnancy prevention and teen parenting, child daycare, child protection, children affected by incarceration, family foster care, group residential care, housing and homelessness, kinship care, juvenile justice, mental health, positive youth development, substance abuse prevention and treatment, and a range of community services that strengthen and support parents and families.

Children and Adults with Attention Deficit/Hyperactivity Disorder (CHADD)

www.chadd.org

CHADD is a national nonprofit organization providing education, advocacy, and support for individuals with ADHD. Parents whose children have this diagnosis will find information relative to IEPs and 504 plans.

Children's Research Triangle

www.childstudy.org

The Children's Research Triangle works extensively with children who are adopted or in the foster-care system and have experienced abuse, neglect, and prenatal alcohol and drug exposure.

Dr. Joseph Crumbley

www.drcrumbley.com

This renowned author on transracial adoption has also produced a series of videos available on his website:

- "Special Needs of Minority Children Adopted Transracially"
- "The Impact of Transracial Adoption on the Adopted Child and Adoptive Family"
- "Parenting Tasks in Transracial Adoptions"
- "Assessing a Family's Ability to Adopt Transracially"

Evan B. Donaldson Adoption Institute

www.adoptioninstitute.org

The institute's mission is to provide leadership that improves adoption law, policies, and practices—through sound research, education, and advocacy—to better the lives of everyone touched by adoption. The site offers adoption professionals a way to stay abreast of cutting-edge research and recommendations pertaining to all facets of adoptees and the adoption process.

International Adoption Medicine Program, University of Minnesota
www.med.umn.edu/peds/iac
This was the first international adoption clinic in the United States, and most others in the country are modeled after it. Dr. Dana Johnson, its founder, is an internationally known physician who has trained thousands of people around the world.

Joint Council on International Children's Services (JCICS)
www.jcics.org
JCICS is the lead voice on intercountry children's services. Its mission is to advocate on behalf of children in need of permanent, safe, and loving families. JCICS promotes ethical child-welfare practices, strengthens professional standards, and educates adoptive families, social-service professionals, and government representatives throughout the world. This site contains a parent section that provides useful information to guide families through the international adoption process. JCICS also puts forth country-specific information for more than fifty countries. The site also includes information about the JCICS annual conference.

KidsHealth
www.kidshealth.org
KidsHealth is the largest and most visited site on the Internet providing doctor-approved health information about children from before birth through adolescence. Created by The Nemours Foundation's Center for Children's Health Media, the award-winning site provides families with accurate, up-to-date, and jargon-free health information they can use. KidsHealth has separate areas for kids, teens, and parents, each with its own design and age-appropriate content. There are thousands of in-depth features, articles, animations, games, and resources—all original and all developed by experts in the health of children and teens. This site is a wealth of information about everything

related to medical illnesses, mental-health issues, school issues, child development, and more.

The Latham Foundation

www.latham.org

Latham is a clearinghouse for information about humane issues and activities, the human companion animal bond (HCAB), animal-assisted therapy, and the connections between child and animal abuse and other forms of violence.

National Child Traumatic Stress Network

www.nctsn.org

NCTSN is a unique collaboration of academic and community-based service centers whose mission is to raise the standard of care and increase access to services for traumatized children and their families across the United States.

National Institute of Mental Health (NIMH)

www.nimh.nih.gov

This site provides thorough coverage of any mental-health disorder listed in the DSM-IVTR. Treatments for different disorders are discussed, and there is much information about the use of medications in the treatment of mental-health disorders. It includes three articles that discuss the adolescent brain:

- "Teenage Brain: A Work in Progress" (2001)
  www.nimh.nih.gov/publications/teenage-brain-a-work-in-progress.shtml
- "Imaging Study Shows Brain Maturing" (2004)
  www.nimh.nih.gov/press/prbrainmaturing.cfm
- "Inside the Teenage Brain," Jay Giedd, interview, *Frontline* (2002)
  www.pbs.org/wgbh/pages/frontline/shows/teenbrain/interviews/giedd.html

National Organization on Fetal Alcohol Syndrome (NOFAS)

www.nofas.org

NOFAS is the leading voice and resource of the Fetal Alcohol Spectrum Disorders (FASD) community. This site provides articles and additional resources for those who are parenting or working with children with FASD. The "Living with FASD" section offers great strategies for helping children with FASD. The tips are organized according to the child's developmental stages.

North American Council on Adoptable Children (NACAC)

www.nacac.org

NACAC promotes and supports permanent families for children and youth in the United States and Canada who have been in foster care or have special needs. NACAC has long been recognized as the preeminent leader in adoption in this country.

Pact, An Adoption Alliance

www.pactadopt.org

This nonprofit organization embraces a mission to serve children of color in need of adoption or who are growing up in adoptive families.

Perspectives Press

www.perspectivespress.com

Perspectives Press has specialized in publishing books about adoption and infertility for twenty-five years. The site provides an overview of each of the books available, and purchases can be made directly through the site. Perspectives Press also features an array of articles written by its authors, as well as the authors' speaking schedules.

RainbowKids.com

www.rainbowkids.com

This online magazine is an excellent source of adoption-related information.

Society & Animals Forum

www.psyeta.org

Society & Animals Forum (formerly Psychologists for the Ethical Treatment of Animals) works with social scientists, mental-health providers, and other animal protection organizations to reduce the suffering and exploitation of animals.

Special Children

specialchildren.about.com

This site offers more than seven hundred links to information for parents.

Tapestry Books

www.tapestrybooks.com

Tapestry Books offers more than three hundred adult and children's books on adoption, infertility, and parenting adopted children. For children, preteens, and teens, topics include understanding adoption, thinking about birth parents, celebrating differences, and being in foster care. For adults, topics include international adoption, transcultural adoption, pre-adoption preparation, talking about adoption, adopting older children/children with special needs, attachment, search and reunion, foster parenting, and infertility. The bookstore may be browsed by topic, author, or title.

Teen Matters

www.teen-matters.com

This site for adolescents addresses suicide, stress, depression, body image, relationship violence, drugs and alcohol, counseling and treatment, and bullying.

Dave Thomas Foundation for Adoption

www.davethomasfoundation.org

This site is dedicated to increasing adoptions. Videos and posters available.

The Trauma Center

www.traumacenter.org

The Trauma Center provides comprehensive services to traumatized children and adults and their families. The executive director is Joseph Spinazzola, PhD, and the medical director and founder is Bessel van der Kolk, MD. These two prominent professionals are part of the group responsible for the creation of the concept of "complex trauma." In addition to clinical services, the Trauma Center offers training, consultation, and educational programming for post-graduate mental-health professionals.

ABOUT THE AUTHOR

G regory C. Keck, PhD, founded the Attachment and Bonding Center of Ohio, which specializes in the treatment of children and adolescents who have experienced developmental interruptions. In addition, he and his staff treat individuals and families faced with a variety of problems in the areas of adoption, attachment, substance abuse, sexual abuse, and adolescence.

Dr. Keck is certified as a diplomate and fellow by the American Board of Medical Psychotherapy and is a diplomate in professional psychotherapy. He is a part-time graduate faculty member in the school of social work at the University of Akron and is involved in training for many agencies, hospitals, and organizations, both nationally and internationally.

His memberships include the Cleveland Psychological Association, the Ohio Psychological Association, the American Psychological Association, and the National Association of Social Workers. From 1991 through 2000, he served on the board of directors of ATTACh, the Association for Treatment and Training in the Attachment of Children. He served as president for two years and was honored by the organization in 2001 with its annual award for outstanding contribution to the field. Dr. Keck was given the Adoption Triad Advocate Award in 1993 by the Adoption Network of Cleveland, Ohio.

He is an adoptive parent and has appeared on numerous television and radio talk shows to discuss a broad spectrum of adoption issues.